CICERO'S ACCRETIVE STYLE

Rhetorical Strategies in the *Exordia* of the Judicial Speeches

Steven M. Cerutti

University Press of America, Inc.
Lanham • New York • London

Copyright © 1996 by
University Press of America,® Inc.
4720 Boston Way
Lanham, Maryland 20706

3 Henrietta Street
London, WC2E 8LU England

Library of Congress Cataloging-in-Publication Data

Cerutti, Steven M.
Cicero's accretive style : rhetorical strategies in the Exordia of the
judicial speeches / Steven M. Cerutti.
p.   cm.
Includes bibliographical references and index.
1. Cicero, Marcus Tullius--Style. 2. Speeches, addresses, etc., Latin--
History and criticism. 3. Latin language--Style. 4. Rome--
Civilization. 5. Rhetoric, Ancient. 6. Oratory, Ancient. I. Title.
PA6357.47 1996   875'.01--dc20   96-23758 CIP

ISBN 0-7618-0438-2 (cloth: alk: ppr.)

PA 6357

C 47

1996

⊖™The paper used in this publication meets the minimum
requirements of American National Standard for information
Sciences—Permanence of Paper for Printed Library Materials,
ANSI Z39.48—1984

For my sister Diana
who gave me my first dictionary
and saved my life one time in New York

Contents

PREFACE

This book owes its origin and inspiration to my first experiences teaching Cicero, and began as a study titled *Character and Transition: Rhetorical Progression in the Ciceronian* Exordium. As I had originally conceived it, the book would examine how Cicero uses the characters in his speeches as rhetorical devices in his *exordia*, specifically as transitional devices or mechanisms controlling the progression of the various components of his opening statements. My original intention had been to argue that the characters of Cicero's speeches play a dual role within the structure of the *exordium*: on the one hand these individuals function as literary figures and act within a narrative progression — they were real people, and Cicero portrays them as such; on the other hand, Cicero uses the *personae* of each speech as thematic engines that drive the *exordium* on a rhetorical level — patterns of action that illustrate specific principles central to the presentation of his case. I soon realized, however, that before I could successfully demonstrate how Cicero incorporated *personae* into the rhetorical framework of his *exordia*, I first had to understand the internal dynamics of that rhetorical framework, and be able to evaluate its chronological development in the context of Cicero's training as an orator and in the perspective of the trajectory of his career. It was not long before I found the focus of my study shifting from a strict analysis of characterization within separate, isolated *exordia*, to a broader analysis of the overall rhetorical style of the Ciceronian *exordium*. While I chose for my models the *exordia* of Cicero's judicial speeches, for these are the most numerous, I began to see certain patterns emerging that could be applied to the *exordia* of other types of speeches as well. In the end, I found that character portrayal is only one of many rhetorical features Cicero uses in what I have come to call the "accretive style" of his *exordia*. While I hope that this study will help future students of Cicero to understand and appreciate what Cicero is doing in his *exordia* on a rhetorical level, it is also my hope that this book will be the opening wedge into further exploration of Cicero's use of character in his *exordia*.

The help I have received in bringing this book to press has come from so many quarters — friends, family, and colleagues — that I cannot possibly make an honest account of all of them here in this brief space. But I should be poor in thanks indeed were I not to acknowledge the signal efforts of a select few individuals, without whose attention and encouragement this book could never have been written. It is my pleasure to thank first and foremost my mentor and friend, Professor Lawrence Richardson, jr, not only for the many drafts of this book he read, and with each reading improved, but also for guiding me patiently *non passibus aequis* through the *opaca locorum* of my years as a graduate student in the Department of Classical Studies at Duke University, and since then for his continued personal commitment to my development as a classicist: the debt I owe, and gratitude I feel, can hardly be appropriately expressed in words, nor ever adequately repaid in deed. I would also like to thank Professor Roger Hornsby, who first suggested that I undertake this project, and who has offered me much guidance and encouragement over the many rewarding years I have known him. Recognition is due to Dr. W. Keats Sparrow, Dean of the College of Arts and Sciences, for establishing classics at East Carolina University, as well as for his generous assistance with matters more practical, but certainly no less invaluable, to the process of the publication of this book. And I cannot forget the support that I have received from all of my colleagues in the Department of Foreign Languages and Literatures, who gave classics a home at East Carolina University, and excused with understanding my frequent absences from departmental meetings while I finished this manuscript. To all of these, and especially to Professor Tony Papalas, whose unconditional faith and friendship has never wavered, I attribute whatever success this book may find; its failures must rest with me.

Finally, I would like to thank my brother Marc, who gave me the computer on which this camera-ready text was produced, and patiently taught me how to use it; and who cheerfully accommodated countless pleas for assistance over the phone and often very early in the morning.

Steven M. Cerutti
Greenville, North Carolina
Independence Day, 1996

INTRODUCTION

Students of Cicero's speeches, and especially neophytes at Latin, know that a reader approaching the text of a Ciceronian speech for the first time will find that one of the most difficult parts of any oration is the *exordium*, or opening statement, for it is always characterized by a highly rhetorical style and often by a philosophical color, and on the surface seems at first reading to have little to do with the actual case itself. This is partly due to the fact that the oral qualities of Cicero's delivery, the pace and emphasis on particular words or phrases, are lost to us, as is any real appreciation of the physical circumstances in which he spoke, and partly due to the format of the judicial process of Cicero's day.

This study examines the nature of the Ciceronian *exordium* and its rhetorical structure and function through a detailed analysis of the specific rhetorical strategies employed in the *exordia* of a succession of six speeches: the *Pro Quinctio* (81 B.C.), *Pro Roscio Amerino* (80 B.C.), *Pro Murena* (63 B.C.), *Pro Milone* (52 B.C.), *Pro Rege Deiotaro* (45 B.C.), and the Second Philippic (44 B.C.). These speeches were selected for study because they span Cicero's career as a forensic orator and offer a wide variety of the rhetorical strategies Cicero uses in the *exordium* to prepare the audience for the speech they are about to hear. But while the rhetorical strategies vary with each speech, the purpose of the *exordium* remained the same for Cicero throughout his career: it sets the tone, creates an atmosphere, and introduces the individuals (*personae*) and the issues (*causae*) involved in the case on trial. In the hope of helping readers of Cicero's speeches to understand and appreciate what Cicero is doing in his *exordia*, particular attention will be paid to the "accretive" development and progression of the arguments within the *exordium*, a technique Cicero employs that stylistically defines and structurally sets the *exordium* off from the rest of the speech, allowing it to function both as a microcosm in its own right and as an introduction or program piece intended to prepare the audience for what is to come. Because Cicero wrote several detailed textbooks in which he discussed the component parts of a speech and their respective functions, one cannot study the *exordium* without also measuring how closely Cicero in practice adhered to the principles he wrote about in theory in his rhetorical works, as well as how and in what circumstances he departed from them.

These pages owe much to the scholarship that the past century has produced on Cicero's rhetorical style. The earliest of these, Theodor Zielinski's ground-breaking work, *Das Clauselgesetz in Ciceros Reden* (Leipzig 1904), focused on prose rhythm in the speeches and is credited with being the first major contribution to the study of final clausulae in Cicero's speeches. Zielinski, particularly in his subsequent work, *Der Constructive Rhythmus in Ciceros Reden* (Leipzig 1914), shows how the rhythmical element in Cicero's speeches is an indispensable part of ancient *Kunstprosa*, that is, how the phrasing and rhythm of the sentence structure in Cicero's speeches, its various cadences, allowed the ancient speaker to emphasize and enhance its delivery.[1] Eduard Fraenkel, building in many ways on Zielinski's work, and in many ways departing from it, studied word grouping, or cola, in Cicero's speeches by employing especially non-rhythmical criteria, and produced a series of scholarly studies that are still widely used and consulted today. They are: *Kolon und Satz I* (Munich 1932), 197-213; *Kolon und Satz II* (Munich 1933), 319-354; *Noch einmal Kolon und Satz* (Munich 1965), Heft 2; and *Leseproben aus Reden Ciceros und Catos* (Rome 1968).[2] A few years after the last of Fraenkel's studies, Giovanni Cipriani produced *Struttura retorica di dieci orazioni ciceroniane* (Catania 1975), in which he combined elements from both Zielinski's and Fraenkel's criteria to arrive at an appraisal of Ciceronian rhetoric

---

1. Another excellent and comprehensive study of the metrics of Latin prose is that of Henri Bornecque (1907), a work that traces the tradition of Latin prose rhythm from the first century B.C. to the sixth century A.C.

2. For an evaluation of Fraenkel's contribution to the study of *Kunstprosa*, its debt to Zielinski's work, and its influence on succeeding scholarship, see E. Laughton's review, *JRS* 60 (1970), 188-194.

through a study of metrical clausulae and a catalogue of rhetorical figures in ten of Cicero's speeches. Cipriani's work is significant in that it also incorporates evaluation of the "Asianic" and "Atticistic" elements of Cicero's prose style into an overall evaluation of Cicero's rhetorical technique.[3] In his approach Cipriani was working within a tradition at least as old as that of Zielinski, which endeavored to demonstrate how and when Cicero abandoned the "Atticistic" rhetorical coloring of his youth for the "Asianic" style of his more mature works. Hauschield, in his dissertation, *De Sermonis Proprietatibus Quae in Philippicis Ciceronis Orationibus Inveniuntur* (Halle 1886), combed the Philippics for any and all evidence of Atticism, as Wilamowitz would in the *Caesariana* some years later in his article "Asianismus und Atticismus," *Hermes* 35 (1900), 1-52. Despite L. Laurand's objection that any argument for or against the notion of "three styles" over which the "Asianic" versus "Atticistic" debate raged was built on sand, scholars such as E. Castorina, *L'atticismo nell'evoluzione del pensiero di Cicerone* (Catania 1952), continued to try to prove that Cicero returned to the Atticism of his youth once he had learned to distinguish between "*due atticismi, uno buono ed uno cattivo*" (p. 229).[4] The debate is still far from laid to rest today.

It was not until the publication of his book *Luxuriance and Economy: Cicero and the Alien Style* (Berkeley 1971), that W. R. Johnson steered the course of scholarship devoted to Ciceronian rhetorical technique out of the morasses of the rhythmical studies of Zielinski and Fraenkel, and the strict categorizing approaches of Hauschield and Castorina, and into the currents of modern rhetorical scholarship based on stylistic analysis of sentence structure in the speeches. This is not to say that Johnson objected entirely to the arguments of his predecessors, only to their methodology. As Johnson observes: "Castorina sees very well that there is a major stylistic change

---

3. There are many good introductory studies that treat the influences of these trends on the history of the study of Roman rhetoric: among the most helpful are Eduard Norden (1918), in particular his section on Roman prose style (156-327); George Kennedy (1972), esp. 149-297; see also M. L. Clark (1953).

4. L. Laurand (1928-1931), 284-286. See also G. L. Hendrickson (1905), 249-290, who attempts to show that the middle style is in effect a combination of the "elaboration" of the grand style and the "pragmatic objectivity" of the plain, or low style.

in Cicero's last years, but he does little in the way of stylistic analysis of the speeches," (p. 1. n.1). In his approach to Cicero, Johnson in many ways opened the field for the study of Ciceronian rhetoric today by putting the findings of Zielinski, Fraenkel, and their successors into proper perspective, focusing on all aspects of sentence structure and composition. Johnson also seems to be the first of this new generation of Ciceronian scholars to pay particular attention to the *exordium*, its rhetorical structure and function, which is the focus of the study presented in the pages that follow.

Perhaps the most important rhetorical study to emerge since Johnson's work, and one whose influence shows on every page of the present work, is Harry Gotoff's stylistic commentary, *Cicero's Elegant Style: An Analysis of the Pro Archia* (University of Illinois, Urbana-Champaign 1979), a sentence-by-sentence rhetorical analysis of the *novum genus dicendi* Cicero admits to employing in the speech. Since Gotoff, many scholars have followed his lead by focusing their analytical skills on single speeches, or single rhetorical elements appearing in several speeches. Among these one may cite Jerzy Axer's *The Style and Composition of Cicero's Speech* Pro Q. Roscio Comoedo: *Origin and Function* (Warsaw 1980), a study that analyzes the style, rhythm, and comic touches of this puzzling speech in order to try to determine a precise date for its delivery and publication; and Holly Smith Montague's unpublished dissertation, *Style and Strategy in Forensic Speeches: Cicero's Caesarians in Perspective* (Harvard 1987), in which she analyzes the *Pro Ligario* both within its Caesarian context and in contrast to the earlier speeches of the orator's career. Most recently has appeared John Kirby's *The Rhetoric of Cicero's* Pro Cluentio (Amsterdam 1990), in which Kirby examines Cicero's longest and most puzzling speech in terms of Cicero's manipulation of Aristotle's tripartite division of a speech among the categories of *ethos*, *pathos*, and *logos*. While Kirby's book is very helpful to understanding a speech that has confounded scholars since antiquity, his organization and presentation often confuses the reader, for he does not proceed in a systematic way through the speech.

Rhetorical analyses of a more general nature are also numerous: C. Joachim Classen produced two important studies devoted to the elements of Cicero's rhetorical style. In the first, "Ciceros Kunst der Überredung," in *Éloquence et rhétorique chez Cicéron* (Fondation Hardt, Geneva 1981), Entretiens Tome 28, 149-184, with discussion, 185-192, Classen analyzes how Cicero's rhetorical style embraces and responds to a combination of legal right under law (*Rechtslage*), the political climate, and the social situation through an analysis of a broad range of Cicero's speeches. The article has many excellent insights, especially in the third part (177-184), where Classen examines certain key terms (*Wortgebrauch*) that Cicero uses in each speech to characterize and define these various conditions. In many ways the study is an introduction to his more detailed work that followed a few years later, *Recht, Rhetorik, Politik: Untersuchungen zu Ciceros Rhetorischen Strategie* (Darmstadt 1985), in which Classen examines six speeches individually along similar thematic lines: the *Pro Cluentio, Pro Murena, Pro Flacco, Post Reditum in Senatu, De Lege Manilia,* and *Contra Rullum.* James May's *Trials of Character* (Chapel Hill 1986) attempts a broad but penetrating and useful rhetorical outline of most of the major speeches of Cicero's life and career. Finally, Christopher P. Craig's recent book, *Form as Argument in Cicero's Speeches* (Atlanta: Scholars Press 1993), a study of "dilemma" in Cicero's speeches, offers one an excellent starting point for understanding the dynamics of Cicero's rhetorical art. But while all these studies touch upon, in more or less detail, the *exordium*, aside from Paul Prill's brief but excellent article, "Cicero in Theory and Practice: The Securing of Good Will in the *Exordia* of Five Forensic Speeches," *Rhetorica* 4 (1986), 93-109, the only studies devoted exclusively to the Ciceronian *exordium* that I have encountered are Margaret Fusco's unpublished dissertation, *From Auditor to Actor: Cicero's Dramatic Use of Personae in the Exordium* (University of Chicago 1988), and Claude Loutsch's recently published dissertation, *L'Exorde dans les discours de Cicéron,* (Brussels: *CollLatomus* 224, 1994).

In her study, Fusco analyzes the Ciceronian *exordium* strictly in terms of the dramatic role of the *personae* introduced in it. And while there are certainly numerous occasions on which Cicero uses *personae* to heighten the drama of the *exordium*, this is only a subordinate rhetorical device dependent upon a larger rhetorical structure which for the most part Fusco loses sight of in the tight focus of her study, but which I am convinced is essential to the understanding of the form and function of the Ciceronian *exordium*. Furthermore, in her evaluation of *persona* as a dramatic element Fusco fails to take into account the important relationship between *persona* and *causa* in the *exordium*, a relationship that was in Cicero's mind indissoluble.

Loutsch's work, on the other hand, seems at times too general. While Loutsch admirably undertakes to analyze some twenty-seven speeches, his study leaves one with only a broad, theoretical

understanding of what the *exordium* is and how it functions in relation
to the rest of the speech. To his credit, Loutsch focuses on the question
of how often Cicero adhered to, or departed from, the theories of his
rhetorical works, but his method is descriptive rather than analytical,
and in the end one is left with barely more than an inventory listing of
the contents of the *exordia* of the various speeches of Cicero that he
treats. Like Fusco, Loutsch also loses sight of, or fails to take into
account, the style of the *exordium*, how it is different from any other
part of the speech, and the accretive progression of the important
rhetorical dynamics of *persona* and *causa* that Cicero manipulates with
sometimes wicked effect within that progression.

Persona et Causa: Cicero's Ratio Exordiendi

In the *Brutus* (290) Cicero describes the scene that should greet the
orator when he rises to speak before the court in a public *iudicium*:

> Volo hoc oratori contingat, ut cum auditum sit eum esse dicturum, locus
> in subselliis occupetur, compleatur tribunal, gratiosi scribae sint in dando
> et cedendo loco, corona multiplex, iudex erectus; cum surgat is qui
> dicturus sit, significetur a corona silentium, deinde crebrae assensiones,
> multae admirationes; risus cum velit, cum velit fletus: ut qui haec procul
> videat, etiam si quid agatur nesciat, at placere tamen et in scaena esse
> Roscium intellegat.

In this passage Cicero defines the potential of the orator in terms of
his *persona*, likening the practiced orator's ability to command the
attention of his audience to that of an accomplished actor in a theatrical
performance — and no less an actor than Cicero's contemporary, the
great comic actor Roscius. Because from the moment he rose to speak
the orator had to focus the attention of his audience on himself and the
client he represented, the *exordium*, or opening statement of an oration,
was in Cicero's view probably the most important part of the speech, for
it was in the *exordium* that he captured and focused the attention of the
audience on what he felt was the central issue, or *causa*, of the trial.

Throughout his career Cicero always preferred to speak for the defense and almost always, if not always, spoke last, after all the other *patroni* had presented their arguments on behalf of the client whom they were collectively representing.[5] This freed Cicero from having to instruct the jury and educate them in terms of many of the technical and legal aspects of the case. In another passage in the *Brutus* (207-209) Cicero actually condemns the custom of his day of employing multiple pleaders for a case, but regardless of how he felt about speaking in coordination with other orators on behalf of a single client, Cicero does seem to have always preferred to speak last. His speeches, therefore, are more often than not the concluding statement and summing up of the combined efforts of the *patroni* — the dessert course, as it were, of the meal — and for this reason alone were probably much welcomed by his audience. Cicero could take advantage of his speaking time to rouse the emotions of his audience and elicit a controlled response, while at the same time entertaining them to a certain degree.

To understand what Cicero is about in his speeches we have to understand the difference between what the first speech in a series was like and what the last speech was like, the one that Cicero usually delivered. While the *Pro Cluentio* is probably our only example of how Cicero handled a judicial case as a single *patronus*, it is not a good example of what the first speech in a series would typically have been like because of the long history of the case and the numerous *praeiudicia* held before the actual trial of Cluentius.[6] Therefore, a good example of the difference between what must have been the first speech in a series and the last — that is, one designed to examine and account for evidence and instruct the jury, and one designed to rouse the emotions of people already familiar with certain details — is to be found in the First and Second Catilinarian orations. In the First Catilinarian, delivered to the senate in the Temple of Jupiter Stator, Cicero had to reveal and examine important and precise information about the Catilinarian conspiracy to his audience, the disclosure of which would compel the senate to declare Catiline *hostis* and drive him

---

5. As he states in the opening sentence of the *exordium* of the *Divinatio in Caecilium: Si quis vestrum, iudices, aut eorum qui adsunt forte miratur me, qui tot annos in causis iudiciisque publicis ita sim versatus, ut defenderim multos, laeserim neminem, subito nunc mutata voluntate ad accusandum descendere...*

6. In the *Pro Cluentio* (199), Cicero proudly proclaims: [*ego*] *qui totam hanc causam vetere instituto solus peroravi.*

and his consprators from the city — what Cicero had wanted. In the Second Catilinarian, delivered to the people on the next day, Cicero was able to give free rein to emotional and entertaining flights of rhetoric, in which we can see him using many of the same elements as in the First Catilinarian, but in a more richly emotionally charged manner.[7] This is not to say that the Second Catilinarian is more impassioned than the First, but rather that the rhetorical strategies Cicero uses differ drastically between the two, and the reason for this is the audience. As the passage from the *Brutus* (290) shows, because Cicero understood the importance of the impact of the orator's first impression on his audience, the *exordium* of a speech was crucial, for this was the moment when the orator had to capture the attention of his audience and secure their *benevolentia*. Because it is in the *exordium* that Cicero must also introduce the principal individuals (*personae*) involved, as well as the central issues (*causae*) of his case, and, if he is defending (as he preferred to do), to counter and correct any negative impression of his client left on his hearers by the prosecution's speeches, the rhetorical strategy he adopts in his handling of the elements of the *exordium* is also crucial to the groundwork of his speech.

Cicero's entire life was devoted to the study and practice of rhetoric. Suetonius (*Rhet.* 1) tells us that he continued to declaim in both Latin and Greek up until the time of his praetorship in 66 B.C., and thereafter in Latin until he was quite old.[8] Through the course of his life Cicero wrote and published no fewer than seven treatises on the relationship of rhetorical theory and oratory. These are: *De Inventione* (c. 91 B.C.), *De Oratore* (c. 55 B.C.), *Brutus, Orator,* and *De Optimo Genere Oratorum* (c. 46 B.C.), *Partitiones Oratoriae* (of uncertain date, but probably of this same period, certainly no earlier than 50 B.C.), and the *Topica* (c. 44 B.C.). Three of these, the *De Inventione*, *De Oratore*, and *Partitiones Oratoriae*, are of particular importance to the study of the Ciceronian *exordium*, for in each work Cicero discusses

---

7. Another parallel might be the orations *Post Reditum in Senatu* and *Ad Populum* or the Third and Fourth Philippics.

8. According to Cicero (*Brut.* 320) it was Hortensius' failure to keep up this practice that accounted for the decline of his rival's oratory. For the practice of declamation, see S. F. Bonner (1949), esp. 1-50. For examples of Roman declamation see Quintilian, *Declamationes Minores*, Shackleton Bailey ed., (1989).

his system of rhetoric based on the main divisions of oratory, and in each he pays specific attention to the *exordium* as one of the most important parts of a speech. In addition to Cicero's rhetorical works, we also have the *Rhetorica ad Herennium*, a textbook of rhetorical theory of unknown authorship but more or less contemporary with the *De Inventione* and covering the same material in nearly the same terms;[9] and Quintilian's *Institutiones Oratoriae* (c. A.D. 96), which contains a complete description of the history of rhetoric and an evaluation of its practitioners down to his own time, with a special emphasis on Cicero's technique in his speeches.[10] Although often in his rhetorical works Cicero admits his debt to the Aristotelian system of rhetoric for his own rhetorical theory (cf. *Inv. Rhet.* 1.9), and in his treatment of *persona* he is clearly following Aristotle's definition of *ethos* and its importance in rhetoric, the present study is not intended to be a comparison of Ciceronian and Aristotelian rhetorical theory.[11] For while Cicero's theories on rhetoric can and have been analyzed and evaluated in an Aristotelian context, they also need to be evaluated on their own merits and in the light of how they contribute to the making of Cicero's unique style of oratory. Cicero himself said of the *De Oratore* that it owed much to the precepts of both Aristotle and Isocrates (*Fam.* 1.9.23), but we can also see the sources for many of Cicero's ideas in the New Academy.[12] And while Cicero himself acknowledged his debt to his Academic training (*Or.* 12), it would be presumptuous to assume that Cicero's work on rhetoric was based on any one source. Rather, as Clark comments, it was a synthesis all his own: "And even if Cicero owed not a little to the contemporary Academy, he also derived much

---

9. For the problematic dating of the *Rhetorica ad Herennium* see L. C. Winkel (1979), 327-332, and for further discussion and bibliography see Kennedy (1972), 126-138.

10. A comprehensive treatment of Quintilian, his life and works, is given by Kennedy (1969), esp. chapter 1. For those interested in Cicero's effect on the study of rhetoric in the centuries after Quintilian, there is Halm (1863).

11. For the Aristotelian elements in the *De Oratore* cf. F. Solmsen (1938), 390-404; (1941), 35-50, 169-190. For Isocratean influences on Cicero see H. Hubbell (1913).

12. See L. C. Montefusco (1988); E. Schuetrumpf (1988), 237-258; see also W. Kroll (1903A), 552-597; (1903B), 681-689.

from his reading in the whole field of rhetorical study. The rhetoric of the schools, the theories of the philosophers, Roman traditions and Cicero's own experience are combined in a synthesis which has sufficient individual quality to allow us to recognize its author as an independent thinker on such matters. And even if none of the ideas or precepts in the *De Oratore* is new — and it was difficult to be original in such a well-worked field — the choice and combination remain Cicero's, as do the force and conviction and the elegance and charm with which they are presented."[13]

Following Aristotle (*Rhet.* 1.3.1-3) Cicero divides oratory into three classes: *genus demonstrativum, genus deliberativum,* and *genus iudiciale* (*Inv. Rhet.* 1.7, cf. *Rhet. ad Her.* 1.2).[14] The first type, epideictic, including panegyric (*exornatio,* as Cicero calls it in the *Part. Or.* 10), is concerned with the praise or censure of an individual; the second, deliberative, is involved with political debate; the third, judicial or forensic, has to do with criminal prosecution and defense, and the conduct of civil suits. This study will focus on analysis of the *exordium* in this last type of speech, the forensic, because it was the most challenging to the orator in that it strove to establish facts or engender an opinion in an audience that was often hostile and often sympathetic to a clearly identifiable opposition.[15] This is also most true of the forensic mode when the orator is speaking for the defense, the position Cicero chose to take most often in his career. While the Second Philippic is not a judicial but an epideictic speech, it is included in this study as a sort of epilogue or conclusion because it allows us to see how Cicero uses many of the elements and rhetorical strategies of his judicial speeches in the *exordia* of other types of speeches.

The strategy of the orator (*officia* or *vis oratoris*), also called the *partitiones* (*Part. Or.* 3), is divided by Cicero into five parts: *inventio, dispositio, elocutio, memoria,* and *pronuntiatio* (*Inv. Rhet.* 1.9; *Rhet ad Her.* 1.3). *Inventio* is defined by Cicero as the marshalling of imagination, conjuring up arguments valid or probable that will make a case appear more plausible; *dispositio* is the arrangement or distribution

---

13. M. L. Clark (1953), 51.

14. For a study of the Aristotelian influence on Cicero's rhetorical theory see A. Michel (1982), 104-147.

15. For Aristotle's comments on this aspect of the forensic speech, see S. Deligiorgis (1971), 311-318.

of the arguments, or the "framework" of the speech; *elocutio* is the presentation, which Cicero says should be *ad inventionem accommodata* (*Inv. Rhet.* 1.9; cf. *Rhet. ad Her.* 1.3). The final two, *memoria* and *pronuntiatio*, mental grasp of matter and words, and control of voice and body, were considered equally important by Cicero but in his opinion stood apart from the first three, being concerns more of the training of the orator than the art of oratory itself (*De Or.* 1.145).[16]

According to Cicero, once the orator established the type of speech his case demanded he then applied the theories of the *officia orationis* to construct the various parts of a speech. Cicero defines these as: 1) the *exordium* or opening statement; 2) the *narratio* or statement of facts; 3) the *divisio* or *partitio*, the particular points which the orator wishes to contest and what he in turn hopes to prove; 4) the *confirmatio*, or examination of the pros and cons raised in the *partitio*, that is the case itself; and 5) the *peroratio* or conclusion. This is the five part division given in the *De Inventione* (1.19) and *Rhetorica ad Herennium* (1.4), but elsewhere Cicero varies the number of parts, as does Quintilian.[17] Because the *exordium* was the first and in the eyes of many, including Cicero, the most important part of the speech, theory dictated that the nature of the case (*genus causae*) should dictate the nature of the *exordium*. The extent to which Cicero followed his own advice here is debatable, but for the purposes of his textbooks he identifies five *genera causae: honestum, admirabile, humile, anceps, obscurum,* and two styles of *exordia* to suit them: *principium* and *insinuatio* (*Inv. Rhet.* 1.20).[18]

Igitur exordium in duas partes dividitur, principium et insinuationem. Principium est oratio perspicue et   protinus perficiens auditorem

---

16. Quintilian (1.22) discusses *memoria* and *pronuntiatio* under the category of *eloquentia*, but at 3.4 includes them in his list of the five parts of oratory.

17. The number often varied, cf. *De Or.* 2.79. In *Part. Or.* 4, 27 Cicero lists four: *principium* or *exordium, narratio, confirmatio,* and *peroratio* (cf. *Top.* 97); Quintilian (3.9.1-3) lists five, for he regards *partitio* as contained in the third part, which he calls *probatio.*

18. For a brief study see F. Solmsen (1938), 542-556; and P. Prill (1968), 93-109.

benivolum aut docilem aut attentum. Insinuatio est oratio quadam dissimulatione et circumitione obscure subiens auditoris animum.

The *principium*, or direct approach, is to be used only when the orator feels confident that his case can be presented clearly and in a straightforward manner (*perspicue et protinus*), that it will be received favorably by his audience, and that he is arguing from a position of strength; *insinuatio*, the indirect approach, is to be used in those cases where the orator feels that, because the issues of his case cannot be explained clearly (*obscure*), he is at some disadvantage with his audience and therefore must talk around things or sidestep issues. But if Cicero felt the need to make such distinctions between two main types of *exordia* in his rhetorical writings, this distinction becomes blurred in practice, as every speech would have to be tailored to the particular individuals (*personae*) and specific circumstances (*causae*) of the case, and therefore there would be much overlapping between *principium* and *insinuatio*. In her dissertation Fusco attempts to make clear distinctions between the occasions when Cicero uses *insinuatio* and when he uses *principium* in the *exordium*, following the conclusions of Christes that Cicero uses *insinuatio* more often than *principium*.[19] But to focus on such distinctions invites too strongly a conclusion that is misleading, for often, if not always, Cicero uses both the direct (*principium*) and indirect (*insinuatio*) approach within the same *exordium*. In fact, one could say that the ability to move easily between the two types of *exordia* was one of Cicero's particular rhetorical strengths and a trademark of his style.

Let us now turn to the *exordium* as Cicero's defines it in his rhetorical works, starting with his earliest treatise, the *De Inventione* (1.20):

Exordium est oratio animum auditoris idonee comparans ad reliquam dictionem; quod eveniet si eum benivolum, attentum, docilem confecerit.

Cicero goes on (1.22) to identify the strategy for securing the *benevolentia* of his audience:

Benevolentia quattuor ex locis comparatur: ab nostra   persona, ab adversariorum persona, ab iudicum persona, a causa.

---

19. J. Christes (1978), 556-573.

To this we can compare the nearly identical definition in the *Rhetorica ad Herennium* (1.8):

> Benivolos auditores facere quattuor modis possumus: ab nostra, ab adversariorum nostrorum, ab auditorum persona, et ab rebus ipsis.

According to Cicero and the author of the *Rhetorica ad Herennium*, the primary means of securing *benevolentia* in the *exordium* was either through the portrayal of character (*quattuor personae*), or through examination of the circumstances or issues peculiar to the case itself (*causa*). What we should focus on in an analysis of Cicero's rhetorical strategy in the *exordium*, therefore, is how in each case Cicero constructs the *exordium* to suit the specific needs of his client, the issues of the *causa*, including such external factors as the political atmosphere, and the personality and motivations of the opposition as well as the identity and character of the *iudices* or, where there is a single *arbitrator*, the *iudex*. When we compare Cicero's description of the *exordium* in the *De Inventione* to the following passage from the *De Oratore* (2.182), we see that his approach to the *exordium* remained for the most part consistent over time:

> Valet igitur multum ad vincendum probari mores et instituta et facta et vitam eorum, qui agent causas, et eorum, pro quibus, et item improbari adversariorum, animosque eorum, apud quos agetur, conciliari quam maxime ad benevolentiam, cum erga oratorem tum erga illum pro quo dicet orator.

In the above passage Cicero again stresses the use of character portrayal to secure the *benevolentia* of the *iudices*, and then goes on to say that *persona*, if handled properly, is often more effective than the *causa* itself (*De Or.* 2.183):

> Horum igitur exprimere mores oratione, iustos, integros, religiosos, timidos, perferentes iniuriam, mirum quiddam valeat; et hoc vel in principiis vel in re narranda vel in peroranda tantam habet vim, si est suaviter et cum sensu tractatum, ut saepe plus quam causa valeat.

These two passages show that even after acquiring the experience of almost three decades of public speaking, Cicero still defined the strategy of the *exordium* in the same terms as he did as an *adulescens* in the *De Inventione*, emphasizing that character portrayal (*personae*) was at least as important as, and often more important than, the issues (*causa*) of the case itself. And at a later point in the *De Oratore* (2.318-321) Cicero stresses the importance of the relationship between *persona* and *causa* in the *exordium*:

> [Principia] autem in dicendo non extrinsecus alicunde quaerenda sed ex ipsis visceribus causae sumenda sunt; sed cum erit utendum principio, quod plerumque erit, aut ex reo aut ex adversario aut ex re aut ex eis apud quos agetur sententias duci licebit.

And in the *Partitiones Oratoriae* (28), written years after the *De Oratore*, Cicero continued to stress the importance of the relationship between these same two elements of the *exordium*:

> Faciam, et a principiis primum ordiar, quae quidem ducuntur aut ex personis aut ex rebus ipsis; sumuntur autem trium rerum gratia: ut amice, ut intellegenter, ut attente audiamur. Quorum primus locus est personis nostris, disceptatorum, adversariorum, e quibus initia benevolentiae conciliandae comparantur aut meritis nostris efferendis aut dignitate aut aliquo genere virtutis, et maxime liberalitatis, officii, iustitiae, fidei, contrariisque rebus in adversarios conferendis, et cum eis qui disceptant aliqua coniunctionis aut causa aut spe significanda: et si in nos aliquod odium offensiove collocata sit, tollenda ea minuendave aut diluendo aut extenuando aut compensando aut deprecando.

Cicero stresses three primary aims of the *exordium* (*trium rerum gratia*): that the orator's speech may be received in a friendly way (*ut amice*), that his audience understand what he is saying (*ut intellegenter*), and that he hold their attention (*ut attente audiamur*).[20] Cicero sums this aim up with one word, *benevolentia*, and says that this can be achieved through a manipulation of *persona* and *causa* (*ex rebus ipsis*). Quintilian, following Cicero, also recognized the important interdependence between *persona* and *causa*:

> Benivolentiam aut a personis duci aut a causis accepimus. Sed personarum non est, ut plerique crediderunt, triplex ratio, ex litigatore et adversario et iudice. Nam exordium duci non numquam etiam ab actore causae solet (4.1.6).

---

20. As Cicero concludes the *exordium* of the *Pro Cluentio* (8): *quaeso ut me, iudices, sicut facere instituistis, benigne attenteque audiatis.*

Quintilian argues that *benevolentia* is won through a combination of *persona* and *causa*, and just as Cicero he acknowledges that the *exordium* must contain characterizations of all the parties involved in the case. The *triplex ratio* of tradition consists of: [*personae*] *ex litigatore*, *ex adversario*, and *ex iudice*; Quintilian then adds as especially important the *persona* of the orator (*ab actore causae*). Quintilian is not adding this as an afterthought, as the discussion that follows makes clear the importance of the ethos of the orator himself and its place of importance especially in the *exordium* (4.1.6-11). Quintilian, like Cicero, recognized the importance of the personality of the orator in what Aristotle called the "ethical" appeal of the art of persuasion, and in the *exordia* of Cicero's speeches we can observe how Cicero establishes his own *persona* in various ways depending upon whom he is representing, the nature of the opposition, and the overall conditions of the *causa*. And the way Cicero moves through the various developments of the *persona* and *causa*, the two most important and inextricable elements of the *exordium*, is at the heart of what we may call for the purposes of this study Cicero's "accretive" style.

Cicero's Accretive Style

As we have seen, Cicero defines the *exordium* as a series of "arguments" (*loci*) or "appeals" (*preces, obsecrationes*) through which the orator tries to prejudice the *iudices* for and against the various individuals involved in the case by delineation of their character (*persona*) and through a manipulation of the particular issues (*causae*) of the case. But because the *exordium* had to be short in proportion to the rest of the speech, to the point, and generally without intrusive rhetorical ornamentation (*De Or.* 2.318, 320; cf. *Inv. Rhet.* 1.18), there was little opportunity for formal transition from one tactical position or argument to the next. For this reason Cicero believed that movement within the *exordium* had to be governed by the most important elements of the *exordium*:

> Haec autem in dicendo non extrinsecus alicunde quaerenda sed ex ipsis visceribus causae sumenda sunt...ita momenti aliquid afferent, cum erunt

paene ex intima defensione deprompta et apparebit ea non modo non esse
communia nec in alias causas posse transferri sed penitus ex ea causa quae
tum agatur effloruisse. (*De Or.* 2.318-319)

Cicero tells us that the movement, or gathering force (*momentum*), of
the *exordium* depended upon the most fundamental elements, which
Cicero maintains were the portrayal of *persona* and *causa*. Analysis of
Cicero's technique in the *exordia* of the speeches that follow shows that
all share the common stylistic characteristic that I call the "accretive
style," and no other part of the speech bears this trademark as much as
the *exordium* does. It is here that we can most readily observe how
Cicero establishes conflict in the opening sentence or sentences by
introducing certain key themes, or by characterizing key individuals,
through "concept words" or phrases, which he then carries forward and
develops into a thematic struggle between the defense and the
prosecution. The accretive style of the *exordium* keeps the *momentum*
of the arguments moving in a swift and meaningful progression that
almost always culminates with the appeal *a iudicum persona*, where
Cicero reduces the elements of *causa et persona* to a juxtaposition of
the "concept words" which he has introduced and developed throughout
the *exordium*; the result of this is generally a depersonalization of the
issues of the case that transforms the oration from simply the defense
(or prosecution) of a certain individual to an elevated disquisition of
universal appeal. An excellent example of how Cicero uses "concept
words" to achieve polarity occurs in the *peroratio* of the Second
Catilinarian, where he characterizes the individuals involved on both
sides of the conspiracy:

> Ex hac enim parte pudor pugnat, illinc petulantia; hinc pudicitia, illinc
> stuprum; hinc fides, illinc fraudatio; hinc pietas, illinc scelus; hinc
> constantia, illinc furor; hinc honestas, illinc turpitudo; hinc continentia,
> illinc libido; hinc denique aequitas, temperantia, fortitudo, prudentia,
> virtutes omnes certant cum iniquitate, luxuria, ignavia, temeritate, cum
> vitiis omnibus; postremo copia cum egestate, bona ratio cum perdita,
> mens sana cum amentia, bona denique spes cum omnium rerum
> desperatione confligit. (*Cat.* 2.25)

In this passage we can see how Cicero uses "concept words" to
characterize the conflict between Cicero's supporters (*hinc*) and the
supporters of Catiline (*illinc*): the struggle becomes thematic as Cicero
contrasts *pudor* with *petulantia*, *pudicitia* with *stuprum*, *fides* with
fraudatio, *pietas* with *scelus*, *constantia* with *furor*, *honestas* with

turpitudo, continentia with *libido, aequitas* with *iniquitas, temperantia* with *luxuria, fortitudo* with *ignavia,* and *prudentia* with *temeritas.* In short, *virtutes omnes certant...cum vitiis omnibus.* Through this very select and normative vocabulary Cicero isolates his opposition by characterizing it in terms that are the antithesis of those he uses of his own side. In a similar fashion Cicero uses loaded terms to establish conflict and contrast in the *exordia* of the speeches that follow, where we will see many of these same terms recur with frequency. In the *exordium,* as opposed to the *peroratio,* however, Cicero is introducing these terms for the first time and therefore incorporates them into the rhetorical fabric of his opening statement slowly, accretively. By exploiting such terms as are appropriate to describe or set the tone of the social or political situation of the trial, Cicero builds a rhetorical foundation from which he can move through the various arguments or *loci* of the *exordium.* Cicero achieves this end through the accretive style, by introducing a term and then carrying it forward and combining it with something new, all framed within a kind of antithetical rhetorical structure dependent upon the relationship between *persona* and *causa.* In this way, as we shall see, Cicero uses the vocabulary of the *causa* to "characterize" the central *personae* and portray them as either its victims or champions.

The Text of the Speeches

Although the dramatic flourishes and gestures that Cicero must have used when speaking in public are lost to us, as are also the pace and intonation of his delivery, fortunately the rhetorical means by which he manipulated his audience survives in the published form of the speeches as we have them. But whenever one attempts to analyze Cicero's oratory as it has come down to us, the question of the relationship between the "published" version that we read today and the "delivered" version that Cicero gave in the forum must be addressed.[21] Ancient testimony on this point offers little illumination. Cicero implies (*Brut.* 91; *Tusc.* 4.55) that he published his speeches much as he

---

21. See L. Laurand's introduction (1928-1931), 1-17.

delivered them, but according to Asconius (*In Corn.* 54, Stangl p. 50) Cicero turned the *Pro Cornelio* into two published speeches; although Nepos, quoted by Jerome (*Ep.* 72), observes that the published work was much the same length as the original. Pliny the younger, however, in a letter to Tacitus (1.20), addresses the question of the relationship between the delivered and published versions of Cicero's speeches, and from what he says we get the impression that the speech Cicero delivered and the speech Cicero published often varied greatly.[22] And while any attempt to answer this question would cause this study to stray far afield from its intended parameters, I have tried to address it on a case-by-case basis whenever doing so will help us appreciate and understand better what Cicero is accomplishing, or striving to accomplish, in the *exordium* and why.[23] But the focus of the analysis remains a purely literary one with the emphasis on vocabulary and sentence structure and the way Cicero manipulates these elements to convey theme and contrast in order to evoke a particular response from the audience. We need not concern ourselves with the question of how accurately the published speeches represent the delivered speeches in order to evaluate the rhetoric of the Ciceronian *exordium*, for as Quintilian observed (12.10.51), the relationship between the written and spoken word was a close one, the published speech being simply a *monumentum actionis habitae*:

> Mihi unum atque idem videtur bene dicere ac bene scribere, neque aliud esse oratio scripta quam monumentum actionis habitae.

Furthermore, the fact that Cicero continued to write books on rhetoric while he was delivering speeches in the forum and publishing versions of them for a reading audience, and doubtless with an eye to their being used in the schools, indicates that Cicero must have felt his own oratory, especially in its published form, illustrated the precepts of his textbooks regardless of how much the speech he published varied from the speech he had delivered. Therefore the question of how closely the

---

22. For a fuller discussion of the evidence of Pliny and other evidence see A. N. Sherwin-White (1966), 133 n.8.

23. J. Humbert (1925), 12, distinguishes between spoken and written speech, but argues that such distinction is weakened by Cicero's blending of the two styles, making his written works more "oral" and his spoken ones more "literary."

speeches as we have them might have corresponded to the delivered version becomes secondary to this analysis. The reasons that would have led to publishing, or deliberately not publishing a speech, seem to indicate that a published version of a speech had greater impact in Rome than the original delivery, even of a highly successful speech.[24] In his later rhetorical works Cicero often casually cites examples from his own published speeches to support or illustrate his statements, as though these would be familiar to his reader. Quintilian, writing over a century later, follows this same practice, indicating that such references must have been intended for Cicero's readership, for they correspond very closely to the speeches as they survive today. That we possess these orations in the exact form in which they were delivered is certainly not the case; that we possess them in the form in which Cicero had intended that they be read is much more probable and therefore we should feel secure to proceed to analyze them as the rhetorical models that their author intended them to be.

Textual note: The excerpts from Cicero's speeches quoted in the text are from A. C. Clark's Oxford edition (1901-1909) unless otherwise indicated. For Cicero's rhetorical works I have relied upon the Oxford edition of A. S. Wilkins (1901-1902) except for the *De Inventione*, where the text is the Teubner edition of G. Friedrich (Leipzig 1884). For Cicero's correspondence I have used the text of D. R. Shackleton Bailey (Cambridge 1965-1970). For Quintilian's *Institutio Oratoria* I have used the text of M. Winterbottom (Oxford 1970). The text of the *Rhetorica ad Herennium* is that of H. Caplan's excellent Loeb edition (Harvard 1964). Punctuation and capitalization are my own.

---

24. For a discussion of the evidence for and against the publication of speeches see J. W. Crawford (1984), 14-16, 243 n.8.

CHAPTER ONE

Pro Quinctio

Introduction

The *Pro Quinctio* is Cicero's earliest extant speech, delivered in 81 B.C., in the consulship of M. Tullius Decula and Cn. Dolabella (Cicero, *Leg. Agr.* 2.35; A. Gellius, *NA* 15.28.3). This date is also supported by what Cicero says in the speech: Publius Quinctius left Rome in the year in which L. Cornelius Scipio and C. Iunius Norbanus held the consulship (*Quinct.* 24), i.e. 83 B.C., and he returned to Rome before the Ides of September of that year (*Quinct.* 29). But it would be another eighteen months before Sextus Naevius brought him before the praetor to face the charges against him (*Quinct.* 30), i.e. in the spring of 81 B.C. [1]

Cicero was not the first *patronus* to represent Quinctius in his dispute with Naevius. By the time Cicero took charge of the case it had already undergone a number of preliminary hearings, or *praeiudicia* (*Quinct.* 3), in which Quinctius had been represented by M. Iunius

---

1. See *RE* under Cornelius (Münzer, 4.1., 1900, no. 338), and Norbanus (Münzer, 17.1, 1937, no. 5).

Brutus. Cicero's defense of Quinctius seems to be another in this series of *praeiudicia,* for there is no jury present, only the *iudex* C. Aquilius Gallus, acting as arbiter, and his *consilium.*[2] The decision of a *praeiudicium* established the basis (*res*) for all subsequent litigation, so it was not an insignificant proceeding, nor does Cicero seem to treat it as such.[3] In the case of the dispute between Quinctius and Naevius, the *praeiudicium* was necessary in order to sort out the question of the rightful ownership of the property in Gallia Narbonensis that Quinctius inherited from the estate of his brother after his death, which was later seized by Naevius in the course of the legal battle that ensued.

The dispute between Quinctius and Naevius is difficult to understand because Cicero tells us so few details about the case. This may be because he was placed in the uncomfortable position of speaking first and therefore had yet to hear the case of the opposition, which was represented by Hortensius, Cicero's senior by some ten years and at that time the leading orator in Rome (*Brut.* 229). Because this hearing was a *praeiudicium,* it seems that both Cicero and Hortensius spoke alone, although of this we cannot be certain. Nowhere in the speech does Cicero mention anyone else as a colleague on behalf of Quinctius, nor does he mention anyone besides Hortensius as counsel for Naevius. Although at one point Cicero does mention the fact that L. Marcius Philippus, an accomplished orator and a contemporary of Crassus and Antonius, was present at the trial, it becomes clear that he was present only as an *advocatus* (*Quinct.* 72, 77, 80).

When Quinctius' brother died he left Quinctius his share of some property in Gaul that he owned in partnership with Naevius. Along with the property, however, Quinctius also inherited his brother's debts, some of which were owed to Naevius, others to certain individuals in Rome (*Quinct.* 23, 43). In order to resolve the debts Quinctius announced that he intended to sell his brother's share of the property in Gaul, a proposition that did not appeal to Naevius, who claimed it was not a good time to sell (*Quinct.* 16). Instead, Naevius offered to loan Quinctius the money to pay off his brother's debts. Relying on Naevius'

---

2. Aquilius would later go on to be praetor with Cicero in 66 (*Clu.* 147), but he did not go on to stand for the consulship because of his health and the demands made upon him as a jurisconsult (*Att.* 1.1.1).

3. For the *praeiudicium* cf. *Inv. Rhet.* 2.60. The structure of the jury who heard *praeiudicia* seems to have varied; cf. *Clu.* 9: *praeiudicia esse facta ab ipsis iudicibus a quibus condemnatus est.* See also Quintilian 5.2.1.

word Quinctius had already informed his creditors in Rome that he intended to pay off his brother's debts when suddenly Naevius reneged on the offer, refusing to pay Quinctius a single sestertius until they had come to some arrangement about the jointly-owned property in Gaul. Having already committed himself to his brother's creditors Quinctius was left with no other alternative than to proceed with his plans to auction his share of the property in Gaul (*Quinct*. 26). Realizing that Naevius might take offense at his actions, Quinctius attempted to placate him through the intervention of intermediaries, M. Trebellius representing Naevius and Sex. Alfenus representing Quinctius. When still no compromise could be reached, the case went to court. In the meantime Naevius took it upon himself to put up for auction whatever portion of the property in Gaul Quinctius owned in order to satisfy what he felt was owed him.

A date for a hearing was set, and a *vadimonium* was put up by each side. Quinctius, however, continued to postpone the day they were to appear before the praetor, Cn. Dolabella,[4] at which time Naevius left Rome for Gaul (*Quinct*. 22-42). Upon returning to Rome Naevius offered to go to court with Quinctius, but Quinctius again refused and himself left Rome for Gaul. Quinctius' *vadimonium* was still in force, however, and Naevius appeared before Dolabella and won permission to take possession of Quinctius' property by default (*missio in possessionem*). As Naevius proceeded to enforce the *missio* and take possession of Quinctius' property in Rome, he was met with opposition by Sex. Alfenus, Quinctius' agent. When Quinctius returned to Rome and tried to take Naevius to court, Naevius demanded that if Quinctius wanted to go to court he should put up a security (*sponsio*), since his property had already been seized and therefore Quinctius was legally *infamis*. This meant that if his property had been held for thirty days in accordance with the praetor's edict, then Quinctius would be allowed to defend himself against the claim Naevius was making only if he furnished additional security.[5] Quinctius argued that his property had been seized illegally and therefore he should not have to furnish additional security. Dolabella disagreed, but consented to hear the case.

---

4. The praetor urbanus of 81, see *RE* under Cornelius (Münzer, 4.1, 1900, no. 135).

5. See A. H. Greenidge (1894); J. M. Kelly (1966), 24-26; W. W. Buckland (1963), 9-15; F. Schulz (1951), 72-79.

Such a compromise, however, did not satisfy Quinctius, and he continued to try to delay the proceedings, at which time Quinctius' counsel, M. Iunius Brutus, found a pretext to drop the case (*Quinct.* 3), and Cicero took it up. The point contested was whether Naevius had actually taken possession of Quinctius' property legally. This placed Cicero more or less in the position of *accusator*, and therefore he had to speak first. Although Quinctius' property was already in Naevius' hands, Cicero contends that it had been seized by him illegally.[6]

Commentary

In the opening sentence of the *Pro Quinctio* Cicero identifies the conflict between his side and the opposition and establishes the main themes of his defense:

1.1-3: Quae res in civitate duae plurimum possunt, eae contra nos ambae faciunt in hoc tempore, summa gratia et eloquentia; quarum alteram, C. Aquili, vereor, alteram metuo.

Cicero begins by naming immediately what he feels to be the main obstacles confronting himself and his client: *summa gratia et eloquentia*.[7] The bipartite construction of the opening sentence is odd, for it is an example of the *vitiosa expositio*, a strategy the author of the *Rhetorica ad Herennium* (2.34) warns against using, particularly in the *exordium*:

Item vitiosa expositio est quae constat ex falsa enumeratione, si aut cum plura sunt pauciora dicamus, hoc modo: "Duae res sunt, iudices, quae omnes ad maleficium impellant: luxuries et avaritia." "Quid amor?" inquiet quispiam, "quid ambitio? quid religio? quid metus mortis? quid

---

6. *Bona possessa non esse;* see W. Stroh (1975), 101-103.

7. Cf. Cicero's use of *invidia* in the *exordium* of the *Pro Cluentio* (1.1): *Animum adverti, iudices, omnem accusatoris orationem in duas divisam esse partis, quarum altera mihi niti et magno opere confidere videbatur invidia....*

imperii cupiditas? quid denique alia permulta?" Item falsa enumeratio est
cum pauciora sunt et plura dicimus, hoc modo: "Tres sunt quae omnes
homines sollicitent: metus, cupiditas, aegritudo." Satis enim fuerat dixisse
metum, cupiditatem, quoniam aegritudinem cum utraque re coniunctam
esse necesse est.

According to Quintilian (4.1.11), on the other hand, praise of these very
qualities in your opponent was an advisable strategy to pursue in the
exordium:

Etiam partis adversae patronus dabit exordio materiam, interim cum
honore, si eloquentiam eius et gratiam nos timere fingendo, ut ea suspecta
sint iudici, fecerimus...

It is curious that Quintilian in this passage does not cite as an example
the *Pro Quinctio*, since all the elements, including respect (*honos*),
which Cicero feels, or professes he feels, for Hortensius' *eloquentia*,
and his fear of it, are brought out in the very first sentences of the
exordium.   That Cicero seems to be violating the rule of the *ad
Herennium* while acting in accordance with Quintilian's strategy shows
that the procedure Cicero followed was dictated by the practicalities of
the case.   He is purposely introducing the two terms, *gratia* and
eloquentia, separately, taking what Quintilian maintains was a stock
maneuver to be used against the *partis adversae patronus*, and using it
against both the *patronus* and his client. While this construction is used
by Cicero elsewhere in different speeches, it occurs only in the
exordium of this speech.[8]   Through this innovation he draws his
audience in and holds their attention as he begins to define these terms
and assign or identify them in the next passage. Furthermore, Cicero
creates suspense through the two synonyms *vereor* and *metuo* ("I fear"
and "I dread"), as the audience must have wanted to know what the
cause of this fear was.

    Eloquentia and *gratia* were both very important weapons in the
orator's arsenal.   For Cicero there was no greater power than *eloquentia*
for the orator, and he lists it as one of the best ways to win *gloria* in
general, even over military accomplishments (*Off.* 2.48); furthermore,
because of its ability to persuade, its possession allowed for the

---

8. Cf. e.g. *Cael.* 51; *Red. Sen.* 33; *Sest.* 96; *Vat.* 10.

building of considerable political power.[9] *Summa gratia* was also for
Cicero a very important part of the *potestas* of the orator, as he states in
the *Pro Murena: Magnus dicendi labor, magna res, magna dignitas,
summa autem gratia* (*Mur.* 29); and while he acknowledged its
importance, he did not approve of its being used as a tool of the
prosecution: *nolo accusator in iudicium adferat...non nimiam gratiam*
(*Mur.* 59). In the present context these terms cry out for explanation,
but Cicero makes his audience wait until the next sentence, where he
specifically assigns these two elements to Hortensius and Naevius,
cancelling out what the author of the *Rhetorica ad Herennium* felt was
a faulty start because it was too general and left too much room for
question. Such an opening allows Cicero the opportunity to use
eloquentia and *gratia* in order to make a clear distinction between
himself and the opposition in anticipation of the appeals *a nostra
persona* and *ab adversariorum persona*. It is important for Cicero to
establish the character of both sides and the clear nature of the conflict
between them immediately so that he can prepare the ground for
presenting the case to the *iudices* (that is, Aquilius and his *consilium*) in
the important appeal *a iudicum persona*, the culmination of the
exordium. To this end Cicero uses one appeal to lead into the next; he
characterizes the opposition and then introduces first the antithesis
between himself and Hortensius, and then that between Quinctius and
Naevius. The order is important for it is the conflict between Quinctius
and Naevius that Cicero is trying to bring out, and by delaying it he can
do so in the most dramatic way possible. He builds dramatic tension on
several levels. The syntactic expectation raised by the relative *quae*
clause is not resolved until the end of the sentence with *gratia* and
eloquentia, which Cicero adds as appositives to *res*. The periodic
structure gives dramatic emphasis to the two nouns, and more
important, makes a transition to the second sentence where Cicero
introduces Quinctius.

    Gratia and *eloquentia* were for Cicero powerful forces (*plurimum
possunt*), and he uses them to characterize Hortensius and Naevius in
order to establish for his audience the nature of the *potestas* that is on
the side of the opposition. *Potestas* is one of the main themes of
Cicero's case, and in the *exordium* alone *potestas* and its cognates occur
16 times. Although a word of broad scope ("possibility," "control," as

---

9. Cf. *De Or.* 1.15, 30-34, 2.33; *Inv. Rhet.* 1.5; *Tusc.* 1.5; *Mur.* 22-24; *Man.* 1-
2; *Cael.* 46.

well as "power" and "influence") *potestas* is used in this speech as synonymous with *eloquentia* and *gratia*. Cicero is using all these terms rather easily and freely in his opening, throwing them out faster than his audience can fully comprehend them in their present application or context: they must listen and wait as he develops them in the *exordium*, until he defines them.

The intensity, and even the genuineness, of Cicero's reaction to his opponents' *gratia et eloquentia* must be questioned, for Cicero's praise (*honos*) of Hortensius' ability over his own seems to be stated elsewhere almost ironically (cf. *Quinct.* 77).[10] But regardless of whether Hortensius was Cicero's superior at this point in his career and just how sincere his respect for the *eloquentia* of his senior opponent was, the point is, rather, how Cicero chooses to portray this relationship in this speech for the specific rhetorical purpose of character exploitation. Cicero uses the *eloquentia* of Hortensius to contrast his character with his opponent's in order to introduce the conflict between Quinctius and Naevius. The point of contrast, *potestas*, becomes the central theme of the speech. By portraying himself and Quinctius as helpless victims confronting the respective juggernauts of *potestas* that Hortensius and Naevius represent, he effectively reverses his role from *accusator* to *defensor*, an important factor in winning the sympathy of the court.[11]

Cicero establishes his own fear (*vereor, metuo*) in the face of the *potestas* of the opposition, and then uses the antithesis created by the bipartite construction of the first sentence to introduce Quinctius in the second:

> 1.4-6:   Eloquentia Q. Hortensi ne me in dicendo impediat, non nihil commoveor, gratia Sex. Naevi ne P. Quinctio noceat, id vero non mediocriter pertimesco.

Cicero begins by contrasting how the *eloquentia* of Hortensius affects him and the *gratia* of Naevius threatens Quinctius. The distinction Cicero makes through the phrases *non nihil commoveor* and *non mediocriter pertimesco* is an amplification of the distinction

---

10. H. V. Canter (1936), 457-464, esp. 461. But cf. J. C. Davies (1969), 156-157, who argues otherwise. The debate is picked up by T. E. Kinsey (1970), 737-738.

11. As Cicero states below (8-9), he is forced to speak first although Quinctius is the true defendant in the case.

between *vereor* and *metuo* in the opening sentence. The sentence is transitional, first, because Cicero carries forward the concept of *potestas* from the opening sentence while also carrying forward the theme of fear; second, it introduces the characters of Cicero and Quinctius and establishes their relationship to the opposition while defining the nature of the conflict between them; third, it anticipates the next passage, where Cicero characterizes himself and Quinctius in similar terms. Cicero develops the theme of fear in the two parallel clauses that correspond to the parallel clauses of the *alteram...alteram* construction in the previous sentence. Cicero addresses the *eloquentia* of Hortensius first, the lesser of his two fears, in order to delay what he makes out to be his primary concern, the *summa gratia* of Naevius and its effect on Quinctius, until the end of the sentence for emphasis. The dramatic resolution of the sentence is reinforced through the verbs *commoveor* and *pertimesco*, both of which are elaborated compound forms of *vereor* and *metuo* from the previous sentence.

This sentence is a good example of how Cicero uses thematic elements in conjunction with character as a transitional device in its most basic and unembellished form. Cicero begins with the appeal *ab adversariorum persona*, characterizing both Hortensius and Naevius in terms of their respective spheres of *potestas*: *eloquentia* and *gratia*; he then uses this dual characterization to shift ($\Rightarrow$) from the appeal *ab adversariorum persona* to *a nostra persona* in the following parallel *ne* clauses. Periodic resolution is achieved at the end of each clause with two parallel verbs in which the final antithesis is exposed, in this case the conflict between Quinctius and Naevius that arises out of Cicero's fear:

[Thematic: *power*] Eloquentia

[Attribution: *persona*] Q. Hortensi

[$\Rightarrow$ a nostra]   ne me in dicendo impediat

[Resolution: *fear*] non nihil commoveor

[Thematic: *power*] Gratia

[Attribution: *persona*]   Sex. Naevi

[⇒ a nostra] ne P. Quinctio noceat

[Resolution: *fear*] id vero non mediocriter pertimesco

Antithesis and parallel periodic construction are an integral part of Cicero's transitional technique as well as his overall rhetorical strategy. In this case he also uses litotes to describe his fear both of Hortensius' *eloquentia* and Naevius' *gratia* (*non nihil commoveor* :: *non mediocriter pertimesco*), yet despite the parallel use of understatement, which helps link the two clauses, the verb *pertimesco*, introduced by *id vero*, is indeed more emphatic and produces a better clausula than *commoveor*, with the internal rhyme (*mediocriter pertimesco*) adding to the cadence.[12] Cicero is clearly making a distinction between the nature of the *potestas* of his two opponents, implying through a rhetorical relationship that the *gratia* of Naevius poses a greater threat to his client than the *eloquentia* of Hortensius. Because it is the *gratia* of Naevius that affects his client, Cicero clarifies this distinction in the two parallel *ne* clauses, in which he describes the *eloquentia* of Hortensius as a mere obstacle for himself (*impediat*), but the *gratia* of Naevius as a real threat (*noceat*) to Quinctius. The focus of the appeal *ab adversariorum persona* is on identifying the dangerous and ruthless power of the opposition; the focus of the appeal *a nostra persona* is to show how that power affects Cicero and his client. Cicero's purpose is to prejudice the judge and audience against the opposition by building up in their minds the idea that without their support and sympathy he and his client are powerless (*impotens*) in the face of the *potestas* of the opposition:

2.6-12: Neque hoc tanto opere querendum videretur, haec summa in illis esse, si in nobis essent saltem mediocria; verum ita se res habet, ut ego, qui neque usu satis et ingenio parum possum, cum patrono disertissimo

---

12. For *vero* taking up an idea with emphasis see Leumann-Hofmann 2.2.2, 494-495.

comparer, P. Quinctius, cui tenues opes, nullae facultates, exiguae amicorum copiae sunt, cum adversario gratiosissimo contendat.

Cicero carries forward the theme of *potestas* as the central point of contrast between his side and that of the opposition, and through chiasmus uses it to unite himself and Quinctius (*haec summa in illis...si in nobis mediocria*) while using the disparity (*summa :: mediocria*) to offer some hope for his side in the *si* clause. Through the two parallel relative clauses that follow Cicero returns to his initial characterization of himself and Quinctius contained in the parallel *ne* clauses of the previous sentence and explains the reasons behind his fear of the opposition. Again Cicero uses the contrast between himself and Hortensius as a transitional device to introduce through contrast the greater danger that Quinctius faces:

CICERO: qui neque usu satis et *ingenio parum possum*

HORTENSIUS: cum patrono *disertissimo*

[RESOLUTION]: *comparer*

QUINCTIUS: cui *tenues opes, nullae facultates, exiguae copiae sunt*

NAEVIUS: cum adversario *gratiosissimo*

[RESOLUTION]: *contendat*

The theme of *potestas* remains the central point of contrast between the appeals *a nostra* and *ab adversariorum persona* as Cicero describes himself as *parum possum* with respect to his own *ingenium* (an appropriate synonym for *eloquentia*), because he is matched (*comparer*) with a *patronus disertissimus*; likewise, Cicero characterizes Quinctius in terms that are the complete antithesis of those used to describe Naevius. *Opes* and *facultates* are synonymous for material resources, and the phrase *exiguae amicorum copiae* completes the picture, for *copiae* not only qualifies *amicorum*, but also balances *opes* and *facultates*: material resources and friends are the basis of *gratia*, hence the contrast with *gratiosissimo*. Cicero chooses his words carefully: both *comparer* and *contendat* convey a strong sense of physical struggle, the former used of the pairing of gladiators, the latter of military struggle, and this is picked up by the shift in emphasis of the parallel prepositional phrases (*cum patrono :: cum adversario*).[13] The military metaphor is a common feature of the Ciceronian *exordium*, and Cicero uses it here to emphasize the *certamen iudici*.

Parum possum recalls the phrase *plurimum possunt* that Cicero used of the *potestas* of the opposition in the opening sentence, and as well sets up the verb *comparer* which he is about to use in order to show his own inequality as compared with his opponent. Furthermore, *gratiosissimus* recalls the *summa gratia* of Naevius. We should, however, regard the disclaimer of *ingenium* with suspicion, for throughout his career it was this quality that Cicero, a master at choosing strategy, was most often modest about in himself, and which he reserved as the grounds for the highest praise of others.[14]

In the opening two sentences of the *exordium* Cicero establishes the central themes of his defense and uses them to establish character and conflict: the *potestas* of the opposition works against him and his client not only because it is a very powerful weapon in their hands (*plurimum possunt*), but also because Cicero is unable to match it (*parum possum*), and furthermore the political color of the times (*in hoc tempore*) allows this type of influence to prevail over *veritas* and *aequitas*. The disparity between the two sides of the *certamen iudici* becomes a primary element in the structure of the *exordium*, as Cicero illustrates with the introduction of *veritas* and *aequitas* in contrast to the *potestas* of the opposition. This is the central contrast Cicero chooses as the basis of his defense and one which he will soon use to introduce the appeal *a iudicum persona*.

In the next section Cicero takes a new angle on his lack of *potestas*: the case has been thrust upon him at the last minute and he has not had sufficient time to prepare:

4.19-3: Ita quod mihi consuevit in ceteris causis esse adiumento, id quoque in hac causa deficit. Nam, quod ingenio minus possum, subsidium

---

13. For *comparo*, cf. *Quinct.* 58, 93; *QFr.* 3.4.2, and *Pis.* 27; for *contendo*. cf. Caesar, *BGall.* passim.

14. Cf. e.g., *Balb.* 1; *Sest.* 1; *Rosc. Am.* 1.

mihi diligentia comparavi; quae quanta sit, nisi tempus et spatium datum
sit, intellegi non potest.

The inadequacy Cicero confessed in the previous passage (*ingenio
parum possum*) he restates here (*ingenio minus possum*), but now he
clarifies the term *ingenium* by contrasting it with the term *diligentia*:
because he has not been given sufficient time to prepare his case
(*comparavi* echoing *comparer*) he is at a double disadvantage.
Preparation (*diligentia*) is his only means of making up for what he
lacks in natural ability (*ingenium*), and because this has been denied
him he has been unable to get a firm grasp on the issues of the *causa*
(*intellegi non potest*). There is no doubt that both of these qualities
were important to the orator, but as with Cicero's initial modesty about
his *ingenium*, we should also receive his complaint about *diligentia*
with caution. [15] According to him (*Inv. Rhet.* 1.25) *diligentia* should be
concealed from the audience because the orator runs the risk of losing
their sympathy should he let on that he has had time for extensive
preparation. It was not advisable to give the impression of having
enjoyed the luxury of *diligentia* in preparing one's case, but important
to complain of not having had the opportunity for it. Therefore, despite
the truth of the claim, evoking the sympathy of his audience is clearly
his reason for stating that his customary *diligentia* has not been
permitted him, which allows him an effective means of transition from
the appeal of ethos (*a nostra persona*) to the appeal of pathos (*a
iudicum persona*). Although elsewhere in the *exordium* he ignores the
consilium and addresses Aquilius alone, here Cicero addresses both,
Aquilius directly and his *consilium* in the third person:[16]

> 4.3-5: Quae quo plura sunt, C. Aquili, eo te et hos qui tibi in consilio sunt
> meliore mente nostra verba audire oportebit, ut multis incommodis veritas
> debilitata tandem aequitate talium virorum recreetur.

---

15. Cf. *De Or.* 2.147; also *Div. in Caec.* (37-43), where Cicero calls both
Caecilius' *diligentia* and *ingenium* into question.

16. In his final appeal to the bench (10) Cicero is careful once again to include
the *consilium*, although Aquilius alone is addressed. The members of Aquilius'
consilium, whom Cicero does not name until section 54, are: P. Quinctilius
Varus, M. Claudius Marcellus, and L. Lucilius Balbus.

In his appeal *a iudicum persona* Cicero draws a parallel between himself and Aquilius in terms of his lack of *ingenium* and *diligentia*: despite having little *ingenium* to start with, he has been given even less chance to compensate for that with *diligentia*; Aquilius, on the other hand, although *veritas* is undermined *multis incommodis*, does have the opportunity to compensate through *aequitas*. Up to this point, Cicero has been stressing the disparity between his side and the opposition in quantitative terms (*plurimum, parum, tantus...quantus, minus, deficit*). With the phrase *aequitate talium virorum*, applied to Aquilius and his *consilium*, Cicero introduces the element of quality in contrast to quantity: although the opposition has greater *potestas* than Cicero or his client, Aquilius and his *consilium* have their own *potestas*, namely their *auctoritas*, i.e., what they themselves are capable of bringing about. Cicero contrasts this with the *potestas* of Naevius, which is based on *gratia*, or what he is able to achieve only through his influence with others. For Cicero, the scope of an individual's *potestas* was defined by the amount of *gratia* and *auctoritas* he possessed.[17] Cicero then picks up on this basic conflict between Aquilius' *aequitas* and the *gratia* of Naevius as he portrays Aquilius as being in the same position as he himself. Cicero devotes the central portion of the *exordium* to developing the contrast between Aquilius and Naevius in these terms:

5.6-11: Quod si tu iudex nullo praesidio fuisse videbere contra vim et gratiam solitudini atque inopiae, si apud hoc consilium ex opibus, non ex veritate causa pendetur, profecto nihil est iam sanctum atque sincerum in civitate, nihil est quod humilitatem cuiusquam gravitas et virtus iudicis consoletur.

A standard feature of the appeal *a iudicum persona* is the depersonalization of the argument, in which Cicero often omits the names of the parties involved and identifies them only by the character traits or concept words he has developed through accretive progression

---

17. Cf *Planc.* 32: *pater...tueri vel auctoritate sua vel gratia possit?*; 47: [*Plancius*] *in operas plurimos patris auctoritate et gratia miserit....* In its most basic sense *gratia* was defined by Cicero as the basis for *amicitia*: *gratiam [eam appellant] quae in memoria et remuneratione officiorum et honoris et amicitiarum observantiam teneat* (*Inv. Rhet.* 2.66); the state of being *in gratia* between *amici* depended upon a reciprocal observance of the interests of the other: *gratia [est] in qua amicitiarum et officiorum alterius memoria et remunderandi voluntas continentur* (*Inv. Rhet.* 2.161). Cf. also *Att.* 4.16.5.

from the beginning. Here Cicero reduces the conflict between Quinctius and Naevius to a conflict of *inopia* and *veritas* versus *opes* and *gratia*, in which he picks up on and further develops the parallel between Quinctius and Aquilius established in the previous passage. This contrast becomes central to Cicero's defense, and he returns to it in his summation at the end of the *confirmatio*, as well as throughout the *peroratio.*[18]

The compound protasis restates the conflict established through the opening characterization, and here Cicero maintains the military imagery by portraying Aquilius (*tu iudex*) in the first *si* clause as the only *praesidium* that can protect Quinctius (*inopia*) from Naevius (*gratia*). Cicero introduces the image of *praesidium* immediately, but suspends the datives *solitudini atque inopiae* to which it corresponds until the end of the clause and after the phrase *contra vim et gratiam.* Cicero uses *inopes* to emphasize the contrast between Quinctius' isolation and the support behind Naevius' *gratia*;[19] furthermore, through the double dative construction, which brackets *vis* and *gratia*, Cicero further emphasizes the conflict between Naevius and Quinctius as well as the imperative that Aquilius (= *praesidium*) must intervene. Cicero employs parallel hendiadys (*vim et gratiam...solitudine atque inopiae*) to emphasize not only the power of the opposition, but also the destitution of the defense. In the second *si* clause Cicero shifts his focus from Aquilius to *apud hoc consilium* in order to introduce the contrast between *opes* and *veritas* as he characterizes the struggle between influence and honesty, removing it from a personal to a philosophical contest, a contrast that echoes, and is meant to parallel, the juxtaposition of *gratia* and *inopia* in the previous clause. Yet the parallel is not equally clear on the two sides of the equation. While *opes* and *gratia* do share a common denominator, there is very little that is patently common between *veritas* and *inopia*, which seems to suggest

---

18. Cf., *Omnia sunt, C. Aquili, eius modi quivis ut perspicere possit in hac causa improbitatem et gratiam cum inopia et veritate contendere* (*Quinct.* 84); *Obsecret obtestetur P. Quinctius...ut cum veritas cum hoc faciat, plus huius inopia possit ad misericordiam quam illius opes ad crudelitatem* (*Quinct.* 91); *Non comparat se tecum gratia P. Quinctius, Sex. Naevi, non opibus, non facultate contendit* (*Quinct.* 93).

19. For this usage of *inopes*, cf. *Att.* 1.1.2: *Thermus cum Silano contendere existimatur. Qui sic inopes ab amicis et existimatione sunt mihi videatur non esse.*

that Cicero is attempting to bring ethical arguments to Quinctius' defense in spite of their lack of similarity. Cicero's choice of *veritas*, however, might be dependent upon what is to come in the compound apodosis, where he continues to reduce the issues of the case to an impersonal struggle between power and helplessness and warns that if *gratia* succeeds over *inopiae*, or *opes* prevail over *veritas* (i.e. if Naevius wins), it will be potentially very harmful for the state (*nihil est iam sanctum atque sincerum in civitate*). But in the second *nihil* clause Cicero introduces *virtus* into the equation, a new element and one to combat the *vis* of the opposition.

Virtus is traditionally represented on coins as an armed goddess with her counterpart *Honos*, and for Cicero represented praiseworthy achievement especially in upholding and defending the standards of the *res publica*; [20] yet it is especially used by Cicero as a force to counter the force of *vis*, and is most often used by Cicero in this context.[21] By invoking the image of *virtus* here, Cicero is in effect reminding Aquilius and his *consilium* that they must uphold the government, that they are armed with the power of the law and they must use it.[22] Cicero is continuing to use military imagery in order to draw clear lines of conflict between the *virtus* of Aquilius and his *consilium* and the *vis* of the opposition. Cicero reminds the court of the humble circumstances of his client (*humilitatem*), and because he continues to generalize (*cuiusquam*), the argument has further universal appeal. By implying that the fate of Quinctius will determine the future of the court system

---

20. See Crawford, *RRC,* 403/1. There were two temples to *Honos et Virtus* in Rome: one *ad portam Capenam* dedicated originally to *Honos* by Q. Fabius Maximus Verrucosus in 234 B.C., then duplicated to contain both by M. Claudius Marcellus (Livy 25.40.2-3, 27.25.7-9, 29.11.13), the other one built by Marius; outside the porta Collina was another temple possibly dedicated only to *Honos* (Cicero, *Leg.* 2.58).

21. For the meanings of *virtus* cf.: *Tusc.* 2.43; *Leg.* 1.25; for usage, especially with *vis*, cf.: *Red. Sen.* 19; *Red. Pop.* 19; *Sest.* 86, 136-38; *Arch.* 25; *Man.* 36; *Cael.* 41; *Verr.* 2.5.181; *Balb.* 51; *Mur.* 17; *Mil.* 101; *Phil.* 3.34, 4.13, 5.2,4; 8.23, 13.5; *Deiot.* 26; Caesar, *BGall.* 1.1.

22. For studies on the concept of *virtus* as a Roman virtue see D. C. Earl (1966), 5-40; (1967), 20-35. A. Ernout (1946), 255-260. P. Kuklica (1975-76), 3-23. J. Ferguson (1958), 159-178. J. Sarsila (1978), 135-143. W. Eisenhut (1973).

Cicero attempts to impress upon Aquilius and his *consilium* that their welfare as well depends on that of his client.

> 5.12-14: Certe aut apud te et hos qui tibi adsunt veritas valebit, aut ex hoc loco repulsa vi et gratia locum ubi consistat reperire non poterit.

For the moment Cicero has effectively transformed this case from a civil dispute between two individuals to a universal struggle between the forces of good and evil in the state, the outcome of which will determine not only the fate of Quinctius, but possibly the future integrity of the court system. But Cicero is careful not to appear to question the integrity of Aquilius and the members of his *consilium* or their ability to judge fairly. Therefore he stresses his confidence in them through the correlative *aut...aut* construction. In the first alternative he confirms their *auctoritas* by stating his confidence in their integrity (*veritas*), taking care to address this remark both to Aquilius and to his *consilium* (*certe aut apud te et hos qui tibi adsunt veritas valebit*); but in the second he reminds them of the possible consequences should they fail to bring their *auctoritas* to bear at this juncture; again, Cicero describes the situation in military terms: *aut ex hoc loco repulsa vi et gratia locum ubi consistat reperire non poterit.*[23] By coupling *vis* and *gratia* here, Cicero uses synonymy to define the two terms and contrast them with the *virtus* of Aquilius. Cicero goes on to reassure Aquilius of his confidence in his ability to judge fairly in this case:

> 5.15-18: Non eo dico, C. Aquili, quo mihi veniat in dubium tua fides et constantia, aut quo non in his quos tibi advocavisti viris lectissimis civitatis spem summam habere P. Quinctius debeat.

Cicero continues to reinforce what he said above, that he does not doubt Aquilius' *fides et constantia*, nor ought Quinctius to hesitate to place his complete trust (*spem summam*) in the members of his *consilium*, whom he is careful to portray as *viri lectissimi civitatis*. By coupling *fides et constantia* in a formulaic phrase that recalls *gratia et eloquentia*, Cicero defines the *veritas* of Aquilius and his *consilium* upon which he and his client must rely:[24]

---

23. For *locus* in its military context cf. Cicero, *Clu.* 128; Caesar, *BGall.* 5.34.1; See also D. Packard (1968), vol. 3, s.v. *locus*.

24. Cf. *Off.* 1.23: *fides est dictorum conventorumque constantia et veritas.*

6.18-24:   Quid ergo est? Primum magnitudo periculi summo timore hominem adficit, quod uno iudicio de fortunis omnibus decernit, idque dum cogitat, non minus saepe ei venit in mentem potestatis quam aequitatis tuae, propterea quod omnes quorum in alterius manu vita posita est saepius illud cogitant, quid possit is cuius in dicione ac potestate sunt, quam quid debeat facere.

The question *quid ergo est?* is rhetorical and often used by Cicero to introduce a recapitulation of the points covered thus far, as in the *peroratio,* where he also uses the phrase *periculi magnitudo* (91). But because a true summation at this point would be premature, Cicero uses the question to allow him the opportunity to enlarge upon the idea of Quinctius' dependence upon the *fides et constantia* of the court. By using the term *homo* ("any man") Cicero is still generalizing, but, of course, through the references to fear and danger Cicero continually puts his audience in mind of Quinctius' particular situation. This approach is reminiscent of Cicero's initial characterization of himself and Quinctius at the beginning of the *exordium*: the *magnitudo periculi* has affected Quinctius with *summo timore*. Cicero now introduces the noun *potestas* itself for the first time and attributes it to Aquilius, repeating the word in parallel clauses in which he attempts to show that Quinctius' particular situation (i.e. his dependence upon the *fides et constantia*, or *potestas*, of the court to defend him against the *gratia et eloquentia*, or *periculum,* of men such as Naevius) is in fact a characteristic shared by all men (*omnes*), of whom he is only one (*uno*).

QUINCTIUS:

    (A_1) quod uno iudicio de fortunis omnibus decernit

      (B_1) idque dum cogitat

        (C_1) non minus saepe ei venit in mentem potestatis quam
                                        aequitatis tuae

ALL MEN:

(A₂) propterea quod omnes quorum in alterius manu vita posita
                                                        est

(B₂) saepius illud cogitant

(C₂) quid possit is cuius in dicione ac potestate sunt quam
                                            quid debeat facere

Up to this point Cicero has characterized Naevius and Hortensius
as the epitome of power whose *gratia et eloquentia* (= *potestas*)
threatens Quinctius, but now Cicero challenges that power by
introducing the *fides et constantia* (= *potestas*) of Aquilius and his
consilium. Cicero uses nearly parallel correlative grammatical structure
within the two clauses to define the *potestas* of Aquilius and his
consilium here in terms of their *aequitas et dicio*, a variation on the
theme of *fides et constantia*. In the first *quod* clause ($A_1 - C_1$) Cicero
draws a balance between *potestas* and *aequitas* through comparison
(*non minus saepe potestatis...quam aequitatis*), and in the second ($A_2 -$
C_2) through hendiadys (*dicione ac potestate*): Aquilius' *potestas* lies in
his sense of justice (*aequitas*) and his jurisdiction (*dicio*) because he is
iudex.
        Having established the central issues of the case through the
introduction of thematic or concept words, which he used to
characterize the *personae* of the case, and then by generalizing and
reshaping the conflict between these *personae* into a struggle
represented purely in terms of these concept words, Cicero now
reintroduces Quinctius and Naevius, addressing the issues of the case
with them specifically in mind:

> 7.24-2: Deinde habet adversarium P. Quinctius verbo Sex. Naevium, re
> vera huiusce aetatis homines disertissimos, fortissimos, florentissimos
> nostrae civitatis, qui communi studio summis opibus Sex. Naevium
> defendunt, si id est defendere, cupiditati alterius obtemperare quo is
> facilius quem velit iniquo iudicio opprimere possit.

Because here *deinde* does not signal the final element in a series, as it
normally does, nor does it carry forward the argument from the

previous sentence, it therefore informs the audience that Cicero is bringing the *exordium* to a close; his return to the appeals *a nostra persona* and *ab adversariorum persona* certainly indicates as well that a *conclusio* is close at hand. Although those elements are present, Cicero is not just recapitulating; rather, he keeps the attention of his audience by introducing a new element in the conflict. Cicero focuses on Naevius' *advocati*, whom he identifies as the real basis of his opponent's *gratia* through the antithesis of the *verbo...re vera* construction.[25] The superlatives Cicero attributes to Naevius' *advocati* correspond to the thematic terms he has been using to characterize the opposition. *Disertissimus* and *florentissimus* correspond to *eloquentia* and *gratia* which Cicero used in his initial characterization of Hortensius and Naevius, and *fortissimus* strikes a contrast with the weakness of Quinctius. Possibly Cicero may even be using this term with Naevius' *advocatus* Philippus in mind, but if he is, it is doubtful that Cicero is referring to his oratory. Although in this speech (72) Cicero alludes to Philippus' oratorical ability as the equal of Hortensius (*pro me pugnabit L. Philippus, eloquentia, gravitate, honore florentissimus civitatis, dicet Hortensius, excellens ingenio, nobilitate, existimatione...*) these are words put into Naevius' mouth by Cicero; elsewhere (*De Or.* 3.4) Cicero describes Philippus as *vehementi et diserto et in primis forti ad resistendum*, but in the *Brutus* (173) Cicero's praise for Phillipus is somewhat less than enthusiastic. Furthermore, because he uses both *florentissimus* and *floreo* of Philippus on two occasions in this speech (72, 80), but never *fortissimus*, perhaps *fortissimus* is simply meant to be general and applicable to all; it is certainly meant to be ironic. Philippus, present only as an *advocatus*, was not going to speak for Naevius, and Cicero clearly states that Naevius' *advocati* are only supporting him because they share his greedy nature and no doubt expect to profit from their loyalty (*communi studio summis opibus Sex. Naevium defendunt*). At the same time Cicero condemns Naevius' *advocati* for their *studium* by questioning the sincerity of their support with the insertion of a corrective conditional clause (*si id est defendere*) that alerts the audience that they should question the integrity of Naevius' *patroni* and the motives behind their support. Cicero also seems to be deliberately

---

25. A favorite formula for antithesis, which Cicero employs often and in various forms, cf. *Quinct.* 56; *Rosc. Am.* 123, 137; *Verr.* 3.33, 5.63, 87; *Caec.* 21, 59; *Imp Pomp.* 52; *Agr.* 2.10; *Cael.* 40; *Phil.* 2.11, 14.24.

mysterious about the purpose and character of these men, many of whom probably were not present at the trial and therefore could not be counted among his *advocati*. Cicero characterizes them as creatures subservient to Naevius' greed (*cupiditati*) and who are abusing the legal system (*iniquo iudicio*). *Fortissimus* will prove to be even more ironic shortly, when Cicero addresses the issue of having to speak first with the metaphor of a doctor who must heal wounds that have not yet been inflicted by the opposition (8.9-14):

> 8.2-8:   Nam quid hoc iniquius aut indignius, C. Aquili, dici aut commemorari potest, quam me qui caput alterius, famam fortunasque defendam, priore loco causam dicere? cum praesertim Q. Hortensius qui hoc iudicio partis accusatoris obtinet, contra me dicturus, cui summam copiam facultatemque dicendi natura largita est.

Nam introduces a continuation, or explanation, of the previous argument, in this case the idea that the trial is an *iniquum iudicium*. Cicero now uses the comparative adjective *iniquius* to pose a rhetorical question which also helps bring out the irony of his use of *fortissimus* in the previous passage: although Cicero is in effect speaking in defense of Quinctius, he has been put in the position of speaking first before he has heard the charges of the opposition. Cicero all but calls the opposition the *accusator*, a term which, though it might loosely apply to the *petitor* or *actor* in a civil case (as this is), is properly used of the prosecutor in a criminal trial (*Part. Or.* 11). Having emphasized his fear of Hortensius' *eloquentia* at the start of the *exordium* Cicero now uses it to his advantage by complaining that he is disadvantaged not only because he must speak first in defense (*priore loco causam dicere*) before he has had the opportunity to hear the charge of the *accusator*, but also because in this case the *accusator* is a superior orator (*cui summam copiam facultatemque dicendi natura largita est*). Cicero uses the chagrin he feels at the injustice of his present situation (*iniquius aut indignius*) as a means of transition to the next passage, in which he portrays this injustice in a dramatic metaphor:

> 8.9-14: Ita fit ut ego, qui tela depellere et volneribus mederi debeam, tum id facere cogar cum etiam telum adversarius nullum iecerit, illis autem id tempus impugnandi detur cum et vitandi illorum impetus potestas adempta nobis erit, et, si qua in re, id quod parati sunt facere, falsum crimen quasi venenatum aliquod telum iecerint, medicinae faciendae locus non erit.

Having assigned to Hortensius the role of *accusator* in the previous passage, Cicero can now describe him and the other members of the opposition as an aggressive enemy (*telum iecerit*) on the attack (*impugnandi*), a strong military metaphor that recalls the past military imagery Cicero has been careful to use throughout the *exordium* up to this point (note the use of *locus* here and above). Using imagery that must have been a common metaphor for the perils of the court, Cicero describes his own defensive tactic (*tela depellere*) against the offensive weapons of the *accusatores*;[26] but Cicero does not stop here, rather he adds a new element to the metaphor in order to raise the pathos of the appeal by describing himself not only as on the defensive, but in fact as a doctor (*volneribus mederi debeam*) forced into the absurd position of providing care for wounds that have not yet been inflicted (*tum id facere cogar cum etiam telum adversarius nullum iecerit*). At the center of the passage is the issue of *potestas* which Cicero uses once again to characterize the opposition in contrast to himself (*[ut] illis autem id tempus impugnandi detur cum et vitandi illorum impetus potestas adempta nobis erit*). Through this metaphor Cicero reinforces the picture of himself as the *defensor* and Hortensius as the *accusator*, the holder of *potestas*, whose intent is not only hostile, it is immoral and treacherous (*falsum crimen quasi venenatum aliquod telum iecerint*). Cicero does not hesitate to make the point that the *telum* of the opposition is in fact a *falsum crimen*, for which poison there will be no chance of a remedy (*medicinae faciendae locus non erit*). Cicero concludes by restating his role as the doctor, but avoids repeating *mederi* through the periphrastic construction.[27]

Although Cicero has made much of the disadvantage of being forced to speak first, he pauses momentarily to impute this injustice to Cn. Dolabella, the praetor in charge of the case:

9.14-19: Id accidit praetoris iniquitate et iniuria, primum quod contra omnium consuetudinem iudicium prius de probro quam de re maluit fieri, deinde quod ita constituit id ipsum iudicium ut reus, ante quam verbum accusatoris audisset, causam dicere cogeretur.

---

26. Cf. *Part. Or.* 14: *non eadem accusatores et rei, quod accusator rerum ordinem prosequitur et singula argumenta quasi hasta in manu collocata vehementer proponit.*

27. Cf. *De Or.* 2.186 for a similar construction.

Cicero's first objection is that the praetor decided that Cicero should first answer the charge of whether Quinctius was *infamis* or not in respect to Naevius' seizure of the property (*de probro*), because Quinctius had not appeared in court after having giving a *vadimonium*. But Cicero would rather address the case itself (*de re*), that is, the underhanded way in which Naevius seized the property. To add insult to this *iniuria*, he must also speak first.[28] Cicero uses this passage as a transition to the *conclusio* of the *exordium*, as he insinuates that he has been forced to speak first and address the matter of Quinctius' *infamia* first, because of the influence of the *advocati* who support Naevius:

> 9.19-24: Quod eorum gratia et potentia factum est, qui, quasi sua res aut honos agatur, ita diligenter Sex. Naevi studio et cupiditati morem gerunt et in eius modi rebus opes suas experiuntur, in quibus, quo plus propter virtutem nobilitatemque possunt, eo minus quantum possint debent ostendere.

Quod (causal) continues the thought from the previous sentence. Cicero began the *exordium* by using the *eloquentia* of Hortensius to focus on the *gratia* of Naevius, what he claimed was the real threat to Quinctius. Now he focuses on that quality alone, *gratia*, defining it through hendiadys (*gratia et potentia*) as the true *potestas* at work for the opposition.[29] Cicero unites the two terms to expose the greed of Naevius' *advocati*, whom he again characterizes as acceding to Naevius' greed (*cupiditati*); who, like Naevius, are the antithesis of Quinctius and Aquilius, and who use their resources (*opes*) to support him as if they were serving their own interests (*quasi sua res aut honos agatur*). Cicero characterizes Naevius' *advocati* with the term *virtus*, the same term he used of Aquilius and his *consilium*, only here Cicero is using these terms against the opposition by asserting that they are perverting this admirable quality by exploiting it under the present circumstances (*quo plus propter virtutem nobilitatemque possunt, eo minus quantum possint debent ostendere*): because of their *virtus* and high birth they are more advantaged to the extent that they ought the less to make a show of that potential.

---

28. For the definition and implication of *infamia* as it applies to Quinctius, see T. E. Kinsey (1971), appendix I, 217-218.

29. Cicero uses this same combination in relation to Chrysogonus, the antagonist of the *Pro Roscio Amerino* (*Rosc. Am.* 122).

10.25-3: Cum tot tantisque difficultatibus adfectus atque adflictus in
tuam, C. Aquili, fidem, veritatem, misericordiam P. Quinctius confugerit,
cum adhuc ei propter vim adversariorum non ius par, non agendi potestas
eadem, non magistratus aequus reperiri potuerit, cum ei summam per
iniuriam omnia inimica atque infesta fuerint, te, C. Aquili, vosque qui in
consilio adestis, orat atque obsecrat ut multis iniuriis iactatam atque
agitatam aequitatem in hoc tandem loco consistere et confirmari patiamini.

In the final sentence of the *exordium* Cicero brings together all the
themes he has developed up to this point and in a series of symmetrical
clauses demonstrates the central conflict between Quinctius and
Naevius, and the significance that it has for Aquilius as *iudex*.
Quinctius is the victim (*adfectus atque adflictus*) who has sought refuge
(*confugerit*) in the *fides*, *veritas*, and *misericordia* of Aquilius, the three
primary defining attributes of a *iudex*. The theme of the inequality of
potestas between Quinctius and the opposition also emerges (*propter
vim adversariorum non ius par*), recalling the military description of
the *certamen* of the opening sentence (*comparer*), and further
emphasizing the disparity between the two sides. Cicero is also careful
to describe the *aequitas* of Aquilius in similar terms (*aequitatam in hoc
tandem loco consistere*).

The sentence is constructed around a series of interlocking main
(M) and dependent (D_{1-4}) periodic clauses in which Cicero summarizes
the main points of each of the three main appeals *a nostra, a iudicum,*
and *ab adversariorum persona*:

(D_1) cum tot tantisque difficultatibus adfectus atque adflictus in
      tuam, C. Aquili, fidem, veritatem, misericordiam P.
      Quinctius confugerit

(D_2) cum adhuc ei propter vim adversariorum
         non ius par
           non agendi potestas eadem
             non magistratus aequus reperiri potuerit

(D_3) cum ei summam per iniuriam omnia inimica atque infesta
                                     fuerint

(M) te, C. Aquili, vosque qui in consilio adestis orat atque
                                                    obsecrat

(D_4) ut multis iniuriis iactatam atque agitatam aequitatem in hoc
       tandem loco consistere et confirmari patiamini

Of the five symmetrical clauses that make up this sentence, the first
dependent *cum* clause (D_1) is devoted to Quinctius' predicament and his
reliance upon Aquilius to protect him, a theme picked up in the third
dependent clause (D_3) and the subsequent main clause (M). These two
pairs of dependent clauses (D_1 and D_3) bracket the central *cum* clause
(D_2), in which Cicero uses a tricolon to illustrate the central thesis of
the *exordium*:   the *gratia* of Naevius is so powerful that it has
threatened the possibility of a fair trial for Quinctius.   In the second
member of the tricolon of D_2 Cicero focuses on the theme of *potestas*
(*non agendi potestas eadem*), which is then picked up in the final
member (*potuerit*).   The tricolon of D_2 then reflects the tripartite
superstructure of the first three *cum* clauses (D_{1-3}), through which
Cicero reveals the *potestas* of the opposition.

Throughout the sentence we can find an abundance of alliterative
and paranomastic effects reinforced with verbal echoes and word play
consisting of internal rhyming schemes and paranomasia. The opening
cum clause of the sentence begins with confident and lively alliterative
effects (*tot tantisque*) to which Cicero also adds word play (*adfectus
atque adflictus*) and an internal rhyming scheme and homeoteleuton
(*difficultatibus adfectus...adflictus*). This corresponds to the closing
ut-clause (D_4), in which Cicero employs the same devices (*iactatam
atque agitatam aequitatem...tandem*) with the minor homeoteleuton (-
am... -am...-em...-em), and although these would probably have been all
elided on delivery except the last, nonetheless the effect would have
been dramatic. In the main clause (M) Cicero begins by addressing
Aquilius (*te, C. Aquili*), echoing the first dependent clause (*in tuam, C.
Aquili*) where he employed a chiastic homeoteleuton (*tuam...fidem
veritatem misericordiam*) that corresponds to that of the closing *ut*
clause (D_4) discussed above. In the third *cum* clause (D_3) we also get
an emphatic instance of elision and homeoteleuton (*summam per
iniuriam omnia inimica atque infesta*), and in the final periodic
resolution of the *ut* clause (D_4) Cicero seems to be avoiding a dramatic
ending with the absence of any strong cadence or other rhetorical
device aside from minor alliterative and homeoteleutonic effects
(*consistere et confirmari patiamini*). The note Cicero closes on is not

Quinctius, however, but the abstract *aequitas*, for that is what Cicero would have his *iudex* believe to be the real issue at stake here: not the fate of one man, but of the integrity of the entire judicial system. One of Cicero's main objectives in the *exordium* has been to demonstrate through characterization that the disparity between Quinctius and Naevius, which centers around the issue of *potestas*, also presents a threat to the *aequitas* of Aquilius (*non magistratus aequus reperiri potuerit*); because of this threat everything is suffering (*omnia inimica atque infesta*).

Conclusion

In the *exordium* of the *Pro Quinctio* Cicero immediately focuses on the *potestas*, or *potentia*, of the opposition and the disadvantage he and his client face because of their lack of it. Cicero identifies the components of the *potestas* of the opposition as the *gratia* of Naevius and the *eloquentia* of Hortensius. Both of these terms are vague and general, but in the context of the *exordium* are highly judgmental and demand an ethical evaluation of Hortensius and Naevius in comparison with Cicero and Quinctius. This is exactly what Cicero wants, for he would have his audience believe that both he and Quinctius are at a considerable disadvantage in comparison to Hortensius and Naevius. Although neither *gratia* nor *eloquentia* has anything to do with the facts of the case itself, Cicero is stressing *persona* to impress upon his audience that the issues of the *causa* are ethical ones, and therefore demand not an understanding of the facts of the case, but an insight into human character and a basic perception of right and wrong. Because the occasion for the *Pro Quinctio* was not an actual trial, but a pre-trial hearing, or *praeiudicium*, Cicero's initial approach to the *exordium* is puzzling. The issues raised in the *praeiudicium* ought to address the question of rightful possession and ownership which arose from the legal wager (*sponsio*) agreed upon initially by Naevius and Quinctius, not Cicero's own personal criteria for passing ethical judgments against the *personae* of his opposition. The focus of the hearing should be *res*, not *persona*. And while in the body of the speech Cicero does get around to addressing the specific facts of the *sponsio*, by beginning with his characterization of the opposition in terms of their *eloquentia et gratia*, which he uses to establish the conflict between the appeals *a nostra persona* and *ab adversariorum persona,* Cicero emphasizes *persona* over *causa* in this *exordium.*

Because he had yet to defend Roscius of Ameria, who had influential friends among several of Rome's leading families, notably the Metelli, the Servilii, and the Scipiones, Cicero must not have felt in confident possession of such advantages himself. Although Cicero does not name them in the speech, Quinctius must not have been without his own connections as well, for otherwise Cicero probably would not have accepted the case.[30]

Cicero's approach to this *exordium* may betray a lack of self-confidence on his part, but this is not necessarily the case. We should question the sincerity of Cicero's reaction to Hortensius' *eloquentia,* because his praise (*honos*) of his rival's oratorical ability is phrased later in the speech almost ironically (cf. 77).[31]   But regardless of whether at this point in his career Hortensius was Cicero's superior, the point is, rather, how Cicero chooses to portray this relationship in the *exordium* of this speech for the specific rhetorical purpose of character exploitation. Cicero uses the *eloquentia* of Hortensius to juxtapose his own character with his opponent's in order to sharpen the conflict between Quinctius and Naevius. Cicero uses *gratia* and *eloquentia* to establish conflict not only between himself and the opposition, but also between the opposition and Aquilius and his *consilium,* whom he characterizes in terms of their *fides et constantia.* By portraying himself and Quinctius as helpless victims confronting the *potestas* of the opposition, Cicero effectively reverses his role from *accusator* to *defensor,* an artificial distinction, but one that allows him then to complain about having to speak first — a further disadvantage and another important factor in winning the sympathy of the court. By portraying himself as crippled by the *eloquentia* of his rival Hortensius, Cicero displays considerable self-confidence through his eagerness to engage him in a *contentio dicendi,* an admirable quality that would have endeared him to his audience. As we shall see in the *exordium* of the *Pro Roscio Amerino,* delivered just a year after the *Pro Quinctio,* the relationship between *persona* and *causa* can be an even closer one than

---

30. Cf. F. Hinard (1975), 88-107, who analyzes the political implications of Cicero's decision to undertake Quinctius' case before Aquilius and the members of his *consilium.*

31. H. V. Canter (1936), 457-464, esp. 461. But cf. J. C. Davies (1969), 156-157, who argues otherwise. The debate is picked up by T. E. Kinsey (1970), 737-738.

Cicero makes it in the *exordium* of this speech. But this may be due to the nature of the difference between the two cases, the *Pro Quinctio* being a civil suit, the *Pro Roscio Amerino* a capital trial, and perhaps the first murder trial to be heard under the new organization of the Sullan courts.

CHAPTER TWO

Pro Roscio Amerino

Introduction

In 80 B.C., in the consulship of the dictator L. Sulla and Q. Caecilius Metellus (A. Gellius, *NA* 15.28; Quintilian, 12.6.4), a year after his defense of Publius Quinctius, Cicero defended Sextus Roscius of Ameria. He was twenty-seven years old. Roscius had been charged with the murder of his father (*parricidium*), and in the wake of the proscriptions of 81 B.C., following Sulla's appointment as *dictator legibus faciundis et rei publicae constituendae,* his was to be one of the first murder trials held under the jurisdiction of Sulla's newly established *quaestio de sicariis et veneficis.*[1] According to Cicero (*Inv. Rhet.* 2.58) it was not uncommon for a case involving parricide to be

---

1. Sulla was named dictator on the proposal of L. Valerius Flaccus, interrex, shortly after the closing of the proscription lists in June 81 B.C. The *lex Valeria* of 81 B.C. ratified all of Sulla's enactments, past, present, and future (Vell. Pat. 2.28; Plutarch, *Sulla* 33; Appian, *BCiv.* 1.98; cf. Livy, *Epit.* 89).

taken *extra ordinem* because of its heinous nature; therefore, it is possible that Roscius' trial was the first held under Sulla's newly organized *quaestio*, and if this was the case, it must have attracted a great deal of public attention.[2]

Sextus Roscius was born into a wealthy, influential family of the *municipium* of Ameria, a town in Umbria some fifty miles north of Rome. The family estates of the Sexti Roscii included thirteen farms, almost all of which bordered on the Tiber (*Rosc. Am.* 20). Roscius *pater*, an active socialite among the aristocracy in Rome, had managed to avoid the axe of Sulla's proscriptions probably either by supporting the reforms of the new regime, or through the influence of his friends and associates, most notably the Metelli, the Servilii, and the Scipiones. During his frequent trips to Rome he enjoyed the hospitality of members of these families, many of whom were present as *advocati* at his son's trial (*Rosc. Am.* 15).[3] It was on such a trip to Rome, returning one evening from a dinner party, that Roscius *pater* was murdered near the Pallacinian baths (*Rosc. Am.* 18).[4]

At the time of the murder Roscius *filius*, the defendant, was in Ameria overseeing the family estates. Roscius *filius* was one of two sons; his brother had died sometime before the trial (*Rosc. Am.* 42). According to Cicero, the case of the accusers was based, in part, on the fact that Roscius *pater* favored the deceased son, which caused friction between Sextus Roscius and his father (*Rosc. Am.* 40). Cicero admits that Sextus Roscius, the defendant, the sole surviving son of the society-loving father, was a *homo incautus et rusticus* (*Rosc. Am.* 20), and was perhaps not as close to his father as his brother had been; but Cicero rejects the suggestion that there was any estrangement whatsoever between them. Roscius *pater* may have enjoyed the *hospitium* of many

---

2. But see T. E. Kinsey (1982), 39-40.

3. The heads of these families played no active role in the trial of Roscius, but younger members did appear as *advocati*. The Scipio Cicero mentions was very likely the son of P. Scipio Nasica (pr. 93 B.C.). The Metellus was probably either Q. Metellus Celer (cos. 60 B.C.), or Q. Metellus Nepos (cos. 57 B.C.). According to Cicero (*Rosc. Am.* 149) Valerius Messala prepared and managed the defense. This was either M. Valerius Messala Rufus (cos. 57 B.C.), or M. Valerius Messala Niger (cos. 61 B.C.).

4. Somewhere in the vicinity of the Porticus Minucia Vetus in the Campus Martius, in the neighborhood of the Area Sacra di Largo Argentina (*Rosc. Am.* 132).

influential friends in Rome, but in Ameria he was the protagonist in a long-standing *inimicitia* with two relations, Titus Roscius Magnus and Titus Roscius Capito (*Rosc. Am.* 17), both of whom, according to Cicero, were men of low character.

At the time of the murder Magnus was in Rome, and according to Cicero he sent Mallus Glaucia, a freedman, to Ameria to deliver the news of the death of Roscius *pater*. But upon reaching Ameria, Glaucia did not report to Sextus Roscius the son, but to Magnus' relation and confederate in crime, Capito. Word was also sent to L. Cornelius Chrysogonus, a powerful freedman of the dictator Sulla, who was at Sulla's camp at Volterra (*Rosc. Am.* 20).[5] The property of the Sexti Roscii may have been considerable and was apparently well known, for immediately following the murder a conspiracy among Chrysogonus, Capito, and Magnus was formed to seize it, and to this end they added the name of the murdered father to the proscription lists (although the proscriptions lists had by then been officially closed).[6] By adding Roscius *pater*'s name to the list of the proscribed Chrysogonus was able to buy the family property from the state for a fraction of its actual worth (*Rosc. Am.* 6, 21).[7]

Chrysogonus dispatched Magnus to Ameria as his agent in the seizure of the property; Sex. Roscius was forced to flee (*Rosc. Am.* 23). So outraged was the community of Ameria at this that a delegation of local *decuriones* was dispatched to Sulla's camp at Volterra to complain to the dictator of the seizure of Roscius' property by Magnus, and to seek its restoration (*Rosc. Am.* 25). Chrysogonus, however, intercepted the embassy and, claiming to be acting for Sulla, assured them that the property would be restored to Sextus Roscius, and sent them back to Ameria without an audience with the dictator (*Rosc. Am.* 26). According to Cicero, immediately upon the departure of the delegates (among whose number was Chrysogonus' instrument Capito),

---

5. Sulla manumitted more than 10,000 slaves of proscribed persons, and enrolled them in the plebs, selecting the youngest and the strongest for his army (Appian, *BCiv.* 1.100); all these took the *nomen* Cornelius. Pliny (*HN* 35.200) mentions Chrysogonus in a list of certain former slaves who had been glutted with the blood of Roman citizens.

6. For the proscription of Roscius' father see T. E. Kinsey (1980), 173-190; and (1981), 149-150.

7. For the question of the legality of the sale see T. E. Kinsey (1988), 325-332.

Chrysogonus, Capito, and Magnus began devising a plot to murder Roscius, realizing that only after his elimination could they enjoy his wealth (*Rosc. Am.* 26).

Meanwhile, Roscius had fled to Rome where he took refuge in the house of Caecilia, the daughter of Q. Caecilius Metellus Balearicus (cos. 123 B.C.), sister of Metellus Nepos (cos. 98 B.C.), and second cousin to Q. Caecilius Metellus Pius, who fought for Sulla in the final struggle against Marius and was consul with him in 80 B.C., the year of the trial (*Rosc. Am.* 27). Although Cicero does not exploit the connection between Sulla and the Metelli in this speech, it was probably the involvement of this very potent political relationship that might have ultimately induced Sulla to withdraw his support of Chrysogonus. Cicero probably did not have to exert himself over much to obtain the acquiesence of the dictator. According to Plutarch (*Crass.* 6.8) Sulla had expressed some displeasure with the excessive profiteering of his subordinates, and Chrysogonus himself, Cicero alleges, was aware that he could not count on the dictator's support.[8]

Foiled in their attempt to destroy Roscius, and fearing that because of Roscius' present association with Caecilia Sulla might learn of their plot, Chrysogonus, Capito, and Magnus decided to do away with Roscius by accusing him of his father's murder. Relying on Chrysogonus' influence with the dictator, and the fact that it had been so long since the last murder trial had taken place, they believed that they could prosecute Roscius on a charge of parricide, and that if they did, he would be unable to find anyone to defend him, and even if he could, the trial, held in Sulla's new *quaestio*, would be a political circus and a legal sham (*Rosc. Am.* 28).[9]

Chrysogonus chose C. Erucius to conduct the prosecution. Although we do not have Erucius' speech, we can form an idea of what it contained from the main points that Cicero addresses in his speech. We should, for example, infer that Erucius addressed the fact that Roscius was not in Rome at the time of the murder, and therefore in order to have carried out his father's murder, he would have had to work through assassins. But on the basis of what Cicero says in his speech Erucius explored none of these points, building his case primarily on Roscius' motive for wanting to murder his father, the evidence for

---

8. *Chrysogonus et ipse ad eos accedit et homines nobilis adlegat qui peterent ne ad Sullam adirent* (*Rosc. Am.* 25; cf. 109-110).

9. Cf. Plutarch, *Cic.* 3; also T. E. Kinsey (1966), 270-271.

which amounted to exaggerated allegations of strained relations between the father and his son. So weak was Erucius' speech, in fact, that in his oration Cicero makes the following observation (*Rosc. Am.* 82):

[crimina] ... quae mihi iste visus est ex aliqua oratione declamare, quam in alium reum commentaretur; ita neque ad crimen parricidii neque ad eum, qui causam dicit, pertinebant.

In his defense of Roscius, Cicero meets the prosecution squarely on the issue of motive and turns the argument against them, charging that Chrysogonus was driven by greed first to seize Roscius' property, then to try to rid himself of Roscius, and to this end to accuse Roscius of the murder of his father. While Cicero used a similar strategy in the *Pro Quinctio* in exposing the greed of Naevius and his *advocati* by characterizing them as *cupidi* (*Quinct.* 71), in this speech Cicero also offers greed as the prime motivation of his opponent.

Chrysogonus was no doubt relying on his well-known influence with Sulla for success in the trial. But it was Cicero's relentless rhetorical efforts in the speech to turn the case into a political watershed that no doubt brought about Sulla's withdrawal of his support of Chrysogonus, and ultimately won Roscius' acquittal. Acquittal on the charge of parricide was all Cicero asked in the *exordium* (*Rosc. Am.* 7); Roscius' property, it seems likely, was never restored to him. Chrysogonus had purchased it with Sulla's sanction, which had the force of law.

According to Plutarch (*Cic.* 3.4-7), immediately following the trial Cicero left Italy fearing reprisal from Sulla. There may be some truth in what Plutarch says, but because there is no documented evidence for Sulla's reaction to the case, there is room for doubt. We know, for instance, that Cicero was still active in Rome in 79, perhaps even 78 B.C. (Cicero, *Caec.* 97), and later Cicero tells us (*Brut.* 312-315) that his success in defending Roscius brought him many more cases in quick succession, and that it was the strain of such forensic activity that forced him to leave Rome on an extended tour of Greece and Asia in order to restore his health and refine his rhetorical skills.

But Cicero knew the risk he was taking in attacking Chrysogonus, that in doing so he could be seen as implicating the dictator Sulla (Cicero, *Off.* 2.14.51). Therefore, the only way for Cicero to proceed against Chrysogonus was to prove, or get the jury to believe, that Chrysogonus had been plotting against the life of his client without the knowledge or consent of the dictator. This would not be easy, for Cicero could not defend Roscius without attacking Chrysogonus and therefore exposing the social and political corruption brought on by Sulla's dictatorship. In the *exordium* alone, Cicero alludes to the proscriptions and their effect on the judicial process six times, though he mentions Sulla by name only once. Indeed, in the *exordium* the *iniquitas temporum* emerges as a central theme that underlies the entire speech. Just as he uses *potestas* and *potentia* in the *Pro Quinctio*, here Cicero uses the *iniquitas temporum* to characterize Chrysogonus and his confederates, as well as to rivet the attention of his audience by showing that Roscius was not the only potential victim of the injustice that the opposition represents. Whereas the integrity of the courts hung in the balance of the *Pro Quinctio*, here Cicero would have his audience believe that the future of the entire state is in question. In doing this Cicero is applying the rhetorical rules he set down in the *De Inventione* (1.23), where he emphasizes the importance of showing how the *causa* concerns the *summa res publica*.

Given the subtle dangers Cicero was forced to skirt in this oration, the triumphant success of his defense indicates that the speech he delivered must have been some of his best rhetorical work. Thirty-six years later, in the *Orator* (107), Cicero would write of the speech: *Quantis illa clamoribus adulescentuli diximus de supplicio parricidarum, quae nequaquam satis defervisse post aliquanto sentire coepimus: "Quid ... conquiescant."*[10] Although he goes on to admit that the speech was in many ways a flawed product of his youth (*sunt enim omnia sicut adulescentis non tam re et maturitate quam spe et exspectione laudati*), looking back as late as 46 B.C. apparently he was still proud of his performance.

According to Cicero (*Rosc. Am.* 28) Sextus Roscius was charged with the murder of his father (*de parricidio*). The exact meaning of the word *parricidium* is elusive, but its legal etymology seems to indicate that it developed from the general to the more specific. The word *paricidas* (nominative singular) first occurs in a law attributed to Numa (*Lex reg.* [*Font. iur.* p. 10]; cf. Festus, s.v. *parricidium*), in which it signifies the willful murder of any free citizen who had not been condemned to death. But in the *De Inventione* (2.58) Cicero uses the term *parricidium* specifically in reference to the murder of a parent. The murder in question there had been carried out by poison, but

---

10. The passage Cicero quotes is from *Rosc. Am.* 72. Cf. also Quintilian, 12.6.4.

because it involved the murder of a parent (*de parricidio*), the trial was heard before a special court. This account indicates that at least a decade prior to the trial of Roscius cases *de parricidio* were tried by courts formed specifically for that crime, that they were separate from the court *de veneficis*. Further evidence for the distinction between the different murder courts lies in what we can trace of the history of the courts.

As early as 142 B.C. crimes *inter sicarios* seem to have been tried by a *quaestio extraordinaria*;[11] C. Claudius Pulcher (cos. 92 B.C.) held the position of *iudex quaestionis de veneficis* sometime between his aedileship (99 B.C.) and his praetorship;[12] in 101 B.C. Publicius Malleolus was convicted of matricide — whether the case was heard by a *quaestio de parricidiis* or in the public assembly is unclear[13] — but in the *Pro Roscio Amerino* (64-65) Cicero makes reference to a recent (*non multis annis*) murder trial (*de parricidio*), which seems to indicate that sometime between 101 and the mid 80s B.C. a *quaestio de parricidiis* was in operation. Whether or not this is the same trial mentioned at *De Inventione* 2.58, there is sufficient evidence to indicate that prior to the time of Sulla the procedures *de veneficis, de sicariis,* and *de parricidiis* were always independent of one another. Among the judicial reforms carried out by his *leges Corneliae* of 81 B.C., Sulla established the new *quaestio de sicariis et veneficis* under whose jurisdiction fell murder cases of all three descriptions.[14] It was in this newly established court that Cicero delivered the *Pro Roscio Amerino*.

---

11. At least on one occasion when, according to Cicero (*Fin.* 2.54), L. Hostilius Tubulus presided over this court as praetor. For other references to Tubulus, cf. *Fin.* 4.77, 5.62; *Nat. Deor.* 1.63, 3.74; *Att.* 12.5.3).

12. *CIL* 1² p. 200 (*aed. cur. iudex. q. veneficis pr. repetundis*). Cf. his *elogium*, (*ILS* 45); Cicero, *Clu.* 147-148, 151, 157; *Digest*, 1.2.2.32.

13. Oros. 6.16.23; Livy, *Epit.* 68; cf. *Rhet. ad Heren.* 1.33.

14. Sulla enacted new statutes for the existing courts of extortion, treason, and murder under the *leges Corneliae repetundarum, maiestatis, de sicariis et veneficis*; he also established what appear to be two new courts for electoral canvassing and for forgery under the *leges Corneliae de ambitu* and *testamentaria* or *de falsis*, as well as a *lex Cornelia de iniuriis*. An excellent review of the evidence for the formation and history of these courts is given by E. Gruen (1968), 258-264; see also G. Rotondi (1912), 352-363.

The magistrate who generally appears with the title of *iudex quaestionis* belongs to the murder court alone. The trial of Sextus Roscius was presided over by the praetor M. Fannius, the *iudex quaestionis* appointed by the same *lex Cornelia* that established the court (Cicero, *Clu.* 148; cf. *Digest* 48.8). Nothing is known of Fannius except what Cicero says of him in this speech, that he had presided over a similar court at an earlier date (*Rosc. Am.* 11), probably one of the independent murder courts in operation prior to Sulla's judicial reforms.[15]

The case against Sextus Roscius of Ameria was heard by a select jury comprised of senators whose appointment was as notorious as the *quaestio* for which they were impaneled; therefore brief mention of the *iudices* who were present at the trial of Roscius is in order. In 81 B.C. Sulla restored control of the *iudicia* to the hands of the senate, after it had been shared with the *equites* since the passage of the *lex Sempronia* of C. Gracchus in 122 B.C.[16] In order to increase the membership of the senate, whose numbers had been severely reduced by the civil war and the proscriptions, Sulla added some three hundred new members taken from the ranks of the equestrians.[17] Though it would not be until his prosecution of Verres a full decade later that Cicero enjoyed their full support, the former equestrians in the jury that heard Roscius' trial were a factor that worked in Cicero's, favor thanks to his own equestrian background. The background of the case of Roscius, especially the seizure of his property by Chrysogonus, also worked in Cicero's favor in his efforts to win the support of the jury. Throughout the *exordium* Cicero takes every opportunity to stress Roscius' material loss, hoping to strike a resonant chord in the hearts of the property-minded equites.

---

15. Previous to Fannius, C. Claudius Pulcher was *iudex quaestionis de veneficis*, and the aedile C. Iunius succeeded Fannius as the *iudex quaestionis* who presided over the court that condemned Oppianicus in 74 B.C. (*Clu.* 89), followed by C. Iulius Caesar, who after his aedileship took over the same office in 64 B.C. (*Clu.* 89; *Brut.* 264).

16. Sources on Sulla's law: Cicero, *Verr.* 1.37-38, 1 47-49, 2.2.77; *Clu.* 55; Vell. Pat. 2.32-3; Tacitus, *Ann.* 11.22; Ps-Ascon. 189, 219, 222 (Stangl); Schol. Gronov. (Stangl, p. 326); *Digest.* 1.2.2.32.

17. Cf. the contrasting reports of Appian, *BCiv.* 1.100; Livy, *Epit.* 89; Sallust, *Cat.* 37; Vell. Pat. 2.32; Tacitus, *Ann.* 11.22; Dion. Hal. 5.77.

Commentary

Cicero begins the *exordium* with an *apologia*, a proleptic explanation of why he of all people has undertaken the defense of Sextus Roscius, which Cicero frames in the form of a question. This approach will become typical of many of the opening sentences of the *exordia* in this study, especially under unusual circumstances, or the *insolentia*, of the trial at hand. Cicero uses the approach not only to project his own *persona*, but also to build suspense into his opening statement:

> 1.1-4: Credo ego vos, iudices, mirari quid sit quod, cum tot summi oratores hominesque nobilissimi sedeant, ego potissimum surrexerim, qui neque aetate neque ingenio neque auctoritate sim cum his, qui sedeant, comparandus.

Periodic word order elevates the dramatic tension of the opening sentence, and adds to the suspense. Cicero begins by immediately establishing the antithesis between himself and Roscius' silent *advocati*, the *summi oratores*, through chiasmus (V PN PN V), at the center of which is the juxtaposition of himself, who understands, and they, who wonder (*credo ego vos...mirari*). By addressing the *iudices* in the second person Cicero immediately involves them in the conflict he is attempting to establish between the different *personae* involved in the trial. Cicero's approach is aimed at introducing himself to his audience, and in particular to the *iudices*, and ingratiating himself with them. He is careful to engage their attention from the outset by opening with a question directed at them. The approach is subtle, but as he continues to develop antithesis a larger agenda will emerge.

Credo, often used sarcastically by Cicero, or parenthetically with no effect on the rest of the construction, is here employed in an emphatic position in the sentence, governing the indirect statement whose verb (*mirari*) in turn governs an indirect question (*quid sit quod*): why are the orators sitting and watching silently when they should be up and doing what Cicero is doing?[18] Cicero lets the *iudices*

---

18. For *credo*, cf., e.g., Cicero, *Rosc. Am.* 60.5; *Verr.* 2.178, 4.7, 8, 43, 5.149; *Phil.* 1.11. 10.18, 11.11; *Att.* 6.1.15. See also A. Haury (1955), 76.

ponder this question while he draws attention to the visual contrast between himself (standing and speaking) and the others (sitting and silent). It must have made an effective impression on his audience. The antithesis of the opening sentence revolves around three main points of contrast between Cicero and the silent orators: position, number, and character (*dignitas*); the arrangement of the clauses is chiastic:

(A₁) ORATORS: [position] sedeant

                       [number] tot

                       [character] summi...nobilissimi

(B₁) CICERO: [position] surrexerim (1st period)

                       [number] ego potissimum

(B₂) CICERO: [character] qui neque aetate
                                    ingenio
                                    auctoritate sim cum his ⇒

(A₂) ORATORS: [position] qui sedeant

                              ⇒ comparandus (2nd period)

Cicero suspends the resolution of the indirect question (*quid sit quod*) introduced by *mirari* with the *cum* clause (A₁) in which he introduces the *summi oratores* whom he describes as: 1) sitting (*sedeant*); 2) many (*tot*); and, 3) eminent and distinguished (*summi...nobilissimi*). The contrast is immediately struck in the following clause (B₁), the main clause of the indirect question, where Cicero describes himself as: 1) standing (*surrexerim*); and, 2) alone (*ego potissimum*). Character, or *dignitas*, the third point of contrast raised by the *cum* clause (A₁), and here the most important, is resolved in the following *qui* clause (B$_2$) modifying Cicero. The perfect tricolon of B$_2$ (*neque aetate neque ingenio neque auctoritate*), in which Cicero expands the length of each individual element by a single increment, corresponds to the bipartite description of the silent orators (*summi oratores hominesque nobilissimi*) in A$_1$, and through antithesis (note the emphatic repetition of the connector *neque*) illustrates the disparity between his own *dignitas* and theirs. The resolution of B$_2$ (*comparandus*) is in turn delayed by the insertion of a second relative clause (A$_2$), where Cicero returns to the image of the seated orators (*sedeant*) with which he began (A$_1$). Cicero's use of *comparo* here, particularly with the preposition *cum*, has the connotation of the matching of opponents for physical combat, and recalls the *exordium* of the *Pro Quinctio* where Cicero employed a similar construction (*ut ego, qui neque usu satis et ingenio parum possum, cum patrono disertissimo comparer*). This suggests that what Cicero is doing is engaging the silent orators in a *contentio dignitatis*, a bold move for one as inexperienced as Cicero claims to be, but strategically astute, for it no doubt endeared him to his audience for his admirable, selfless courage.

The image of the silent orators is a striking visual metaphor for the nature of the crisis at hand: justice has been silenced. The question, of course, is why? In answer, Cicero immediately introduces the theme of *iniquitas temporum*, the cause of the silence of Roscius' *advocati*, as well as Cicero's own frustration and isolation. In this way Cicero reverses the opening antithesis by showing that both he and the orators are moved, albeit to opposite courses of action, by the same external forces. This reversal anticipates Cicero's transition to the appeal *a persona nostra*, as well as his transition to the argument *ab adversariorum persona*.

1.4-7: Omnes hi, quos videtis adesse in hac causa, iniuriam novo scelere conflatam putant oportere defendi, defendere ipsi propter iniquitatem temporum non audent.

Cicero keeps the focus on the silent orators, who are all but on display (*Omnes hi quos videtis...*). Through the chiastic arrangement of the main clause (*putant oportere defendi, defendere...non audent*), strengthened by asyndeton, Cicero shows how the *iniquitas temporum* has rendered the *summi oratores*, men whose moral compass allows them to see clearly the legal right of the accused to be defended (*putant oportere defendi*) against what is clearly injustice (*iniuriam*), and therefore should be the backbone of the legal system, paralyzed and mute. Cicero attributes this to an as yet unnamed and mysterious force, whose sinister nature he only hints at here (*novo scelere conflatam...propter iniquitatem temporum*). Although he will not use this term again when referring to the orators in the speech, *nobilissimi* has suddenly taken on a slightly ironical color. Cicero goes on to explain the paradox of the silent orators:

> 2.13-17: Quia, si qui istorum dixisset, quos videtis adesse, in quibus summa auctoritas est atque amplitudo, si verbum de re publica fecisset, id quod in hac causa fieri necesse est, multo plura dixisse, quam dixisset, putaretur.

As Cicero accounts for the orators' silence (*quia*), he repeats the phrase *quos videtis adesse* from the previous sentence, as though it were the silent orators who were on trial here, and in a way they are. The reason Cicero gives for their silence is the *iniquitas temporum*, introduced in the previous sentence and elaborated upon here. The irony is supported, or at least embellished, by the alliterative effects of this passage which contain a definite *susurratio* (*si...dixisset, quos videtis adesse ... summa auctoritas est ... si ... fecisset ... necesse est ... dixisse...dixisset...*), through which Cicero seems to be suggesting that the men who possess *auctoritas, amplitudo*, and, in short, greater *dignitas* than he, are afraid to speak out; they are reduced to a whispering mass of huddled fear, unable to find a voice for what he alone has the courage to come out and say. In the two conditional clauses Cicero stresses that speech is what is necessary to remedy the situation and what is required of those who are present but silent because they fear the risk they will run if they do speak out. The compound protasis (P_{1-2}) builds to the periodic resolution of the apodosis (A), or main clause, in which Cicero dramatically exposes the cause of their fear:

(P_1) si qui istorum dixisset

    quos videtis adesse

        in quibus summa auctoritas est atque amplitudo

(P_2) si verbum de re publica fecisset

id quod in hac causa fieri necesse est

(A) multo plura dixisse, quam dixisset, putaretur

The subject of the first clause of the protasis (P_1), *qui istorum*, looks forward to the *quos* clause, which, in turn, is modified by a second relative clause (*in quibus*) describing the silent orators, this time in terms of their *summa auctoritas* and *amplitudo*, a restatement of Cicero's initial characterization of them in the opening sentence (*summi ... nobilissimi*), as well as a sharp contrast to Cicero's initial admission of his own personal insignificance (*neque auctoritate*).[19] Such praise of the orators is, at least in the present context, as ironic as his earlier use of *nobilissimi*. The anaphora *qui...quos...in quibus* has no precise parallel in the second conditional clause (P_2), where Cicero makes no attempt at symmetry or balance. Through *variatio* (*verbum fecisset* = *dixisset*) the second protasis appears to restate the point made in the first, but in fact it does more by introducing a new factor into the argument, the *res publica*. With the addition of *de re publica*, Cicero has opened a new door in the oration, one that, once opened, he cannot close until he leads the entire audience through it to whatever concluson he has in mind. This broadens the scope of the impact of the *iniquitas temporum*, adding a link to the chain of obligation by implying that there is much more at stake here than simply the defense of one man: it (the *causa*) ought (*oportere*) to be fought, and, if fought, must include (*necesse est*) some mention of the political situation (*de re publica*), yet no one is willing to do this. Why? Cicero answers this question in the apodosis (A), where he makes no attempt to equal in length the compound protasis; rather, through the periodic construction, which delays the resolution of *putaretur* by the accusative and infinitive of the indirect statement (*plura dixisse*), Cicero shows that he sympathizes with the dilemma of the orators: were they to speak on behalf of the defense, they would run the very real risk of being perceived (*putaretur*) as doing exactly what Cicero is doing, *viz.* attacking the prosecution, and for some reason (not yet disclosed), this is a dangerous thing.

---

19. Cf. Cicero, *Inv. Rhet.* 2.166: *amplitudo [est] potentiae aut maiestatis aut aliquarum copiarum magna abundantia.*

In this passage Cicero uses the silent orators in order to illustrate the stifling effect of the *iniquitas temporum* on free speech.[20] Cicero's repetition of the verb *dico*, along with the idiom *verbum facere*, emphasizes the silence of the other orators and insinuates that they have chosen to remain silent out of fear of political reprisal. Cicero, of course, is not out to condemn the orators for their silence, but to use that silence as a foil to expose and convict the source of this political reprisal, which, we get the impression, is inextricably linked to the prosecution.

In the next two sections (3-4) Cicero explains at length why he, at this early stage in his career, has less to lose by coming forward than do the *summi oratores*. Cicero then sums up these arguments and gives his explanation for why he alone has undertaken the defense of Roscius:

> 5.11-15: His de causis ego huic causae patronus exstiti non electus unus, qui maximo ingenio, sed relictus ex omnibus, qui minimo periculo possem dicere, neque uti satis firmo praesidio defensus Sex. Roscius, verum uti ne omnino desertus esset.

Cicero turns what was at first his weakness into a source of rhetorical strength: not despite, but *because* of his youth, inexperience, and lack of reputation, Cicero is able to assume the role of Roscius' *patronus* and speak freely without the fear of reprisal that has paralyzed the silent orators. *Exstiti* reinforces the bold declaration of *surrexerim* from the opening sentence: building on his initial self-characterization as a man isolated by the danger of the times (*potissimum*), Cicero now explains that he is representing Roscius not because he is the best choice of all possible *patroni* (*non electus unus*), but because he is Roscius' last and only chance (*sed relictus ex omnibus*), and that it is he alone who runs the least risk by speaking out (*qui minimo periculo possem dicere*). Cicero emphasizes his isolation through antithesis and interlocking word order reinforced by alternating instances of homeoteleuton (*non electus unus...maximo ingenio...sed relictus ex omnibus...minimo periculo*).

In the two parallel purpose clauses dependent on *exstiti*, Cicero strategically shifts the focus from his own situation to that of Roscius. Once again, through antithesis and interlocking homeoteleuton (*...neque uti firmo praesidio...defensus...verum uti ne omnino desertus Sex. Roscius*) Cicero shows Roscius' isolation is similar to his own. This

---

20. Cf. Cicero, *Planc.* 35, for a similar tactic.

shared isolation is the focal point of Cicero's transition to the appeal *a persona nostra*. The bipartite passive construction Cicero uses to describe Roscius' predicament echoes the antithesis he used to describe himself in the main clause (*non electus ... sed relictus*), and the word-play on *defensus ... desertus* also recalls Cicero's characterization of the silent orators and their predicament over taking an active or passive role (*defendi, defendere*).[21] Cicero makes Roscius the subject of passive verbs in order to emphasize that his client is indeed a victim of the *iniquitas temporum*, a parallel not only to himself, but to the silent orators as well. Cicero deliberately delays Roscius' name until near the end of the sentence to indicate to his audience that the focus of the sentence is no longer himself but Roscius — an important shift in the argument and key to the accretive progression of the *exordium*.

In his transition from the appeal *a persona nostra* to *ab adversariorum persona* Cicero anticipates the important characterization of Chrysogonus. This is a crucial appeal because in it Cicero will finally identify and denounce those responsible for the *iniquitas temporum*. Cicero delays the introduction of Chrysogonus until he has prepared his hearers for what will be a brief and decisive condemnation of his adversary's character not only by identifying him as the true evil that drives the prosecution, but also by portraying him as the true force behind the *iniquitas temporum*. Typically, Cicero shapes his transitions accretively, by drawing on previous elements introduced in the *exordium*; here he carries forward his portrayal of the silent orators in a manner that is no longer ironic or sarcastic but sincere and even pathetic:

5.16-19: Forsitan quaeratis, qui iste terror sit et quae tanta formido, quae tot ac tales viros impediat, quo minus pro capite et fortunis alterius, quem ad modum consueverunt, causam velint dicere.

Up to this point Cicero has characterized the orators as silent and apprehensive, a foil for his own bold ethos, and there has been more than a hint of contempt in his portrayal of them. But it must be kept in mind, as no doubt Cicero was keenly aware, that these silent orators are present as Roscius' *advocati*, valuable and needed allies of Cicero's

---

21. The use of the same word in close juxtaposition but in different senses is mentioned by Cicero in the *Orator* (155) as one of the ornaments of style (cf. *Causis ... causa* in this passage).

client. Therefore, as he prepares to reveal the reason for their fear and silence (*iste terror...tanta formido*), he also reveals that they are victims of the *iniquitas temporum* just as he and Roscius are. Although Cicero's initial description of the orators as *viri nobilissimi*, possessing *summa auctoritas atque amplitudo*, came across as ironic or paradoxical because of their passivity and silence, now Cicero invites his audience to entertain a different interpretation of that reluctance. For if terms such as these acurately describe the silent orators, then what is the significance and implication of their silence? That these men are afraid to speak despite their station and qualifications is Cicero's best illustration that the *terror* he now mentions is as menacing as he suggests: men such as these are so intimidated by this *terror* that they are unable to defend a man who ought to be defended. Cicero has shifted the focus of the orators' puzzling silence: it is no longer a foil for his surprising and bold defense, but for the menace that the accusation against Roscius represents.

In his transition to the argument *ab adversariorum persona*, Cicero anticipates the appeal *a iudicum persona*, with which he typically concludes his *exordia*. The description *tot ac tales viros* is a phrase Cicero usually reserves for the *iudices*,[22] not fellow orators, and therefore in the present context he may very well be alluding to the members of the jury, adumbrating their dilemma in his characterization of the silent orators. We saw how winning over the *iudices* by including them in the dilemma of the defense was an integral element of Cicero's rhetorical strategy in the *exordium* of the *Pro Quinctio*. By first inviting his audience to see the silent orators as guilty of failing in fulfilling their *officium* despite their *nobilitas* and *amplitudo*, Cicero was merely executing a feint. Cicero's intention was not to criticize or to alienate his silent colleagues — indeed, he is well aware that Roscius needs all the *advocati* he can get; on the contrary, as we saw in the opening sentences of the *exordium*, Cicero went to great lengths to make examples of the silence of the *summi oratores* first as evidence of the danger that faced the entire state, and then as a means of winning the support of the *iudices*. By showing that there is justifiable cause (*iste terror*) for the fear that prompted their silence, Cicero now directs the court's attention away from himself, Roscius, and the silent orators, and focuses it on the source of the *terror*, Chrysogonus. The emotions Cicero is attempting to stir in the *iudices* are similar to those he used to

---

22. Cf. *Rosc. Am.* 54; see also *Div. in Caec.* 51, *Quinct.* 81, *Clu.* 186.

exhort the *oratores nobilissimi* at the beginning of the *exordium*: duty versus expediency, *officium* versus *oportere/necesse est debere, defendere* versus *tacere*. But before he names the source of the *terror*, he takes one further step to win the *benevolentia* of the *iudices* and secure a united front against the opposition:

> 5.19-21:   Quod adhuc vos ignorare non mirum est, propterea quod consulto ab accusatoribus eius rei, quae conflavit hoc iudicium, mentio facta non est.

Cicero furthers his attempts to forge an alliance between himself, Roscius, the silent orators and the *iudices*, by suggesting that the prosecution has deliberately avoided mentioning the real reason why Roscius has been brought to trial. The implication, following on the previous sentence, is that the *iudices* have been kept ignorant of the cause of the mysterious terror by the prosecution because they, the prosecution, are the ones who are responsible for it. Only now can Cicero identify L. Cornelius Chrysogonus, the powerful freedman of the dictator Sulla, as the driving force behind the *terror* and the *iniquitas temporum*, the true criminal in the proceedings. With this revelation Cicero begins the argument *ab adversariorum persona*, toward which he has been subtly but methodically building:

> 6.21-26:   Quae res ea est?   Bona patris huiusce Sex. Rosci quae sunt sexagiens, quae de viro fortissimo et clarissimo, L. Sulla, quem honoris causa nomino, duobus milibus nummum sese dicit emisse adulescens vel potentissimus hoc tempore nostrae civitatis, L. Cornelius Chrysogonus.

Cicero keeps his audience engaged by beginning with yet another rhetorical question, but this one is directed at the heart of the case, and in his answer Cicero builds swiftly to the dramatic disclosure of Chrysogonus.   He begins with the direct object (*bona*) of the main clause, emphasizing gain as the motive of the prosecution;   Cicero is equally emphatic in his identification of the *bona* in question as the *patrimonium* of Roscius (*patris huiusce Sex. Rosci*).   Cicero delays the subject of the main clause, Chrysogonus, until the very end of the sentence with the insertion of three relative clauses, the first two of which modify *bona*;   in the first Cicero states the value of Roscius' property (6,000,000 sesterces), and in the second he reveals the token sum (2,000 sesterces) that Chrysogonus paid for the property, as well as the source of the sale — none other than the dictator Sulla.

Cicero's introduction of Sulla, the only mention of the dictator in the *exordium*, is curious and unexpected, especially since it is Chrysogonus whom he is trying to expose and, more important, isolate. Although in the third relative clause Cicero explains parenthetically that he is mentioning Sulla *honoris causa*, there is more going on here.[23] By mentioning Sulla as the man from whom Chrysogonus bought Roscius' property, Cicero must have known he was taking the chance of implicating the dictator in Chrysogonus' criminal activity, a risky maneuver. But as his audience must have known, many of whom no doubt profited from the proscriptions as well, any property seized in the proscriptions and bought at state auction could be said to have been purchased *de Sulla* — that is, as representative of the state, for according to Cicero *Sulla unus omnia poterat* (*Rosc. Am.* 139).[24] It seems more to the point that Cicero address Chrysogonus' relationship with Sulla, which must have been well-known despite the fact that Sulla had freed thousands of slaves (Appian, *BCiv.* 1.100), in order to dissociate the dictator from his freedman by implying that Sulla was yet another person (like Roscius) of whom Chrysogonus had taken advantage.[25] That the syntactic resolution of the main clause of the sentence awaits the name of Chrysogonus is, no doubt, a deliberate effort on Cicero's part to divert his audience's attention away from Sulla and any association Cicero could be thought to be drawing between Chrysogonus and the dictator. The language Cicero uses in his characterization of Sulla and his characterization of Chrysogonus supports this conclusion. Cicero describes Sulla as a *vir,* and Chrysogonus as an *adulescens*, the contrast between these two terms apparent. The distinction Cicero makes between the dictator and his

---

23. Although the phrase *honoris causa nominare* is formulaic, it seems to have been sincere (cf. Cicero, *Phil.* 2.30).

24. The best commentary on the situation is found in Cicero, *Verr.* 3.81: *Unus adhuc fuit post Romam conditam, cui res publica se totam traderet, L. Sulla. Hic tantum potuit, ut nemo illo invito nec bona nec patriam nec vitam retinere posset: tantum animi habuit ad audaciam, ut dicere in contione non dubitaret, bona civium Romanorum cum venderet, se praedam suam vendere.*

25. For Chrysogonus' abuse of his position, see V. Buchheit (1975), 193-211; and (1975), 570-591.

freedman with his choice of adjectives, however, is less obvious, but more telling. Sulla is *clarissimus et fortissimus*, but it is Chrysogonus whom Cicero calls *potentissimus*. The superlative attributed to Chrysogonus could be interpreted as ironic, were it not for the insertion of the adverb *vel* and the phrase *hoc tempore nostrae civitatis*, a specific, serious, and direct reference to the *iniquitas temporum*.[26] At worst, Cicero seems to be implying that Sulla may be responsible for the advent of the *iniquitas temporum* (a point Cicero wisely does not elaborate upon), but it is Chrysogonus alone who is exploiting it for his own personal gain at the expense of men like Sextus Roscius, a point to which Cicero will return in the course of the speech (cf. 21-22).

The emphasis given by the position of L. Cornelius Chrysogonus' name at the end of this long sentence must have produced a dramatic response among his audience. His *praenomen* and *nomen*, Lucius Cornelius, which Cicero does not fail to mention here, identify him unmistakably as a freedman of Sulla, but his *cognomen*, simply for the fact that it was a Greek word, must have had an especially repulsive ring, and the mention of his name in the present passage elicited a profound reaction from Chrysogonus himself, as Cicero states in the *partitio* of the speech:

59.3-60.8: Peroravit aliquando, adsedit; surrexi ego. Respirare visus est, quod non alius potius diceret. Coepi dicere. Usque eo animadverti, iudices, eum iocari atque alias res agere, antequam Chrysogonum nominavi; quam simul atque attigi, statim homo se erexit, mirari visus est.

In contrast to his portrayal of Roscius as a passive victim (*defensus...desertus* [5.14-15]), Cicero makes Chrysogonus the subject of an active verbal construction (*dicit emisse*). This rhetorical antithesis reinforces the point that it is Chrysogonus, not Roscius, nor even Sulla, who is the true aggressor, indeed the guilty party, in this case. Furthermore, by using indirect statement (*dicit emisse*) to attribute the source of the sale of the property to Sulla, Cicero helps to distance the dictator from responsibility for what happened.

The argument *ab adversariorum persona* leads into the appeal *a causa*, in which Cicero employs rhetorical elements similar to those he used in his initial characterizations in order to emphasize the contrast between Roscius and Chrysogonus. Perhaps because the case of the

---

26. Cf. *vel indignissimum* (8), *vel nobilissima* (21), *vel maxime* (69), and *vel maximam partem* (124) where the force of the adverb is strictly emphatic.

prosecution seems to have been based primarily on Roscius' motive for murdering his father, Cicero now addresses Chrysogonus' motive for seeking Roscius' life: his client's *patrimonium*.   In the following passage, Cicero explains that Chrysogonus is asking the court to condemn Roscius for the murder of his father not because Roscius is guilty, but because only with his elimination could Chrysogonus enjoy Roscius' *patrimonium*.   The sentence is divided into two parts: in the first, Cicero states what Chrysogonus wants; in the second, he gives the reasons why:

> 6.26-5: Is [Chrysogonus] a vobis, iudices, hoc postulat, ut, quoniam in alienam pecuniam tam plenam atque praeclaram nullo iure invaserit, quoniamque ei pecuniae vita Sex. Rosci obstare atque officere videatur, deleatis ex animo suo suspicionem omnem metumque tollatis; sese hoc incolumi non arbitratur huius innocentis patrimonium tam amplum et copiosum posse obtinere, damnato et eiecto sperat se posse, quod adeptus est per scelus, id per luxuriam effundere atque consumere.

The governing verb of the first part of the sentence, *postulat*, establishes the tone of the sentence as Cicero once again casts Chrysogonus in the active role.   The resolution of the *ut* clause, dependent upon *postulat*, is delayed by the insertion of two *quoniam* clauses that explain why Chrysogonus is seeking Roscius' removal. Grammatically, *quoniam* normally requires the indicative,[27] yet Cicero uses the subjunctive in both clauses (*invaserit* in the first and *videatur* in the second) in order to fasten an imputation of effrontery on Chrysogonus, strongly confirmed by the phrase *nullo iure*.[28]   Cicero describes Roscius' property, the object of *invaserit*, as *pecuniam tam plenam atque praeclaram*.   The wording of this phrase is significant; although *pecunia* is used elsewhere by Cicero of property,[29] the adjective *plena* is striking in this context and Cicero no doubt chose it

---

27. Cf. Leumann-Hoffman, 2.627.

28. *Invadere* was technically used of the seizure of landed property as opposed to movables or cattle (cf. Cicero, *Phil.* 2.75; Lucilius, 260; Justinian, *Inst.* 4.2.1).

29. According to the scholiast (Gronov., Stangl p. 303): *id est, in alienum patrimonium. Pecuniam dicit universitatem rei familiaris.* Cf. *Rosc. Am.* 23, 86, 110; *Verr.* 2.61. The word may also be used in the plural with the same sense as at, e.g., *Mil.* 76.

for the sake of its alliterative effect which, in conjunction with an extended homeoteleuton, no doubt made this phrase ring in the ears of the audience. In the second *quoniam* clause Cicero carries forward the idea of *pecunia* but adds a new element, the *vita Sex. Rosci*, which hinders Chrysogonus from enjoying his ill-gotten wealth (*obstare atque officere videatur*). Through periphrasis (*vita*, where the name *Sextus Roscius* would normally be expected), Cicero implies that Chrysogonus does not simply want Roscius removed so that he might enjoy his *patrimonium*, he wants his life taken away. This is an important shift in the argument, for although it is Roscius who stands accused of murder, Cicero is implying that it is Chrysogonus who, if granted his wish, would be the true murderer. The verbs of the *ut* clause (*deleatis, tollatis*) maintain the harsh tone of the present characterization.

The second half of the sentence is a bipartite construction with two parallel clauses in which Cicero uses antithesis to focus on Roscius' helplessness. The contrast between Roscius and Chrysogonus sets the tone and context for the transition to the closing appeal *a iudicum persona*. Again Chrysogonus is the subject of the two main clauses, both of which introduce indirect accusative and infinitive statements. In the first Cicero emphatically introduces the pronoun *sese* (cf. *is* above [6.26]), the subject of the infinitive *posse obtinere*, even before *non arbitratur*, the governing verb. In the second clause, as in the first, Cicero sustains periodicity by introducing the pronoun *se*, the subject of *posse* dependent upon *sperat*, thereby postponing the resolution of *effundere atque consumere*. Nearly all the verbs Cicero attributes to Chrysogonus (*obtinere, adeptus est, effundere atque consumere*) emphasize his initiative, and recall those of the first part of the sentence (*postulat, invaserit* [6.26-28]); furthermore, the description *patrimonium tam amplum et copiosum* echoes *pecuniam tam plenam atque praeclaram*, which serves to remind the audience that greed is the primary motive of the prosecution; *per scelus* restates *nullo iure* (6.28), while *per luxuriam* adds a further dimension to the condemnation of Chrysogonus' depraved character. Furthermore, the repetition of *posse* (6.3-4) reinforces the power that Chrysogonus either has, or aspires (*sperat*) to have.

In contrast to Chrysogonus' greed and aggressiveness, Cicero emphasizes Roscius' impoverishment, innocence, and victimization through a combination of anaphora and alliteration. It is unusual for Cicero to use an ablative absolute (*hoc incolumi*) that refers to a noun otherwise mentioned in the sentence (*huius innocentis*),[30] but the repetition of *huius* after *hoc* is highly emphatic, enhanced by the alliteration of the dependent adjectives *incolumi* and *innocentis*. *Hoc incolumi* corresponds to the ablative absolute (*damnato et eiecto*) that begins the second sentence, and strengthens the asyndeton and balance between the two clauses. Cicero is choosing his words carefully here: *damnatus* and *eiectus* are legal terms, and in using them Cicero is no doubt responding to the words of Erucius' initial charge in which he must have asked for Roscius' "condemnation" and "banishment."[31] Through the juxtaposition of Roscius and Chrysogonus Cicero anticipates his transition to the final and most important appeal of the *exordium*, the appeal *a iudicum persona*. In order to do this effectively Cicero first reminds the *iudices* that Chrysogonus needs their help in order to eliminate Roscius, and warns of the consequences should they allow this to happen:

> 6.5-8:   Hunc sibi ex animo scrupulum qui se dies noctesque stimulat ac pungit ut evellatis postulat, ut ad hanc raedam tam nefariam adiutores vos profiteamini.

In this passage Cicero focuses on the relationship between Chrysogonus and the *iudices* for the first time, and makes clear the consequences should they favor Chrysogonus in this case. Roscius has all but dropped from the picture, and Cicero describes him here as nothing more than an annoying pebble (*scrupulum*) in Chrysogonus' sandal. Cicero is not discounting the significance of his client's case, rather he is showing the threat that Chrysogonus' actions represent to the future of the state. Cicero is trying to convince his audience that the case against Roscius is emblematic of a fundamental crisis that goes beyond the defense of a single man: it is about the struggle between good and evil, and what is at stake is the very existence of the state. If they as *iudices* do not condemn Chrysogonus' actions, they are in effect condoning them and by so doing become his confederates.

Having stated what Chrysogonus demands (*postulat*) from the court, Cicero proposes an alternative course of action that the *iudices* should consider:

---

30. But cf. Caesar, *BG.* 2.22: *cum diversis legionibus aliae alia in parte hostibus resisterent.*

31. For similar use of these terms by Cicero, cf. *Cat.* 3.3; *Verr.* 1.98.

7.9-11: Si vobis aequa et honesta postulatio videtur, iudices, ego contra brevem postulationem adfero et, quo modo mihi persuadeo, aliquanto aequiorem.

In this transition Cicero's choice of language is carefully sarcastic as he uses the phrase *aequa et honesta postulatio* to describe Chrysogonus' demands before introducing his own *postulatio* which he describes as "modest" (*brevis*) and somewhat more reasonable (*aequior*).

7.11-15: Primum a Chrysogono peto, ut pecunia fortunisque nostris contentus sit, sanguinem et vitam ne petat; deinde a vobis, iudices, ut audacium sceleri resistatis, innocentium calamitatem levetis et in causa Sex. Rosci periculum, quod in omnes intenditur, propuletis.

In this climactic passage Cicero contrasts the demands of the prosecution with the demands of justice. The antithesis between the two is polar and obvious, but the distribution of its elements in parallel isocola is uncharacteristic for Cicero and therefore in the present context emphatic. The construction is straightforward: the main point of antithesis focuses on Chrysogonus in the *primum* clause and Roscius in the *deinde* clause. Parallel word order prevails throughout both clauses with minimal variation until the final clause of the sentence, where Cicero brings in a new element that introduces the transition to the next appeal, *a iudicum persona*.

Peto is the main verb of both the *primum* and *deinde* clauses, and in both instances it governs parallel purpose clauses. In the *primum* clause, where Chrysogonus is the focus, the issue is plain: money and fortune in exchange for a man's life. The construction *pecunia fortunisque* of the *ut* clause is balanced antithetically by *sanguinem et vitam* in the *ne* clause, the verbs of both clauses (*contentus sit, petat*) following their objects (note the repetition of *peto...ne petat*). Cicero's use of *vita* in this passage recalls the periphrasis at 6.29 (*vita Sex. Rosci*), but with the addition of *sanguis* Cicero produces a hendiadys the obvious effect of which is to emphasize the fact that Chrysogonus seeks the death of Roscius as a solution to his embarrassment.[32]

In the *deinde* clause Cicero shifts the focus of the argument back to Roscius, using Chrysogonus' character as a foil for that of his client. An

---

32. Cf. Cicero, *Quinct.* 39: *sanguinem vitamque*; also *Quinct.* 76: *non pecuniam, sed vitam et sanguinem petere.*

understood *peto* governs a tripartite *ut* construction, the first two clauses of which are arranged by asyndeton but set off from the third by the connector *et*. Cicero arranges the elements of the first two clauses in an isocolon similar to the *ut* and *ne* clauses of the *primum* clause: *audacium sceleri* stands in parallel antithesis to *innocentium calamitatem*, and the verbs of both clauses (*resistatis, levetis*) follow their objects. But the third and final part of the *ut* clause marks a transition, for it is coupled to the previous series by an *et* and no *et* has preceded: the first two clauses represent the contrast between Chrysogonus and Roscius, but the third points the argument in a new direction and forms the opening wedge of the transition between the present appeal *ab adversariorum persona* and the coming appeal *a iudicum persona*.

The transition hinges on the word *periculum*: the danger posed by Chrysogonus extends beyond Roscius to all men (*in omnes intenditur*); therefore it is the responsibility of the *iudices* to repel it (*propulsetis*). Cicero's use of *periculum* recalls his use of the *iniquitas temporum* in his characterization of the silent orators at the beginning of the *exordium,* but it also shows the *iudices* that their own interests are involved in the case. By including the *iudices* Cicero attempts to do more than win their *benevolentia*, he wants to get them personally and emotionally involved.

Cicero uses the appeal *a iudicum persona* to take advantage of the character of the jury in both specific and general terms. First, by specifically addressing those members of the jury, many of whom are of equestrian background, Cicero attempts to arouse sympathy for Roscius' financial predicament; second, Cicero's general characterization of the *iudices* as a unified body dedicated to upholding the law serves to pit them against the lawless machinations of the prosecution.

> 8.27-4: Qui ex civitate in senatum propter dignitatem, ex senatu in hoc consilium delecti estis propter severitatem, ab his hoc postulare homines sicarios atque gladiatores, non modo ut supplicia vitent, quae a vobis pro maleficiis suis metuere atque horrere debent, verum etiam ut spoliis ex hoc iudicio ornati auctique discedant.

Cicero begins by addressing indirectly the equestrian component of the jury, those members who had been recently conscripted into the senate (*ex civitate in senatum*) under Sulla's extensive judicial reforms of 81 B.C.[33] Cicero's purpose in the present context is to appeal to the

---

33. For a description of these see Rotondi (1912), 352-362.

property-minded sensibilities of the equites, those among the jury best able to understand and sympathize with the significance of Roscius' financial loss. Cicero anticipated this feature of the final appeal when characterizing Chrysogonus at key points in the *exordium* by his avaricious seizure of Roscius' property (*pecuniam...invaserit* [6.27-28]; *patrimonium...obtinere* [6.2-3]; *per scelus...per luxuriam effundere et consumere* [6.4-5]), while at the same time stressing the personal ruin that Roscius faced as a result of losing it (*damnato* [6.3]; *innocentium calamitatem* [7.14]).

In his address to the former equestrians Cicero reminds them that they were made senators on account of their personal achievements (*propter dignitatem*), but their selection as *iudices* for this trial (*ex senatu in hoc consilium*) was based on the their moral integrity (*propter severitatem*). Cicero characterizes the *iudices* in terms of their *dignitas* and *severitas* in contrast to his characterization of the prosecution as *homines sicarii atque gladiatores*. Both *sicarius* and *gladiator* are terms that carry criminal connotations, but by using the term *gladiator* Cicero levels a double-edged assault on the moral character of the prosecution. A *sicarius* is literally a man who makes his living by the dagger (*sica*), and through common usage denotes an assassin of any sort who uses a weapon;[34] but the term *gladiator*, while it too describes a man of violent criminal nature who, like the *sicarius*, lives by the sword (*gladius*), can also convey the insinuation of sexual perversion.[35] Both *sicarius* and *gladiator* are terms that Cicero will use again in the course of the speech in connection with Capito, Magnus, and Chrysogonus (cf. 17, 94, 103, 151, 152). By using them here Cicero may also be suggesting that the proceedings at hand resemble more a gladiatorial contest, or mock battle, than a formal trial in a court of law.[36] Cicero sustains the military metaphor by using the term *spolia* for the rewards Chrysogonus will enjoy if he emerges victorious.

Having characterized the *iudices* as a group, Cicero concludes his appeal *a iudicum persona* by directly addressing the *iudex quaestionis*,

---

34. For the idiom cf. Quintilian 10.12.

35. For the possible sexual implications of *gladiator* see S. Cerutti and L. Richardson jr, (1989), 589-594; see also A. Imholz jr, (1972), 228-230.

36. Six times in the course of the speech Cicero speaks of the trial in terms of a *pugna* or *pugnare* (cf. 16, 17, 28, 35, 89, 108).

M. Fannius (11-12), an unusual tactic. He does not, however, approach Fannius immediately; instead, Cicero inserts a brief transition that contains the elements of a formal *conclusio*:

> 9.5-11: His de rebus tantis tamque atrocibus neque satis me commode dicere neque satis graviter conqueri neque satis libere vociferari posse intellego. Nam commoditati ingenium, gravitati aetas, libertati tempora sunt impedimento. Huc accedit summus timor, quem mihi natura pudorque meus attribuit et vestra dignitas et vis adversariorum et Sex. Rosci pericula.

The elements of this transition conform to the requirements of a *conclusio* as defined in the *Rhetorica ad Herennium* (4.41).[37] Cicero summarizes by briefly touching upon key issues and themes from his previous characterizations in the appeals *a nostra persona, a iudicum persona*, and *ab adversariorum persona*. The three sentences that make up this transition are so dependent upon each other, the elements of each succeeding sentence corresponding to and depending upon those that precede them, that they must be analyzed as a single unit.

The first sentence (9.5-7) is an indirect statement constructed in a perfectly rounded period. The meaning of the prepositional phrase with which Cicero begins is extremely ambiguous: *de rebus tantis tamque atrocibus* refers not only to the specific danger threatening Roscius, but also to the general threat that the *iniquitas temporum* poses to the state. The prepositional phrase functions loosely as the object of the three complementary infinitives (*dicere, conqueri, vociferari*) dependent upon *posse*, the verb of the indirect statement, which in turn depends upon the main verb *intellego*. The emphatic placement of *me*, the subject of *posse*, signals Cicero's return to the self-characterization with which he opened the *exordium*. Through the parallel construction *neque satis...neque satis...neque satis*, which connects the three infinitives and their adverbs (*commode dicere...graviter conqueri...libere vociferi*) in parallel order, Cicero builds to the periodic resolution both of the indirect statement (*posse*) and the main clause (*intellego*).

The second sentence (9.7-8) is closely linked to the first by the conjunction *nam*, signalling some further explanation of what has just been said. Cicero uses a simple double dative construction to explain

---

37. *Conclusio est quae brevi argumentatione ex iis quae ante dicta sunt aut facta conficit quid necessario consequatur.*

the reasons for his inability to combat through mere words the difficult situation in which he finds himself: lack of *ingenium* hinders him from speaking appropriately; his youth (*aetas*) renders any complaint a weak and ineffectual outcry; and finally the *tempora* (= *iniquitas temporum*) prevent freedom of speech. Cicero reinforces the subordination of the second sentence to the first by means of a *figura etymologica*, where the nouns *commoditas, gravitas, libertas* correspond directly to the adverbs *commode, graviter, libere* of the previous sentence. The effect is strengthened by the correspondence of word order between the two sentences: the adverb + infinitive construction of the first (*commode dicere...graviter... conqueri...libere vociferari*) is echoed by the dative + nominative construction of the second (*commoditati ingenium, gravitati aetas, libertati tempora*).

The third sentence (9.8-11) is linked to the previous one by the main construction *huc accedit*, which depends loosely on *impedimento*. The subject of this sentence, *timor* (best translated here as "nervousness" or "apprehension"), serves as the concluding point of the entire transition. Despite the fact that throughout his career Cicero often admits to feelings of *timor* whenever speaking in public, especially at the outset of an oration, here he is using *timor* as a means of transition in order to unite the key elements of the previous characterizations of the *exordium*.[38] By attributing his *timor* to his own *natura* and *pudor*, the *dignitas* of the *iudices*, the *vis adversariorum*, and the *periculum* of Roscius, Cicero summarizes the central themes he has developed in the *exordium* up to this point through his characterizations *a nostra persona, a iudicum persona*, and *ab adversariorum persona*.

The insertion of a *conclusio* at this juncture may seem at first to disrupt the logical progression of the *exordium*, but as a means of transition within the appeal *a iudicum persona* it is effective not only by its dramatic isolation of Fannius from the rest of the *iudices*, but also because Cicero's candor allows him to appeal to Fannius on equally personal terms:

---

38. In the *De Oratore* (1.121) Cicero confesses that on one occasion in his early career he was so overcome with fear upon rising to speak that the hearing was adjourned. It was a condition he suffered from for much of his career (cf. *Div. in Caec.* 41; *Clu.* 51; *Deiot.* 1).

11.21-24: Te quoque magno opere, M. Fanni, quaeso, ut, qualem te iam antea populo Romano praebuisti, cum huic eidem quaestioni iudex praeesses, talem te et nobis et rei publicae hoc tempore impertias.

As he has done on several occasions in the course of the *exordium*, Cicero begins his appeal to Fannius by emphatically placing him at the head of the sentence in a dramatic and emotional address (*te quoque magno opere, M. Fanni*) dependent upon *quaeso*, whose object, the *ut* clause, follows immediately and governs the correlative construction (*qualem...talem*) through which Cicero reminds Fannius of the integrity of his past performance as *iudex quaestionis* before the Sullan revolution (*iam antea*). Cicero's purpose here is to impress upon Fannius what is expected of him in the present circumstances: even under the new legal system (*hoc tempore*) his responsibility to uphold justice remains the same.[39] By repeating the pronoun *te* immediately after each correlative adjective, followed by the parallel phrases *populo Romano* and *rei publicae*, Cicero impresses upon Fannius that the entire state is depending upon him to uphold the traditional principles of justice at this crucial moment, despite the political pressures of the times. The periodic structure of the sentence supports the central argument on several levels: by withholding the verbs of the three dependent clauses (*praebuisti, praeesses, impertias*) until the end of their respective clauses, Cicero creates tension, sustained by the separation of the *qualem* clause from the *talem* clause by the insertion of the *cum* clause. The emphasis of the period ultimately falls on the phrase *hoc tempore*, another direct allusion to the *iniquitas temporum*.

At the heart of Cicero's appeal to Fannius is his desire to inspire and encourage Fannius to use his influence as *iudex quaestionis* to uphold the traditional principles of the court under the new Sullan system. It is therefore not only an appeal to Fannius, but an appeal to the whole court and the *corona*. Cicero, well aware of its impoertance, if Roscius' trial is the first of its kind to come before the new court, is at pains to convince Fannius that the outcome of the trial will help to establish a legal precedent that will no doubt have great influence on the future integrity of the entire legal system (11.24-2).

The *exordium* ends with a second *conclusio*. Such emotional appeals may occur at the end of the *exordium*, or after the *narratio* (cf.

---

39. We do not know what court Fannius presided over as *iudex quaestionis* prior to this trial, but from what Cicero says here (*huic eidem quaestioni*), it was probably *inter sicarios*.

Quinct. 32-34), as well as in the *peroratio* (*Rhet. ad Her.* 2.47). Cicero makes a similar emotional appeal at the end of the *exordium* of the *Pro Quinctio*, but with much more verbal elaboration and without the vivid particulars that he includes here:

12.5-12: Petimus abs te, M. Fanni, a vobisque iudices, ut quam acerrime maleficia vindicetis, ut quam fortissime hominibus audacissimis resistatis, ut hoc cogitetis, nisi in hac causa, qui vester animus sit, ostendetis, eo prorumpere hominum cupiditatem et scelus et audaciam, ut non modo clam, verum etiam hic in foro ante tribunal tuum, M. Fanni, ante pedes vestros, iudices, inter ipsa subsellia caedes futurae sint.

The sentence is one of the longest and most complex of the *exordium*. Cicero begins emphatically with the main verb *petimus*, which recalls *peto* of the appeal *ab adversariorum persona* (7.11-15) where Cicero indirectly addressed Chrysogonus, but the use of the plural here, along with the joint address of Fannius and the *iudices*, signals that closure is near. Through the three consecutive *ut* clauses dependent upon *petimus,* Cicero builds to the conclusion of the sentence by repeating in each clause a word or phrase from the preceding clause before the next word of importance is introduced in order to contrast the criminal, avaricious nature of the prosecution with the moral and social obligation of the *iudices*.[40] Cicero ends the passage as he began, by addressing both Fannius and the *iudices* in the vocative, driving home the point that it is up to the *iudices* to insure the future safety of the state by punishing the truly guilty parties, namely Chrysogonus, Capito, and Magnus.

The series of four *ut* clauses builds dramatically, the absence of connectives helping to increase the climactic tempo of the sentence, which Cicero bolsters by expanding the length of each *ut* clause in succession:

Petimus:

(1) ut quam acerrime maleficia vindicetis

(2) ut quam fortissime hominibus audacissimis resistatis

---

40. For this figure cf. *Rhet. ad Heren.* 4.34 (s.v. *gradatio*), and Quintilian, 9.55-57.

(3) ut hoc cogitetis

    (3A) nisi...ostendetis eo prorumpere hominum
                 cupiditatem et scelus et audaciam

    (3B) ut non modo clam verum etiam hic in foro
           ante tribunal tuum, M. Fanni
           ante pedes vestros, iudices
           inter ipsa subsellia caedes futurae sint

In the first two *ut* clauses Cicero entreats the *iudices* to take action against the prosecution; in the second two he warns them of the consequences if they do not. *Quam acerrime* of the first *ut* clause raises the expectation of *quam fortissime* in the second, and in both clauses Cicero creates tension by separating the adverbial phrases from their respective verbs (*vindicetis, resistatis*) by the insertion of the direct objects. Cicero describes the actions of the prosecution as *maleficia* in the first clause, and the character of the prosecution as *homines audacissimi* in the second. In the third clause Cicero begins to shift construction from the parallel structure of the first two. Like the first two clauses, the third *ut* clause is an object clause dependent upon *petimus*, and at first glance *hoc* appears to be the direct object of its verb *cogitetis* in parallel construction to both *maleficia* and *hominibus audacissimis* of preceding two *ut* clauses. But Cicero is playing with the expectations of his audience: the pronoun *hoc* looks forward to the indirect statement, which is delayed by the insertion of the *nisi*-clause, which in turn contains an embedded indirect question (*qui vester animus sit*) as the object of its verb (*ostendetis*). The final *ut* clause, then, is not an object clause dependent upon *petimus* as the first three are, but a result clause signalled by *eo* in the indirect statement that resolves *hoc cogitetis*.

In the final two *ut* clauses Cicero warns of the *cupiditas, scelus,* and *audacia* that threatens to erupt (*prorumpere*) unless the *iudices* show that their intentions are to combat it (*nisi...ostendetis*). Cicero uses the threat of *prorumpere* to return to Fannius and the *iudices,* contrasting *clam* with *hic in foro, ante tribunal,* with *ante pedes vestros,* in order to bring the terror literally to the feet of the jury. Cicero leaves the *iudices* with the image of bloodshed (*caedes*) threatening the very seats upon which they sit. By mentioning the physical appointments of the *iudices,* Cicero has brought the *exordium* full circle, recalling the opening image of the silent orators who remained seated when he alone rose up to speak

In the final passage of the *exordium* (13.13-22) Cicero uses characterization to review the main points of contrast between the criminal, vicious motives of the prosecution and the innocent, destitute condition of the defense. The terms Cicero chooses to illustrate the conflict between Roscius and Chrysogonus are clearly aimed at winning the support of the largely formerly equestrian jury:

> 13.13-22: Accusant ii, qui in fortunas huius invaserunt, causam dicit is, cui praeter calamitatem nihil reliquerunt; accusant ii, quibus occidi patrem Sex. Rosci bono fuit, causam dicit is, cui non modo luctum mors patris attulit, verum etiam egestatem; accusant ii, qui hunc ipsum iugulare summe cupierunt, causam dicit is, qui etiam ad hoc ipsum iudicium cum praesidio venit, ne hic ibidem ante oculos vestros trucidetur; denique accusant ii, quos populus poscit, causam dicit is, qui unus relictus ex illorum nefaria caede restat.

The passage revolves around a repetitive series of parallel clauses in which the character of the prosecution, introduced by the phrase *accusant ii*, is contrasted with that of the defense, introduced by *causam dicit is*. It is important to note the emphasis Cicero places on speech in this final passage with the verbs *accusare* and *dicere*, recalling the image of the silent *summi viri* with which he began the *exordium*. Cicero then underscores the antithesis between *accusare* and *dicere* by contrasting a plural verb (*accusant*) repeatedly with a singular (*dicit*), which also drives home the point central to Cicero's theme of *potestas*: an individual is up against a conspiracy. Furthermore, the paratactic arrangement of the contrasting clauses, achieved with asyndeton, which Cicero repeats four times, gives a swift and dramatic cadence to the sentence signalling closure. For the purpose of analysis the sentence can be broken down into four main units:

> Accusant ii, qui in fortunas huius invaserunt, causam dicit is, cui praeter calamitatem nihil reliquerunt;

Here Cicero implies that the real criminal in the trial is not the man on trial, but those who bring the charge, Chrysogonus and his confederates. They have wrongfully seized Roscius' property while Roscius, the defendant, is left with nothing except his own *calamitas*.

Cicero repeats key words from previous characterizations of both Chrysogonus (*invaserit* [6.28]) and Roscius (*calamitatem* [7.14]).

> accusant ii, quibus occidi patrem Sex. Rosci bono fuit, causam dicit is, cui non modo luctum mors patris attulit, verum etiam egestatem;

Cicero now reminds the jury of the murder of Roscius' father, the grief of the son, and emphasizes that the individual parties of the prosecution had more to gain from this man's death than the son.

> accusant ii, qui hunc ipsum iugulare summe cupierunt, causam dicit is, qui etiam ad hoc ipsum iudicium cum praesidio venit, ne hic ibidem ante oculos vestros trucidetur;

Cicero introduces the idea that not only have Chrysogonus and his two conspirators taken possession of the younger Roscius' property following the murder of the father, but were even involved in the murder itself. Through homeoteleuton (*ipsum iudicium cum*), Cicero underlines the gravity of the reality that Roscius' only chance for safety was to take refuge with the senate, and even then only in the compnay of a bodyguard (*cum praesidio*).

> denique, accusant ii, quos populus poscit, causam dicit is, qui unus relictus ex illorum nefaria caede restat.

Cicero concludes by stating directly that the accusers are the ones who should be on trial, while his client is the honest man, the one sole survivor of a final round of proscriptions. Cicero has shifted from a specific appeal on Roscius' behalf, to a universal one on behalf of he general population which demands (*populus poscit*) redress and punishment for the major crimes of the proscriptions and the innocent men who were put to death for the sake of their property.[41]

---

41 . Although the allusion may be to the delegation sent from Ameria to Sulla to oppose T. Roscius.

Conclusion

Although Cicero delivered the *Pro Roscio Amerino* just one year after the *Pro Quinctio*, we can see a vast difference in the development of Cicero's rhetorical style. Faced with the *insolentia* created by Sulla's judicial reforms, Cicero turns the situation to his advantage by tapping into the fear already present in his audience and using it to establish a common bond between them and his client Roscius. Although there are similarities between the *exordia* of the two speeches, in this *exordium* Cicero exhibits a broader range of rhetorical possibility than in the *exordium* of the *Pro Quinctio*. This becomes apparent in the opening sentence, where Cicero attempts to enter the minds of the jurors (*credo ego vos...mirari quod sit...*). He is more concerned with commenting on their impression of the situation than expressing his own perception of things, as he did in the *Pro Quinctio* (*quae res in civitate duae plurimum possunt...*). Cicero's approach in this oration is less direct than that of the *Pro Quinctio*; in fact, we can describe the *exordium* of the *Pro Roscio Amerino* as an example of *insinuatio*, or the indirect approach, in contrast to that of the *Pro Quinctio*, which is an example of *principium*, or the direct approach. Cicero's specific agendum in this case is the *iniquitas temporum*, and he focuses on it by planting a question in the minds of the jurors in the first sentence, which he then answers in the second. This philosophical approach marks a clear departure from the straightforward approach that Cicero adopts in the *exordium* of the *Pro Quinctio*. But while the rhetorical strategy Cicero uses in the *exordium* of the *Pro Roscio Amerino* differs from that of the *Pro Quinctio*, both are means to the same end: the use of *persona* to focus the attention of the *iudices* on the issues of the *causa* in order to prejudice them against the opposition.

Cicero begins the *exordium* with an *apologia* for his decision to represent Roscius because he is the least qualified of Roscius' *patroni* in terms of age (*aetas*), talent (*ingenium*), and lack of experience (*auctoritas*). The structure of the *exordium* revolves around a complex set of verbal and structural antitheses in which Cicero establishes conflict through an accretive progression that allows him to move succinctly through the appeals *a nostra persona* and *ab adversariorum persona*, building to the climactic appeal *a iudicum persona*. Because his defense of Roscius is actually an indictment of Chrysogonus, Cicero uses characterization to shape each appeal in order to bring about the defeat of the prosecution by prejudicing the *iudices* against them through blackening of character. While Cicero successfully manages to remove the guilt from his client by transferring it to Chrysogonus, he never makes any explicit charge against his opponent.[42] In his characterization of Chrysogonus Cicero portrays his opponent as a shrewd opportunist, perhaps the most powerful, but certainly the most dangerous man in the state, because he has taken full advantage of the *iniquitas temporum* in order to enrich himself at the expense and ultimate peril of Sextus Roscius.

By characterizing Roscius and himself as victims of an unjust political system created by the likes of Chrysogonus, Cicero uses the oppression of the Sullan regime to establish a bond with his client, which in turn forms the basis of the conflict between the *persona* of the defense and that of the prosecution. Cicero's condemnation of Chrysogonus and his praise of Sulla figure large in the way he uses *persona* as a transitional device to move cautiously between the appeals *a nostra persona, ab adversariorum persona* and *a iudicum persona*. The transitional style of this *exordium* is a variation of the strictly accretive style of the *exordium* of the *Pro Quinctio*. While transitional elements are one of the fundamental parts of Cicero's accretive style, the extent to which Cicero uses them in the *Pro Roscio Amerino* is more comprehensive than in the *Pro Quinctio*. This is largely because in the *Pro Roscio Amerino* Cicero is building to the final appeal to the *iudices*, a factor that is not so important in the *exordium* of the *Pro Quinctio* due to the circumstances of the *praeiudicium*, and the absence of a jury.

---

42. As Quintilian observes (7.2.2). See also the discussion in C. Craig (1993), 27-45, esp. 32; cf. W. Stroh (1975), 59-60; T. E. Kinsey (1980), 173-190, esp. 182-183.

CHAPTER THREE

Pro Murena

Introduction

Toward the end of November 63 B.C. Cicero defended Lucius Licinius Murena, consul designate for 62, on a charge of *ambitus*. In addition to Cicero, Murena was represented by Lucius Hortensius and Marcus Licinius Crassus (*Mur.* 48). The prosecution consisted of Marcus Porcius Cato (Uticensis) and Servius Sulpicius Rufus, and assisting them were two relatively unknown men, Gaius Postumus, and Servius Sulpicius, very likely the son of the prosecutor (*Mur.* 3, 7, 54, 56).[1]

---

1. The date of the publication of the *Pro Murena* presents a problem; in 60 B.C. Cicero writes to Atticus (*Att.* 2.1) that he is sending him a copy of his *orationes consulares*, a total of ten speeches among which the *Pro Murena* is not included. For a discussion of the problem, see A. D. Leeman (1982), 193-228, with discussion, 229-236.

It is important to keep in mind the political atmosphere leading up to and surrounding the trial in order to understand Cicero's technique in the *exordium*. Indeed, the timing of the trial could not have worked less in favor of Cato and Sulpicius or more in favor of Cicero. Cicero had confronted Catiline in the senate on the 8th of November 63 B.C., and delivered the First Catilinarian oration forcing Catiline's flight from the city that night. The next day Cicero delivered the Second Catilinarian *ad populum,* after which the senate declared Catiline *hostis* by a *senatus consultum ultimum (Mur.* 51-53; *Cat.* 2.7).[2] It was at some time between the Second and Third Catilinarian orations that Murena's case came to trial. While it must have presented an inconvenient and unwelcome distraction for Cicero, by the same token he must have embraced the opportunity to defend the consul-elect for the following year, as it would give him yet another opportunity to speak out on the issue of the Catilinarian conspiracy and muster support against the conspirators who were still present in the city.

Cicero always kept in mind that he had a case to win, and therefore he uses the threat to the state that Catiline represents in order to build an effective defense for Murena. One cause fed the other, and in his defense of Murena Cicero exploits the Catilinarian affair by making the most of the fact that Murena had been elected consul primarily because of his military qualifications (*Mur.* 20-25, 83-90), qualifications that, thanks to Catiline, were sorely needed by whoever would assume the office of consul, but were conspicuously lacking in his accusers. Furthermore, all three defenders, Cicero, Hortensius, and Crassus, were *consulares,* a claim that could not be made by any member of the prosecution. Cato was, after all, as yet only *tribunus plebis,* and Sulpicius, while he had followed the *cursus honorum* in step with Murena, had lost the election as Murena's rival for the consulship of 62 B.C. For Cicero the key issue in the trial was that if Murena should be found guilty and disqualified, then the state would have only one consul in office on the first of January and, with Catiline still on the loose, this would be an unthinkable situation (*Mur.* 83-85). Because the specter of Catiline demanded that there be two consuls in office for 62 B.C., Cicero focuses his defense of Murena not on the specific charge of *ambitus,* which he never really addresses, but on the fact that Murena is a consul-elect, a military man, the kind of leader needed to meet and

---

2. For the date of the First Catilinarian, see H. Drexler (1976), 145-151; see also A. Primmer (1977), 18-38.

crush the Catilinarian threat.[3] Cicero clearly recognized that this was the key issue in the trial, as he states in the *Pro Flacco*:

> 98.3-4. Defendi item consul L. Murenam, consulem designatum. Nemo illorum iudicum clarissimis viris accusantibus audiendum sibi de ambitu putavit, cum bellum iam gerente Catilina omnes me auctore duos consules Kalendis Ianuariis scirent esse oportere.

Corruption had taken many forms in the Roman electoral system since 432 B.C. when Livy tells us (4.25.13) that candidates were forbidden to whiten their togas for the purpose of calling attention to themselves.[4] This was followed by the *lex Poetelia* in 358 B.C. (Livy 7.15.12), intended to limit the amount of canvassing allowed a candidate, and in 314 B.C. Livy tells us (9.26.9) that a law was passed that forbade the formation of coalitions between candidates. By the end of the third century B.C., however, it seems that canvassing (*ambitio*) had become an accepted electoral practice, together with bribery (*ambitus*).[5] In 181 B.C. the *lex Cornelia et Baebia* was passed (Livy 40.19.11) as a measure to deal with electoral bribery, but Livy merely mentions its enactment and tells us nothing of its provisions or its effect. We can assume, however, because Julius Obsequens (12) records that the elections of 166 B.C. could be held only after intense canvassing, that this law failed in its purpose. Twenty-two years later, in 159 B.C., the *lex Cornelia et Fulvia* was passed against electoral corruption (Livy, *Epit.* 47; Pliny, *HN* 35.41; Polybius 6.56), but here again we have little information as to its scope and application. In 139 B.C. the *lex Gabinia* introduced the secret ballot, and twenty years later Marius erected bridges to approach the voting urns in the Campus Martius in order to control the voting procedure (Cicero, *Leg.* 3.17; Plutarch, *Mar.* 4-7). On the basis of a passage in the Scholia Bobiensia (*Sulla* 17) it seems safe to assume that Sulla also passed legislation that

---

3. For Cicero's use of Catiline in the *Pro Murena* see Leeman (1981), 193-228, with discussion, 229-236; K. Kumaniecki (1971), 161-179; for a good review of the evidence for and significance of the Catilinarian conspiracy in its political context, see E. G. Hardy (1917), 153-228.

4. For a history of electoral corruption in Rome, see R. W. Husband (1915-16), 535-545; L. R. Taylor (1949), 108, 122, 131-139.

5. For *ambitio* cf. Plautus, *Trin.* 1033; for *ambitus* cf. Varro, *LL* 5.28.

addressed electoral corruption, but the problem seems to have persisted
after the restoration of the democracy following the collapse of the
Sullan constitution, for in 67 B.C. the consul C. Calpurnius Piso passed
the *lex Calpurnia de ambitu*, the principal thrust of which was an
increase in the penalties for this crime (*Mur.* 46).[6] But electoral
corruption seems to have worsened in the years that followed,
especially in the area of organized political *factiones*, which seem to
have been the focus of the *lex Fabia* of 66 B.C. (*Mur.* 71), and in 63
B.C. Cicero was pressed by Cato to pass a new *lex de ambitu* that
imposed penalties that were much more severe than those imposed
under the *lex Calpurnia* (*Mur.* 47), even to the extent that *morbus
sonticus* was no longer an excuse for evading prosecution.[7] The call for
the new law was probably due to the fact that in 63 B.C. Catiline was
running for the consulship a second time, having lost in the previous
year to Cicero and Antonius Hybrida, and electoral corruption was no
doubt an issue.[8] Also standing for the consulship of 62 B.C. were
Decimus Silanus, Servius Sulpicius Rufus, and Lucius Murena. It was
because of the degree of corruption in the elections of 63 B.C. that Cato
is said to have declared that he would prosecute for *ambitus* whoever
was elected (Plutarch, *Cat. Min.* 21.3). It turned out to be Decimus
Silanus and Lucius Murena, but because Silanus was Cato's son-in-law,
Cato apparently decided to confine his charge to Murena alone.

Lucius Licinius Murena came from a plebeian family from the
municipium of Lanuvium (*Mur.* 15, 90), an old Latin town in the Alban
hills south-east of Rome, and home to several of Cicero's better known
clients.[9] While Murena could boast of the praetorships of his
grandfather and great-grandfather, the family had yet to obtain a
consulship. Murena's father, Lucius Murena, had served with

---

6. Cf. also Cicero, *Sulla* 17; *Fin.* 2.19; *Clu.* 36, 98; *Balb.* 25, 57; Sallust,
Cat. 18; Cass. Dio, 36.27, 38.5; Suetonius, *Iul.* 9. (*Schol. Bob.* 361 Stangl, p.
78).

7. This procedure goes back to the Twelve Tables and is explained by Aulus
Gellius (*NA* 20.1.27); cf. Justinian (*Dig.* 42.1.60): a litigant could receive an
extension (*diem differt*) under the special condition of *morbus sonticus*.

8. This is also understandable given Catiline's political history; see E. Gruen
(1971), 54-69, esp. 59-62.

9. Milo and Roscius were also from Lanuvium.

distinction as one of Sulla's *legati* at Chaeronea and Mytilene, and was entrusted with the management of affairs in Asia where, according to Appian (*Mith.* 64), he provoked the second Mithridatic war. According to Cicero (*Mur.* 12), the younger Murena distinguished himself in that war and participated in his father's triumph. Following his return to Rome after the campaign he was elected quaestor (ca. 75 B.C., *Mur.* 18), and immediately after holding that office he returned to Asia in the following year as a member of Lucullus' staff (*Mur.* 20). In 65 B.C. he was elected praetor urbanus, after which he served as propraetor of Transalpine Gaul in 64, before returning to Rome in 63 to stand for the consulship of 62. It is interesting to note that Sulpicius had been Murena's colleague as both quaestor and praetor; therefore Sulpicius' resentment at having lost to Murena in the consular elections is the more understandable.

While the *exordium* of the *Pro Murena* is one of our best examples of Cicero's accretive style, it is unlike that of the *Pro Quinctio* in that there is no single point of contrast or conflict that Cicero introduces and develops in a strictly linear progression, as he does with *gratia* and *potestas* in the *Pro Quinctio*; instead, this *exordium* revolves around a central thematic core, like the *iniquitas temporum* of the *Pro Roscio Amerino*, cast in the form of a *precatio*, an adaptation of the prayer Cicero delivered at the consular election for 62, when Murena was elected consul-designate. In the *Pro Roscio Amerino* the thematic progression of the *exordium* was intended to explain Cicero's role as *defensor* in the light of external political forces that were at work influencing the procedures behind the scenes; in the *exordium* of the *Pro Murena*, Cicero introduces the theme of *officium consulare*, the moral obligation that Cicero as consul feels compels him to defend Murena, consul-elect.

A secondary, though important, function of the *exordium* is to set up the *refutatio* that closely follows it and whose themes, *officium* and *amicitia*, derive naturally from it. In the *refutatio*, Cicero counters the particular objections of each of his two primary opponents, Cato and Sulpicius. In addressing Cato's accusations (3-6), Cicero carries forward and expands upon certain themes that he introduced in the *precatio* with which Cicero began the *exordium*: Cicero contrasts his consular *officium*, which compels him to defend Murena, with Cato's Stoic *officium*, which compels him to prosecute. In his treatment of Sulpicius (7-10) Cicero responds to the charge that by defending Murena he has violated the obligations of *amicitia* that he owes Sulpicius, asserting that were he not to defend Murena, he would be violating the moral obligation of *amicitia* that he owes to Murena, just as he would be violating the moral obligation of *officium* that he has as consul to uphold the safety of the state.

For Cicero the moral obligations of *officium* and *amicitia* were closely linked, the primary distinction between the two being that consular *officium* was a public obligation, and *amicitia* was a private obligation.[10] But in the political world of the late republic, the dividing line between the two was often blurred, and Cicero defines *amicitia* in the *Pro Roscio Amerino* (111) in terms of a shared sense of *officium* (*idcirco amicitiae comparantur ut commune commodum mutuis officiis gubernetur*).[11] *Amicitia*, along with its variants (*societas, coniunctio, necessitudo, familiaritas*) was the substitute term for a political "party," and in campaigns for nomination *amicitia* was the chief basis of support by candidates in office.[12] *Amicitia*, based on mutual interest and mutual services (*officia, studia*), was the glue that held political *factiones* together and therefore could also be used as a political weapon.[13] Because *amicitia* was often based on political *officium*, it was of great importance to the political future of an ambitious individual, and so Cicero found himself in a difficult position — caught between the strong obligations of the consular *officium* he felt toward Murena, and the loyalty that his personal *amicitia* with Sulpicius demanded.[14] Cicero understood the political importance of *amicitia*, but he also felt that there was a difference between *amicitia* as personal friendship (*privatum officium*), and *amicitia* as professional alliance (*publicum officium*), which he defined as: *non amicitia sed mercatura quaedam utilitatum suarum* (*ND* 1.122). Cicero felt strongly about both, and in

---

10. For the distinction between the two cf. Cicero, *Marc.* 14 (*hominem sum secutus privato officio, non publico*).

11. Cf. Sallust's observation of a close political union: *haec inter bonos amicitia, inter malos factio est* (*BJ* 31).

12. Taylor (1949), 7-8.

13. See R. Syme (1939), 157.

14. See P. A. Brunt (1965), 1-20.

the introspective year following the death of his daughter Tullia in 45 B.C. he would devote a separate philosophical essay to each.[15]

The philosophical conflict between *officium* and *amicitia* was one that Cicero understood could not be resolved without some moral compromise. Cicero always maintained that there was a strong relationship between philosophy and oratory, the search for truth through reason being the common purpose of both, and in many ways the *Pro Murena* explores the point at which these two intellectual pursuits meet.[16] Although Cicero acknowledges that philosophers before him, such as Aristotle and Theophrastus, had treated such subjects as *concordia, pietas, amicitia*, and *virtus* — all of which appear in some form in the course of the *Pro Murena* — as philosophical concepts, Cicero felt strongly that it was the orator, and not the philosopher, who brought these concepts to life, understood them in the sphere of human experience, and through rhetoric translated them to his audience:[17]

> Etenim cum illi in dicendo inciderint loci, quod persaepe evenit, ut de dis immortalibus, de pietate, de concordia, de amicitia, de communi civium, de hominum, de gentium iure, de aequitate, de temperantia, de magnitudine animi, de omni virtutis genere sit dicendum, clamabunt, credo, omnia gymnasia atque omnes philosophorum scholae sua esse haec omnia propria, nihil omnino ad oratorem pertinere; quibus ego, ut de his rebus in angulis consumendi otii causa disserant, cum concessero, illud tamen oratori tribuam et dabo, ut eadem, de quibus illi tenui quodam exsanguique sermone disputant, hic cum omni iucunditate et gravitate explicet. (*De Or.* 1.55-56)

For Cicero the principles of the "dialectic" and "ethical" argument made up the philosophical foundation on which he based his forensic

---

15. But the doctrines of the *De Amicitia* were not just the product of Cicero's philosophic studies in old age, for he also treats *amicitia* in the *De Inventione* (2.167, cf. 157).

16. Cicero, *Or.* 14; *De Or.* 1.60; *Arch.* 1, 2; *Fin.* 1.14-15, 5.26-27; *Tusc.* 1.29; *Brut.* 121, 191. See also A. Michel (1960), 445-536.

17. Cf. Cicero, *De Or.* 1.55; *Div.* 2.4.

strategies.[18] And while he always seems to have held in high esteem the precepts of Plato as the leading authority of the Old Academy, it was in the dialectic method of the New Academy that Cicero found the means to bridge the gap between philosophy and forensic rhetoric.[19]

In the *exordium* of the *Pro Murena* Cicero refines the issues of the *causa* to anticipate the main conflict between the defense and the prosecution, which is based on opposing views of *officium* and *amicitia*. In the *De Officiis* (1.4) Cicero defines *officium* as the single most important obligation in any and every facet of life:

> Nam cum multa sint in philosophia et gravia et utilia accurate copioseque a philosophis disputata, latissime patere videntur ea, quae de officiis tradita ab illis et praecepta sunt. Nulla enim vitae pars neque publicis neque privatis neque forensibus neque domesticis in rebus, neque si tecum agas quid, neque si cum altero contrahas, vacare officio potest, in eoque et colendo sita vitae est honestas omnis et neglegendo turpitudo.

But when compared with the moral obligation of *amicitia*, *officium* emerges as the more important when matters of state are concerned:

> Maxime autem perturbantur officia in amicitiis, quibus et non tribuere, quod recte possis, et tribuere, quod non sit aequum, contra officium est. Sed huius generis totius breve et non difficile praeceptum est. Quae enim videntur utilia, honores, divitiae, voluptates, cetera generis eiusdem, haec amicitiae numquam anteponenda sunt. At neque contra rem publicam neque contra ius iurandum ac fidem amici causa vir bonus faciet, ne si iudex quidem erit de ipso amico; ponit enim personam amici, cum induit iudicis. (*Off.* 3.43)

It is important to note that, in consideration of the moral obligations behind both *officium publicum* and *officium privatum*, Cicero gave specific precedence to the former, particularly when it pertained to the defense of a consular colleague. A case in point is Cicero's defense of his colleague C. Antonius Hybrida in March or early April of 59 B.C. on a charge of *maiestas* or *repetundae*, probably for alleged misconduct in his province of Macedonia, and possibly also

---

18. Cicero, *Or.* 12; *Att.* 4.16; *Off.* 1.63; cf. R. L. Enos (1988), 33-58; H. A. K. Hunt (1954), 207.

19. Cicero, *Tusc.* 2.9; *De Or.* 3.79-80; *Nat. D.* 2.1; *Fat.* 4.

for suspicion of his involvement with the Catilinarian conspiracy (cf. Cicero, *Cael.* 15; *Flacc.* 5 and *Schol. Bob.* ad loc.; Cass. Dio 38.10). Antonius was prosecuted by Caelius Rufus (*Cael.* 15, 74, 78), and although Cicero knew or at least had considerable grounds for suspecting that Antonius had been significantly involved in the Catilinarian conspiracy, nevertheless he did defend him.[20] Cicero describes this consular *officium* as a *religio* (*Sest.* 8), an oath he had sworn to uphold despite the fact that he had doubts about Antonius' innocence. It therefore should come as no surprise that Cicero would come to the aid of Murena, whom he saw not as a possible Catilinarian sympathizer, but rather as a determined and uncompromising opponent of the Catilinarian threat.

Commentary

There is some disagreement among scholars as to whether or not the *exordium* extends beyond the *precatio* to include Cicero's *refutatio* of the charges of Cato (3-6) and Servius Sulpicius (7-10). The prevailing view among most editors and commentators, which is not without merit, is that the *exordium* must contain these arguments and therefore runs from sections 1 to 10;[21] while others have suggested that the speech has two *exordia*, the *precatio* (1-2.21) and Cicero's treatment of the arguments of Cato and Sulpicius (3-10), a view that seems to be

---

20. It is hard to determine exactly how Cicero felt about Antonius' involvement in the Catilinarian conspiracy, for at *Flacc.* 5 he describes Antonius as: *condemnatus est is qui Catilinam signa patriae inferentem interemit*, without any mention at all of a possible betrayal of loyalty on the part of his colleague (cf. *Att.* 2.2.3).

21. This view dates back to A. Möbius, *M. Tullii Ciceronis Orationes XII Selectae* (Hahn 1833), and is accepted by most modern editors as well as MacDonald's Loeb edition Cambridge 1976; see also Loutsch's discussion (1994), 308 n. 37.

going too far and is without parallel in Ciceronian oratory.[22]   But stylistically there is such a change from the *precatio* to the *refutatio* that follows it that it seems not only appropriate, but unavoidable to consider the *precatio* an independent unit separate from what follows, especially since Cicero marks the end of the *precatio* with a brief *propositio* (2.22-7) in which he introduces the *refutatio*.   But more important, because it is in the *precatio* that Cicero introduces and develops the theme of *officium*, the springboard from which he launches the main arguments of his defense, and because he develops this theme in the distinctly accretive style that unifies the *precatio* and sets it off from the rest of the speech (one of the trademarks of Cicero's *ratio exordiendi* and something that is absent from sections 3-10), it seems clear that the *precatio* fulfills all of the rhetorical requirements of the *exordium*, both in style and content, in ways that sections 3-10 do not, and therefore cannot be considered part of the *exordium*.

The brief *exordium* of the *Pro Murena* (1-2.21), therefore, is an adaptation of the *precatio* Cicero delivered in the comitia centuriata at the conclusion of the consular elections for 62 B.C., over which he presided and after which Murena was proclaimed *consul designatus*.[23] Although beginning a speech with a formal *precatio* might seem out of place in a judicial setting, according to Servius orators of the century before Cicero, such as Cato the censor and the elder Gracchus, never began a speech without invoking the gods in some way.[24]   In only one other extant speech, however, does Cicero use a similar *precatio* in the *exordium*: that delivered before the people immediately upon his return

---

22. Most recently by J. Adamietz in his commentary on the *Pro Murena* (1989), 83; see also C. Macdonald, (1969) 50-51. Humbert (1925), 119-142, accounts for the dramatic shifts in tone between the *precatio* and the rest of the speech with his theory that the published speech is made up of two different speeches delivered at different stages of the trial.

23. We do not know what the actual form of a *precatio* would have been, but cf. Livy, 29.27.2, 39.15.1, 40.46.9; Macrobius, *Sat.* 3.9.11; Ennius, *Ann.* fr. 102/103 (Skutsch).

24. Servius, *Ad Aen.* 11.301: *Nam maiores nullam orationem nisi invocatis numinibus inchoabant, sicut omnes orationes Catonis et Gracchi.* It was also uncommon for Greek orators, but cf. Demosthenes, *De Corona* 1-8, Aeschines, *Timarch.* 116.

from exile in 57 (*Red. Pop.* 1.1).[25] But the circumstances of that speech were not judicial, and while the similarity between the opening of the *Pro Murena* and the *Post Reditum ad Populum* is striking, Cicero does not sustain the *precatio* in that speech to the length that he does in the *Pro Murena*, nor does it function in the same rhetorical capacity.

Cicero's use of the *precatio* in the *Pro Murena* is at first deceptive: while on the surface it seems meant to recall an antiquated tradition of Roman oratory, as it unfolds Cicero reveals a carefully considered and constructed rhetorical argument that arrests the attention of the jurors and anticipates the arguments that follow:

1.1-10: Quae precatus a dis immortalibus sum, iudices, more institutoque maiorum illo die quo auspicato comitiis centuriatis L. Murenam consulem renuntiavi, ut ea res mihi, fidei magistratuique meo, populo plebique Romanae bene atque feliciter evenerit, eadem precor ab isdem dis immortalibus ob eiusdem hominis consulatum una cum salute obtinendum, et ut vestrae mentes atque sententiae cum populi Romani voluntatibus suffragiisque consentiant, eaque res vobis populoque Romano pacem, tranquilitatem, otium concordiamque adferat.

Through the *precatio* not only does Cicero set the tone for the defense of a man of consular *dignitas*, but he also fulfills what was for him one of the most essential requirements of the *exordium*, as he states in the *De Inventione* (1.23):

Attentos autem faciemus si demonstrabimus ea quae dicturi erimus magna, nova, incredibilia esse, aut ad omnes aut ad eos, qui audient, aut ad aliquos illustres homines aut ad deos immortales aut ad summam rem publicam pertinere.

Cicero captures the attention of the *iudices* by making them aware that what they are about to hear is a matter of great consequence, that it pertains both to the immortal gods (*a dis immortalibus*), and to the welfare of the state itself (*populo plebique Romanae*). Cicero uses the device of the *precatio* in several ways: 1) to establish the consular ethos of his client (*L. Murenam consulem*); 2) to remind the *iudices* of his own (*fidei magistratuique meo*); and, 3) to establish a common connection between himself and Murena based on this "consular" bond.

---

25. Cf. also the *Pro Rabirio Perduellionis Reo* (5); see U. Heibges (1969), 833-849, for a discussion of the *religio iuris iurandi*.

Having established this bond, Cicero then shows that he is bound by oath (*fides*) to honor it because it is based on the office of the consulship. What Cicero is demonstrating to the *iudices* is that together he and Murena wield greater *auctoritas* than the prosecution, none of whom is a *consularis*. Cicero's defense of Murena is largely an ethical one, and therefore establishing contrast with the *personae* of the prosecution is central to his case. *Fides*, however, applies not only to Cicero's consular or *publicum officium* in respect to Murena, but also anticipates his argument for the bond of his *privatum officium* or *amicitia*. Both *fides* and *amicitia* are compelling because *fides*, like its cognate *foedus*,[26] was often used of formal treaties which were ratified with solemn oaths (*sanctus*).[27]

The opening sentence that contains the *precatio* is structured around two parallel clauses, a dependent relative clause preceding the main one. Through a rhetorical shift from the relative clause to the main clause Cicero quickly applies the message of the *precatio* to the specific situation at hand in order to give it rhetorical presence. The shift or pivotal point comes in the tense change between the dependent clause, in which he describes the past occasion when he delivered the *precatio* at the consular elections (*quae precatus...sum...*), and the main clause (*eadem precor...*), in which Cicero shows how the *precatio* is still valid in the present situation:

PAST:

Quae precatus...sum

a dis immortalibus

more institutoque maiorum illo die quo auspicato comitiis
centuriatis L. Murenam consulem renuntiavi

ut ea res mihi, fidei magistratuique meo, populo plebique
Romanae bene atque feliciter evenerit

---

26. For the etymology see Walde-Hofmann (1965)[4], s.v. *fido*.

27. For the metaphor cf. Catullus 109.6: *aeternum hoc sanctae foedus amicitiae*; 76.3: *sanctam violasse fidem, nec foedere nullo*; 87.3: *nulla fides ullo fuit umquam foedere tanta*.

PRESENT:

  eadem precor

    ab isdem dis immortalibus

      ob eiusdem hominis consulatum una cum salute obtinendum

        et ut vestrae mentes atque sententiae cum populi Romani
        voluntatibus suffragiisque consentiant, eaque res vobis
        populoque Romano pacem, tranquilitatem, otium
                    concordiamque adferat

Cicero begins with the significant placement of the relative pronoun (*quae*) which immediately precedes the verb of its clause (*precatus...sum*), looking forward to the object pronoun (*eadem*) of the main clause, which in turn immediately precedes its verb (*precor*); likewise, the prepositional phrase (*a dis immortalibus*) in the past clause is answered by the prepositional phrase (*ab isdem dis immortalibus*) in the present clause. In each clause the prepositional phrase is followed immediately with a reference to Murena the consul-elect (*L. Murenam consulem* :: *ob eiusdem hominis consulatum*); both clauses end with an entreaty (*ut*), the first dependent upon *precatus sum*, the second upon *precor*.

With the change in tense between the dependent and main clause Cicero uses the sentiments expressed within the *precatio* to introduce the themes of his defense of Murena. The opening *quae* clause contains what Cicero said on the day of the elections in the comitia centuriata when he announced Murena's election to the consulship (*L. Murenam consulem renuntiavi*): Cicero prayed to the gods that such an outcome of the elections has turned out well for the state (*populo plebique Romanae bene atque feliciter evenerit*). In the main clause Cicero uses the *precatio* to show that his reason for endorsing Murena's election as consul then, and his reason for endorsing Murena now for acquittal on the charge of *ambitus* are the same. Cicero stresses the relationship between past and present through a series of pronouns in the main clause that correspond to antecedents in the relative clause: he prays for the same things now (*eadem*), from the same gods (*ab isdem*), on behalf of the same man (*ob eiusdem*) and for the same purpose (*ut...ut*).

The argument also advances as Cicero introduces several new ideas in the main clause while he carries forward and develops the ideas and images introduced in the first part of the sentence. By linking Murena's consulship to his acquital (*consulatum una cum salute*), Cicero introduces the relationship between *consul* and *salus*, and establishes the dependence of one upon the other. While the *salus* in this passage is Murena's, Cicero is setting up the relationship between Murena's *salus* (i.e., his acquittal) and the *salus communis*, allowing him to associate the cause of his client with the safety of the state.[28]

The main difference between the two *ut* clauses is that the first is general, while the second is directed specifically at the *iudices*, anticipating the appeal *a iudicum persona*. It is in this clause that Cicero brings the authority of the opening *precatio* to bear on the rhetorical struggle of the *exordium*. In the first part of the second *ut* clause Cicero implores the *iudices* to see to it that their vote as judges agrees with the electoral vote of the Roman people. Cicero uses verbal echoes to reinforce the relationship between the will of the people, which was reflected in their votes for Murena in the election (*voluntatibus suffragiisque*) and those of the *iudices* (*vestrae mentes atque sententiae*). Cicero reinforces the relationship between the jury's vote and that of the people by the play on *sententiae...consentiant*. Furthermore, the *progressio* with which the second *ut* clause concludes (*pacem, tranquillitatem, otium concordiamque adferat*) echoes that of the first (*mihi fidei magistratuique meo, populo plebique Romanae bene atque feliciter evenerit*); but in the second clause Cicero takes the progression one step further by stating specifically how Murena, if allowed to take office, will bring about in his consulship what Cicero alluded to at his election: Murena's consulship will bring about *pax, tranquillitas, otium* and *concordia*. These were loaded words for Cicero's audience,[29] even more powerful when spoken by a consul who was defending a consul-elect, for it was the job of the consul to guarantee these things (*evenerit, adferat*). Cicero knew the force of this

---

28. As Cicero did both in the *Pro Quinctio* (5-6) and in the *Pro Roscio Amerino* (7). As we shall see, this will also be Cicero's primary strategy in the *Pro Milone* (cf. also *Pro Sestio* [14-15] where Cicero compares *a salute nostra* with *salute communi*).

29. Cf. Cicero, *Marc.* 27.1; for representations of *Pax* and *Concordia* on republican coinage, see M. Crawford *RRC*, 494, 457, 466, 494, 510-511, 743, and 511 (Venus Cloacina).

statement, for he used these very same sentiments to support his own position on the occasion when he delivered the *De Lege Agraria* (1.24) immediately after assuming the consulship at the beginning of the year:

> Hoc motu atque hac perturbatione animorum atque rerum cum populo Romano vox et auctoritas consulis repente in tantis tenebris inluxerit, cum ostenderit nihil esse metuendum, nullum exercitum, nullam manum, nullas colonias, nullam venditionem vectigalium, nullum imperium novum, nullum regnum Xvirale, nullam alteram Romam neque aliam sedem imperi nobis consulibus futuram summamque tranquillitatem pacis atque oti, verendum, credo, nobis erit ne vestra ista praeclara lex agraria magis popularis esse videatur.

According to Cicero it was the *vox et auctoritas consulis* that could promise and assure *summam tranquillitatem pacis atque oti*; and at the close of the second oration *De Lege Agraria* (2.102) Cicero again reiterates the point that the ensuring of *pax, tranquillitas*, and *otium* was the job of the consul:[30]

> Ex quo intellegi, Quirites, potest nihil esse tam populare quam id quod ego vobis in hunc annum consul popularis adfero, pacem, tranquillitatem, otium.

Cicero sees his consular *officium* as dedicated to bringing about *pax*, and in the present circumstances the best way he can achieve this is by defending Murena so that Murena can in turn defend the state. In this way through the *precatio* Cicero establishes *officium*, particularly consular *officium*, as the theme of his defense.

In the following sentence Cicero states his wish that if the *precatio* he delivered (then) had any force at all, his defense of Murena (now) will turn out in his client's favor:

> 1.10-15: Quod si illa sollemnis comitiorum precatio consularibus auspiciis consecrata tantam habet in se vim et religionem quantam rei publicae dignitas postulat, idem ego sum precatus ut eis quoque

---

30. Cf. Cicero, *Leg Agr.* 1.24, also, 1.23: *...quae populo grata atque iucunda sunt, nihil tam populare quam pacem, quam concordiam, quam otium reperiemus.* Another parallel can be found at *Cat.* 3.17: *...rem publicam tanta pace, tanto otio, tanto silentio liberassemus.*

hominibus quibus hic consulatus me rogante datus esset ea res fauste
feliciter prospereque evenerit.

In the protasis of the condition Cicero carries forward the notion of
consular authority from the opening sentence, and in the apodosis
Cicero returns to the parallel bipartite structure of the opening sentence
with some *variatio*. Just as in the opening sentence the relative pronoun
(*quae*) of the dependent clause anticipated the object pronoun (*eadem*)
of the main clause, so here the demonstrative pronoun (*illa*) of the *si*
clause, which looks forward to its noun (*precatio*), anticipates the
pronoun that signals the apodosis (*idem*), followed by the emphatic *ego*
sum precatus, another echo of the opening sentence. In the *ut* clause, a
prayer dependent upon *precatus sum*, Cicero introduces a new element
through the correlative *tantus...quantus* construction: the *dignitas rei*
publicae, a concept closely linked to his notion of consular *officium*.
But by raising the issue of *dignitas* here, Cicero is anticipating the
contentio dignitatis (*Mur.* 63) that he mounts between Murena and
Sulpicius, a response to what must have been a particular claim made
by Sulpicius in his speech against Murena, namely that he could claim
greater consular *dignitas* than Murena, and therefore he was more
deserving of the consulship (esp. *Mur.* 21-29).[31] Cicero will use the
contentio dignitatis as a primary means of exposing the shortcomings of
Sulpicius and the qualifications of Murena for the office of consul. By
just raising the issue of *dignitas* here, Cicero prepares his audience for
what is to come.

By delaying any mention of the opposition thus far, and using the
precatio to enhance his own consular ethos as well as that of Murena,
Cicero has already in effect alienated Cato and Sulpicius significantly.
Through verbal echoes Cicero maintains the tone of the *precatio*. The
ending of the main clause of the sentence (*fauste feliciter prospereque*
evenerit) is a direct echo of the ending of the *quae* clause of the
opening sentence (*bene atque feliciter evenerit*) — both being
formulaic prayer endings. The theme of the *di immortales* he introduced
at the beginning of the *precatio* now emerges as the primary means by
which Cicero turns the *precatio* from the appeal *a nostra persona* to the
appeal *a iudicum persona*:

---

31. The *contentio dignitatis* seems to have been a regular feature of *ambitus*
trials, cf. C. P. Craig (1990), 75-81, esp. 77-80.

2.15-21: Quae cum ita sint, iudices, et cum omnis deorum immortalium
potestas aut translata sit ad vos aut certe communicata vobiscum, idem
consulem vestrae fidei commendat qui antea dis immortalibus
commendavit, ut eiusdem hominis voce declaratus consul et defensus
beneficium populi Romani cum vestra atque omnium civium salute
tueatur.

Cicero maintains the strict, almost liturgical parallel structure of the
opening two sentences, but the formulaic *quae cum ita sint*, the direct
address of the *iudices*, and a shift from the first person to the more
impersonal third person, all signal the conclusion of the *precatio*.
Cicero begins with the subordinate *cum* clause, in which he establishes
a bond between the *iudices* and the *di immortales*, to which he parallels
the consular bond between himself and Murena in the main clause
(*idem*). This passage sums up the main themes of the *precatio*: first,
Cicero establishes Murena's consular *dignitas* by reminding his
audience of his own, and what that means to the welfare of the state;
second, he establishes the special *auctoritas* of the *iudices*, which he
elevates to a level with that of the gods (*potestas translata sit ad vos
aut certe communicata vobiscum*). The implication is clear: just as at
the consular elections Cicero entrusted Murena's safety to the auspices
of the gods, so now in his defense of Murena he entrusts his client to the
protection of the *iudices* (*consulem vestrae fidei commendat qui antea
dis immortalibus commendavit*). In the purpose clause (*ut*) dependent
upon *commendat*, however, Cicero goes on to explain to the *iudices* that
with the privilege of being sharers of the *potestas* of the gods comes
also the responsibility of preserving the state, and to do this they must
preserve Murena (*beneficium populi Romani cum vestra atque omnium
civium salute tueatur*). Whereas Cicero began the *prectaio* by using
salus as an allusion to the preservation of Murena (*ob...consulatum una
cum salute obtinendum*), he now concludes with the image of a
universal *salus* (*omnium civium salute*) that can only be assured by
Murena's acquittal. The relentless circular logic of the *precatio* presses
to an inevitable conclusion: the fate of the state and the fate of Murena
are inextricably linked, and only by the preservation of the latter can
they preserve the former.

Conclusion

Cicero's use of the *precatio* is a brilliant strategy combining the rhetorical aims of the *exordium* with the defense of a consul-elect. The primary purpose of the *exordium* is to secure the *benevolentia* of the audience, and through the *precatio* Cicero constructs an argument that fulfills what according to Quintilian (4.1.7) was one of the most important requirements of the orator in an oration:

> Quare in primis existimetur venisse ad agendum ductus officio vel cognationis vel amicitiae maximeque, si fieri poterit, rei publicae aut alicuius certe non mediocris exempli.

According to Quintilian, it was of the greatest importance for the speaker to portray himself as having undertaken a case out of his sense of duty (*officium*) either to a blood relation (*cognatio*) or to a friend (*amicitia*), but especially out of a sense of patriotism (*maximeque...rei publicae*). Through the *precatio* Cicero effectively establishes that his defense will be grounded on a sense of *officium rei publicae* and that the theme of consular *officium* will be the most important and most conspicuous element of it. Cicero uses the *precatio* to emphasize the consular bond between himself and his client, and in the brief *exordium* the term *consul* and its cognates occur six times.

As Cicero moves from the *exordium* to the *refutatio* of the speech (3-10), he will also show that his decision to defend Murena has not arisen from any misplaced sense of *amicitia*, as Sulpicius charges. The *precatio* prepares his audience for the arguments of this next section and, indeed, all the rest of the oration. For just as Cicero must defend his own sense of patriotic *officium* (*publicum*) to answer the charges of the young stoic patriot Cato, so he must also defend his actions against the charge of Sulpicius that by defending Murena he has violated the obligations of *amicitia* (*officium privatum*). Cicero will devote much of the rest of the speech to the conflict between *officium* and *amicitia*, or *officium publicum* and *officium privatum,* two themes that Cicero uses as a wedge to divide Cato and Sulpicius. This approach recalls Cicero's strategy in the *exordium* of the *Pro Quinctio,* where he began by establishing a clear distinction between Hortensius and Naevius in terms of their respective *eloquentia* and *gratia.* But in that early speech, Cicero quickly left the *eloquentia* of Hortensius behind in order to focus on the *gratia* of Naevius. In the *Pro Murena,* however, Cicero gives equal attention to both the *officium* of Cato and the *amicitia* of Servius Sulpicius.

The *exordium* of the *Pro Murena* marks the emergence of Cicero's consular ethos in a judicial speech, and a departure from the *persona* Cicero projected in the *exordia* of the pre-consular speeches examined thus far; but while Cicero's *persona* has changed and matured, his approach to the *exordium* remains remarkably unchanged. As in the *Pro Roscio Amerino*, Cicero must defend his decision to appear on behalf of Murena; but unlike those of the *Pro Roscio Amerino* or the *Pro Quinctio*, the *exordium* of the *Pro Murena* is hardly an *apologia* for what Cicero feels to be his inadequacies. Whereas in his defense of Roscius, Cicero needed to justify his appearance because of his lack of *auctoritas*, in the *exordium* of this speech Cicero is operating from a position of ultimate *auctoritas*, and it is clear that he knows it. It is his consular status that not only qualifies, but even compels, him to speak on Murena's behalf. Cicero begins with a *precatio*, and although its solemn tone stands in stark contrast to the rather informal style of the rest of the speech, it establishes the consular theme of his defense — which in turn brings into relief his own consular ethos and that of his client Murena.

CHAPTER FOUR

Pro Milone

Introduction

In 52 B.C. Cicero defended T. Annius Milo, who had been charged with the murder of P. Clodius Pulcher (*de vi*). At the time of his trial there were laws in existence under which Milo could be charged: Sulla's *lex Cornelia de sicariis et veneficis* (under which Roscius Amerinus was haled into court), and the *lex Plautia de vi* were both options, but as Cicero himself tells us in discussing the *praeiudicia* of the *Pro Milone* (*Mil.* 7-23), Pompey established a special court to hear the case:

13.2-6: Hanc vero quaestionem, etsi non est iniqua, numquam tamen senatus constituendam putavit; erant enim leges, erant quaestiones vel de caede vel de vi, nec tantum maerorem ac luctum senatui mors P. Clodi adferebat, ut nova quaestio constitueretur.

The *nova quaestio* to which Cicero refers was, according to Asconius (Stangl, p. 36), established under Pompey's new legislation (*altera de vi*), and directed specifically at Milo. According to Cicero (*Mil.* 12-13, 31, 44) the passing of the *lex Pompeia de vi* was backed by a *senatus consultum*, and the discussion in the senate included specific mention not only of Clodius' murder, but also of the burning of the Curia, and of the attack on Lepidus' house, acts that Cicero calls *contra rem publicam*:

> 12.15-18:   Sequitur illud, quod a Milonis inimicis saepissime dicitur, caedem, in qua P. Clodius occisus esset, senatum iudicasse contra rem publicam esse factam.[1]

In the Second Philippic (2.27-2) Cicero recalls the court in which Milo was tried and repeats his allegation that it had been put together expressly for the purpose of convicting Milo:

> Quamquam de morte Clodi fuit quaestio non satis prudenter illa quidem constituta — quid enim attinebat nova lege quaeri de eo qui hominem occidisset, cum esset legibus quaestio constituta? — quaesitum est tamen.

Milo was tried before this extraordinary *quaestio* under the *lex Pompeia de vi*, the *lex Pompeia de ambitu*, and a third, the *lex Licinia de sodaliciis*, which dealt with illegal organizations.[2] The *lex Pompeia de vi* was aimed directly at Milo, and despite the pleas of Caelius Rufus that the law was unconstitutional (*Mil.* 37) because it was aimed at a single individual, it was eventually passed.

Milo's chief prosecutors for the charge *de vi* were the two senior Appii Claudii, nephews of the murdered Clodius and members of a very respectable family. In Milo's defense Cicero alone spoke. The first sitting of the court *de vi* was held on the 4th of April 52 B.C. and proceedings lasted for five days, four of which were spent in the examination of witnesses and the selection of a jury. The excitement in the forum was so great during these proceedings that Pompey felt

---

1. Quintilian (5.2.1) cites this passage from the *Pro Milone*, and the decision of the senate against Milo, in his definition of a *praeiudicium*.

2. For a list of Pompey's legislation, see Rotondi (1912), 404-407.

compelled to have on hand a military guard to overawe the multitude. According to Dio (40.53), in at least one instance Pompey's soldiers had to resort to force in order to keep the peace.

On the final day of the trial (8 April, 52 B.C., over a hundred days after Clodius' murder), the speeches of the prosecution and defense were heard. For this occasion Pompey, surrounded by his armed guard, watched from the steps of the Temple of Saturn, having set his curule chair *pro aerario.* The sight of such military force and the assailing shouts from the prosecutors are reported to have so terrified Cicero that he lost his composure and spoke badly, without his usual courage, flair, and boldness (Cass. Dio 40.54).

Cicero's defense did not prevail. Milo was found guilty by a vote of 38 to 13 and the next day he left Rome for Marseilles. Some time afterwards, upon receiving a copy of Cicero's revised *Pro Milone*, Milo is supposed to have made the famous remark that had Cicero delivered such a speech on that fateful day in April, then Milo would never have known the excellent mullets of Marseilles (Cass. Dio 40.54; cf. Juvenal 1.49). Given the *personae* involved in the trial, the *Pro Milone* must have been one of Cicero's most personal speeches. Clodius had been responsible for Cicero's exile in 58 B.C., and during his tribunate of that year Milo had been one of the chief supporters of Cicero's recall.

Regardless of its flawed delivery, it must be remembered that the speech was probably taken down by shorthand writers at the time and subsequently published, with or without Cicero's permission, and that it was read by Asconius and by Quintilian, who uses it to illustrate several rhetorical principles. There is, however, substantial evidence to suggest that the speech Cicero delivered on behalf of Milo was not the one that we read today.[3] The basis for this argument lies in the fact that in the first century A.C. there existed two versions of Cicero's defense of Milo. Asconius (Stangl, p. 37), Quintilian (4.3.17), and the author of the *Scholia Bobiensia* (Stangl, p. 112), all refer to an alternate version, which they identify as the speech Cicero actually delivered for Milo. The story of this tradition begins with the interpretation of a passage in Asconius' commentary (*Mil.* 36.24-4) in which he describes Cicero's *terror* and his inability to deliver the speech he had prepared:

---

3. For a review of the evidence pertaining to the delivery and publication of the *Pro Milone,* see J. Crawford (1984), 210-218.

Cicero cum inciperet dicere, exceptus est acclamatione Clodianorum, qui
se continere ne metu quidem circumstantium militum potuerunt. Itaque
non ea qua solitus erat constantia dixit. Manet autem illa quoque excepta
eius oratio: scripsit vero hanc quam legimus ita perfecte ut iure prima
haberi possit.

Asconius says that Cicero was "seized upon" (*exceptus*) by the
acclamation of the Clodians and was not possessed of his usual
imperturbability, but nevertheless his speech survives (*manet*). The
phrase *excepta...oratio* is puzzling in this context, for it means either
that Cicero's speech was "interrupted" as Cicero himself was, or more
probably that the speech was taken down in shorthand.[4] From what
Asconius says we cannot know whether Cicero even finished the
speech, nor does he tell us anything about the content of the oration, but
except for Asconius' account there is no evidence to suggest that Cicero
was unable to deliver his speech entirely as he intended. Plutarch (*Cic.*
35) and Dio (40.54.2) elaborate upon certain elements of the
circumstances surrounding the trial and imply that Cicero was too
flustered even to finish his speech. But if *excepta* is to be understood as
meaning that the speech was taken down in shorthand, then there must
have been reason for its being copied and surviving down to the time of
Asconius and Quintilian.[5] The *Scholia Bobiensia* (Stangl, p. 112), our
only source for the alternate version of the *Pro Milone*, shed little light
on the content of what we believe was the speech actually delivered by
Cicero:

> ...et ipse Tullius pedem rettulit. Et exstat alius praeterea liber actorum pro
> Milone: in quo omnia interrupta et inpolita et rudia, plena denique
> maxime terroris agnoscas.

If the source of the "first" *Pro Milone* lies in court stenography, we
must wonder how the interruptions that the scholiast mentions were

---

4. See B. A. Marshall (1987), 730-736. Marshall argues that there is no reason
to assume that Cicero was intimidated by the presence of Pompey's soldiers and
the opposition of the Clodians; the phrase *excepta oratio* does not indicate
shorthand but rather the impromptu interruptions of the Clodians.

5. But the origins and state of court stenography at this time are sketchy. For
the possibilities of stenography in Rome in 52 B.C. see A. Mentz (1931), 369-
86. Cf. also Settle (1963), 268-80.

communicated, or how an emotion such as *terror* (obvious enough in delivery) could be transformed into shorthand notes. And while conjectures other than stenography may be offered for the source of the "first" *Pro Milone*, there would seem to have been little literary interest to account for the copying of Cicero's speech for Milo delivered on the 8th of April, given the overall disturbances of the occasion and the fact that Cicero himself did, as in other instances, publish a more polished version for his audience at a later date.[6] Certainly Cicero would not have published the first *Pro Milone* had he intended to publish another. As it stood, the piece certainly was not intended to do honor to Cicero.[7] Therefore, the alternate version, whatever its origin, would not have undergone publication in the same sense as Cicero's other speeches.[8] As for Cicero's performance on the day when the *Pro Milone* was delivered, the evidence for the report of Cicero's impaired delivery has to be questioned. As Cicero states in the *exordium* (1-2), Pompey's troops were stationed in the Forum, and whether their presence was at the request of the Milonians for their and Cicero's protection, as Cicero claims, or to ensure Milo's conviction, Cicero had still functioned well enough in the presence of these same troops during the preceding days of the trial.[9] The picture of Cicero after the trial of Milo is by no means that of a broken man. On the contrary, even after Milo's conviction he proceeded to triumph further over the Clodians by successfully defending M. Saufeius, purportedly a leader in the fracas at Bovillae and an accomplice in the murder of Clodius, who was indicted under the same *lex Pompeia de vi* as Milo (Asconius, *Mil.* 54; Stangl, p. 45). Cicero also went on to prosecute T. Munatius Plancus Bursa (Cass. Dio

---

6. Though not much later, for he would leave for his province shortly after the trial.

7. See Settle (1963), 278, where he suggests that perhaps the first *Pro Milone* was written and circulated by a Clodian expressly to embarrass Cicero.

8. Especially because of the criticism of Pompey: see A. M. Stone (1980), 88-111. Stone argues that Cicero's criticism of Pompey in the published *Pro Milone* would not have been in the original version, and proposes a date of publication sometime shortly after the trial of Plancius, when Cicero was alienated from Pompey.

9. When witnesses for the prosecution were called in to testify (Asconius, *Mil.* 41; Stangl, p. 36).

40.55.1), who had led riots following the death of Clodius and the burning of the Curia Hostilia, on a charge of *vis*. In this, too, he was successful.

Titus Annius Milo Papianus was born in Lanuvium, an old Latin town to the south of Rome; by birth the son of a Papius and an Annia, he was adopted by his grandfather on his mother's side, T. Annius, and made heir to the family's wealth.[10] A man of some substance, he owned a house on the Palatine. Milo's legal name was Titus Annius, but he was generally known by the nickname Milo given to him because his physical build resembled that of the famous athlete of Croton of the same name (*Att.* 6.3). A strategic marriage to Sulla's daughter, Fausta, in 55 B.C. connected Milo with one of the richest and most influential families of Rome and helped advance him on a promising, though short-lived political career that began with the tribunate in 57 B.C. and ended with his exile from Rome in 52 B.C. We know nothing of Milo's career before his tribunate in 57 B.C., but because he stood for the consulship in 53 B.C. his praetorship must have come in 55 B.C., but we know nothing of the events during his tenure of that office;[11] evidently he did not go out to a province afterwards.

Publius Clodius Pulcher enjoyed a notorious political career that began in 68 B.C. when he served on his brother-in-law Lucullus' staff in Asia. In 62 B.C. he won election to the office of quaestor, and it was during the interval between his election and entrance of that office that the infamous Bona Dea scandal occurred which resulted in his lifelong feud with Cicero. It was Cicero who destroyed Clodius' alibi of having been at Interamna (some 90 miles from Rome) on the night of the festival's violation by testifying that he had been called on by Clodius at his house earlier that very evening, and because of this Clodius suffered more trouble as a result of the scandal than he otherwise would have, although his own conduct during the legal proceedings did not help to win sympathy for his position.[12] Although he was acquitted

---

10. See *RE* under T. Annius Milo (Klebs, 1, 1894, no. 67, 2271).

11. We have only Cicero's mention *in petitione praeturae* (*Mil.* 68) to attest to his candidacy for this office.

12. For an excellent article on the reasons for Cicero's testimony against Clodius see D. F. Epstein (1986), 229-235, who argues that Cicero's motivation for testifying was provided by Terentia, who wanted to avenge the humiliation that Clodius caused her sister.

after having bribed the jurors, nevertheless Clodius escaped punishment only at the expense of his public image. For this he would blame Cicero, and he would have his revenge.

It is in the legislative powers of the office of tribune that many of the key factors leading up to the death of Clodius converge, for it was as tribune that Clodius promulgated and eventually passed the *lex de capite civis* that was directed at Cicero, condemning him for the execution of the Catilinarian conspirators in December of 63 B.C. Clodius passed the law in late January or early February 58 B.C., and by mid-March Cicero had fled Rome.[13] It was during Clodius' tribunate that Clodius came into fierce opposition with Milo who was working for Cicero's recall, as Cicero comments in a letter to Atticus (*Att.* 4.3.5) about the situation between Milo and Clodius shortly after his triumphant return to Rome in 57 B.C.:

A. d. VIIII Kal. haec ego scribebam hora noctis nona. Milo campum iam tenebat. Marcellus candidatus ita stertebat ut ego vicinus audirem. Clodi vestibulum vacuum sane mihi nuntiabatur: pauci pannosi sine laterna. Meo consilio omnia illi pueri querebantur, ignari quantum in illo heroe esset animi, quantum etiam consili. Miranda virtus est. Nova quaedam divina mitto, sed haec summa est: comitia fore non arbitror, reum Publium, nisi ante occisus erit, fore a Milone puto, si se in turba ei iam obtulerit occisum iri ab ipso Milone video. Non dubitat facere, prae se fert; casum illum nostrum non extimescit.

Milo's candidature for the consulship of 52 B.C. must have been highly inconvenient to Pompey, who was planning his own political future in which, as Cicero suggests, a dictatorship loomed (*Att.* 4.18.3; 4.1.7; *Fam.* 1.1.3; *QFr.* 3.8.4). To be sure, Pompey had his own candidates to put forward for the consulship of 52 B.C. — Q. Metellus Scipio Nasica, whose daughter Cornelia he married after the death of Caesar's daughter Julia; and Hypsaeus, one of his officers during the third Mithridatic war. Milo was clearly an outsider in the close company of this inner circle. It was Clodius, now suddenly and conveniently on friendly terms with Pompey, who would see to it that Milo's election failed. Clodius, who was in this year a candidate for the praetorship, would not have been displeased to have his political landscape cleared of the shadow of Milo's consular cloud. The bribery,

---

13. Cf. Cicero, *Att.* 3.3. Shackleton Bailey (*Att.* 2, p. 227), suggests the third week of March.

terror, and disorder that preceded the elections of this year were so extensive and bloody that elections could not be carried through. In this eventuality Roman law dictated that an *interrex* be appointed, but at Pompey's insistence, who now saw his dictatorship in sight, no *interrex* was. The chaos continued until the 18th of January, when Milo attended a meeting of the senate and then departed for his native town of Lanuvium, where he held the office of dictator, the chief magistracy of the *municipium*. It was his duty to perform annual sacrifice there and to induct a priest into office. The day before, Clodius had left Rome in order to deliver a speech to the senate of Aricia. His absence from the senate meeting in Rome on the 18th was a curious and conspicuous one, which Cicero capitalizes on in the *Pro Milone* (27).

The fatal encounter between Milo and Clodius happened at Bovillae on the Appian Way, with Milo heading to Lanuvium, Clodius returning from Aricia. While both were escorted by large companies of armed men, the encounter must have been purely accidental. Travel on Roman roads in this period was highly unsafe, and therefore one always traveled in large companies, often with armed guards. The primary sources for the skirmish at Bovillae and the death of Clodius differ greatly; the account given by Cicero in the *Pro Milone* (29) differs significantly from that in Asconius's commentary (Stangl, pp. 30-33). According to Asconius, Milo was attended by a large retinue of *servi*, but he makes special mention of two gladiators, Eudamus and Birria. According to Cicero, this entourage was composed mainly of friends and domestic servants, as well as other intended participants in the ceremonies at Lanuvium, about three hundred members in all. Cicero makes no mention of Eudamus and Birria. Both Asconius and Cicero agree that Milo himself rode in a carriage with his wife Fausta and that Clodius was on horseback without his wife. According to Asconius Clodius was attended by only thirty lightly armed slaves and by three companions, C. Causinius Schola, a Roman eques, and two men of lower rank, P. Pomponius and C. Clodius, one of Clodius' freedmen. Cicero gives no exact figures for Clodius' followers. According to both sources the two companies met close to Bovillae, but Asconius mentions that the confrontation occurred near a shrine of the Bona Dea. This detail must be suspect in Asconius' account, for if such had been the case, we cannot imagine that Cicero would have passed up exploiting such a morsel of information that would have reminded his hearers of Clodius' infamous scandal of 62 B.C.

In the fray that ensued Clodius was killed. Asconius places the event four hours earlier than Cicero. But the most important difference between the two accounts is that in Cicero's it was Clodius' men who instigated the fight and drew first blood, and it was Milo's slaves, and not Milo (who mysteriously disappears from the narrative at the crucial moment of the killing), who committed the murder. According to Asconius, on the other hand, it was Milo's two gladiators who initiated the fracas, with the gladiator Birria being the first to wound Clodius. According to Asconius it was Milo who, upon realizing that Clodius had been wounded, decided that he would be better off with Clodius out of the way completely, for if Clodius survived, he would certainly be brought up on charges of *vis*. Therefore he had Clodius dragged out and murdered. One has to question the cogency of Asconius' argument here, for *vis* was a very common charge in this period, and it seems unlikely that Milo would have committed a capital crime to avoid being charged with a lesser one.

Clodius' body arrived in Rome before nightfall and was taken to his house on the Palatine. The next morning Fulvia, Clodius' wife, in tears displayed the body to the mob, who carried it to the Forum where it was burned. In the course of events the Curia Hostilia also caught fire and burned down. In the aftermath of the rioting and chaos that broke out in Rome in the wake of these events, the elections could not be held. Pompey, who at this time was officially the governor of the province of Spain, was urged to declare himself dictator. A succession of *interreges* were finally elected, but none could carry the elections through. Finally a *senatus consultum ultimum* was passed and, largely through the united efforts of the factions of Pompey and Cato, Pompey was elected sole consul and given power to levy troops.[14] This power to maintain a standing army in Rome must have been an especially welcome privilege to Pompey in view of his tenuous and strained relationship with Julius Caesar at this time. Therefore 60 days after the death of Clodius, Pompey was made consul without a colleague and was given the authority to maintain a standing army in Rome, while continuing to hold his governorship of Spain.[15] All power was his, and he saw his opportunity to get Milo out of the way for good.

---

14. Plutarch, *Pomp.* 54; Cass. Dio, 40.45-50; cf. Cicero, *Att.* 7.1.4, 8.3.3; *Phil.* 1.18; Livy, *Epit.* 107; Vell. Pat. 2.47.3; Val. Max. 6.2.11, 8.15.8; Pliny, *HN* 15.3, 33.14, 34.139.

15. Pompey did secure the election of Metellus Scipio, his father-in-law, as his colleague for the last five months of the year (Plutarch, *Pomp.* 55; Appian, *BC* 2.25; Cass. Dio 40.51).

Commentary

Cicero's defence of Milo is in essence a *deprecatio*, that is, an appeal or petition for pity or clemency through a formal act of *intercessio* (Cicero, *Part. Or.* 131).[16] Cicero does not contest that Milo was at least in some way responsible for the death of Clodius, but he maintains that Milo's actions are a case of *iure fecit*.[17] Although Cicero leads us to believe that he is operating under great pressure in this speech, the style of the *exordium* of the *Pro Milone* is as direct as that of the *Pro Quinctio*, and as bold as that of the *Pro Roscio Amerino*; while much of the confidence that Cicero displayed in the *precatio* of the *Pro Murena* is lost in the shadow of the overwhelming fear he confesses has overtaken him. But this emphasis on fear is also a rhetorical device to play up the drama of the moment and win sympathy for himself and his client.[18] In fact Quintilian (6.1.24) cites Cicero's handling of his own *persona* in the *exordium* of this speech as an example of how the orator himself pleads humility and fear when it would be out of character for the accused himself to do so. According to Cicero, Milo did not even appear for his trial in the dress of mourning customary for a defendant (*Mil.* 95), so we have to wonder, given the apparent connection between the formal procedure of the *deprecatio* and the convention of *vestis mutatio*, if Milo's decision not to wear mourning clothes affected the verdict of the *iudices*. Perhaps

---

16. From what Cicero says at *Sest.* 27, 29, and 32, it seems to have been closely associated with, or involved the *vestis mutatio* of the *deprecator*, but how formal a procedure, if any, was followed is unclear. According to the author of the *Rhetorica ad Herennium* (1.24) this was a strategy rarely used in the courts.

17. Cicero admits as much at *Phil.* 2.21. See M. E. Clark, and J. S. Ruebell (1985), 57-72, who argue that Cicero was not able to justify the use of extreme violence against a *civis*, especially homicide, until after his unsuccessful defense of Milo in 52. It is not until the published version of the speech that Cicero begins to develop the philosophical vocabulary of factional politics.

18. See A. Scaillet (1991), 345-347.

this is why, according to Quintilian (6.1.25), it was Cicero who adopted the *persona* of humility:

> Nam quis ferret Milonem pro capite suo supplicantem, qui a se virum nobilem interfectum, quia id fieri oportuisset, fateretur? Ergo et illi captavit ex ipsa praestantia animi favorem et in locum lacrimarum eius ipse successit.

Quintilian (9.4.74) also quotes the opening sentence of this speech in order to illustrate how the orator can strengthen his *exordium* by beginning with a metrical resolution (*ultima versuum initio conveniunt orationis*). As Quintilian observes, the first words of the *Pro Milone* are the resolution of an iambic trimeter. Quintilian points out, however, that such poetic resolutions are useful only at the beginning of a paragraph, and are generally inappropriate for the resolution of a period; yet in another instance (11.3.47) Quintilian quotes this sentence in order to demonstrate the variety of tone required by an orator when addressing the jury. We may ask, however, if Cicero was using the dramatic meter to enhance the drama of the *exordium*, if only for the purpose of getting the attention of his audience. Cicero certainly makes the most of the dramatic tension of the circumstances surrounding the trial in his opening sentence:

> 1.1-7:   Etsi vereor, iudices, ne turpe sit pro fortissimo viro dicere incipientem timere minimeque deceat, cum T. Annius ipse magis de rei publicae salute quam de sua perturbatur, me ad eius causam parem animi magnitudinem adferre non posse, tamen haec novi iudicii nova forma terret oculos, qui quocumque inciderunt, consuetudinem fori et pristinum morem iudiciorum requirent.

Just as in the *Pro Roscio Amerino*, the opening sentence of the *exordium* of the *Pro Milone* is an exploitation of the extraordinary circumstances (*insolentia*) surrounding the trial. Everything about the trial is new and strange (*haec novi iudicii nova forma*), a veiled reference to the presence of Pompey and his company of armed soldiers. As in the *exordium* of the *Pro Quinctio*, Cicero begins by declaring his fear (*vereor*) under the present circumstances, which he uses on two levels: first, as a foil against which he contrasts Milo's courage (*pro fortissimo viro*); second, as a means of establishing a bond between himself and his audience. One of Cicero's most effective means of winning the *benevolentia* of his audience in the *exordium* of

this speech is to assure them that despite the presence of Pompey's
soldiers, they share the common responsibility of ensuring that justice
must still be served, and furthermore, that because they are on the side
of good men (*boni*), and the Clodians are on the side of evil
(*perditissimi*), the latter have more to fear from Pompey than they
themselves do.

Within the protasis of the *etsi...tamen* construction Cicero
establishes Milo's character by contrasting it with his own through a
series of interlocking clauses. Like *tamen* and *quamquam*, *etsi* in
Cicero takes the indicative, as it does here (*vereor*), for Cicero is
making a general statement of fact.[19]   Cicero applies to himself the
general principles contained in the first two object clauses (*ne turpe
sit...dicere incipientem timere* :: *minimeque deceat...me...adferre non
posse*) which he uses to emphasize the disparity between his *persona*
and Milo's. In both *ne* clauses the emphasis remains on Cicero's fear in
contrast to Milo's courage; in the first, the prepositional phrase *pro
fortissimo viro* depends upon the infinitive *dicere* that follows
immediately but is governed in turn by the participle *incipientem* rather
than the infinitive *timere*, the main verb of the accusative + infinitive
construction, which Cicero delays until the end of the clause. The
rhetorical structure of the first *ne* clause is echoed in the second, where
Cicero uses litotes to avoid strict parallelism (*turpe sit* :: *minime
deceat*): just as Cicero delayed the subject complement of *turpe sit* in
the first *ne* clause with the insertion of *pro fortissimo viro*, likewise in
the second *ne* clause Cicero interrupts the resolution of *minimeque
deceat* with the insertion of the *cum* clause, in which he explains the
phrase *pro fortissimo viro* of the previous clause and identifies the
fortissimus vir as T. Annius, his client: both Cicero and Milo are
afraid, but Cicero fears for himself in his role as Milo's *patronus*
(*vereor, dicere incipientem timere*), whereas Milo fears for the state
more than himself (*magis de rei publicae salute quam de sua
perturbatur*), and is willing to sacrifice himself for it. For this reason,
Cicero is unworthy to represent Milo because of his fear in the present
circumstances of the trial (*me ad eius causam parem animi
magnitudinem adferre non posse*). Cicero's trepidation at speaking on
Milo's behalf will reflect badly upon him because Milo is a man who
deserves to be defended. Cicero plays up the disparity between himself

---

19. Cf. Cicero, *Tusc.* 4.63; *Div.* 2.34; *Att.* 5.16.1, 17.2, 7.12.3, 16.22.2; *Phil.*
2.75; *Fin.* 5.31.

and his client to win the support of the *iudices*, just as he contrasted himself and Quinctius with Naevius and Hortensius in the *Pro Quinctio*, which shows Cicero's ability to adapt his *exordium* to the case at hand. The structure of the protasis is as follows:

CICERO: ne turpe sit ⟹

   MILO: pro fortissimo viro

CICERO: ⟹ dicere incipientem timere (1st period)

CICERO: (ne) minimeque deceat ⟹

   MILO: cum T. Annius ipse magis de re publica salute quam de
                          sua perturbetur

CICERO: ⟹ me ad eius causam parem animi magnitudinem
                 adferre non posse (2nd period)

Cicero makes no attempt in the *tamen* clause to balance the complex, bipartite construction of the *etsi* clause, yet the resolution of the sentence has rhetorical impact because the paradox of the *etsi* clause demands resolution, which comes in Cicero's efforts to show that fear is an emotion that he and the *iudices* together share. In the *tamen* clause Cicero contrasts his own fear of inadequacy in providing a sufficient defense for Milo, the point established in the *etsi* clause, with the very different sort of fear that the jury is experiencing. Cicero is afraid to speak (*timere*) because of his own inadequacies, while the conditions under which the trial is being conducted terrify (*terret*) not only the *iudices* but the entire attendance, including Cicero. Cicero uses chiasmus again to contrast the phrase *novi iudici nova forma*, an emphatic description of the cause of the terror, with the phrase *veterem consuetudinem fori et pristinum morem iudiciorum*, an evocation of the conditions under which Cicero is accustomed to speak. Of course the person responsible for this *terror*, or *insolentia*, is Pompey, for it is the presence of his soldiers that provokes the fear. Cicero emphasizes the visual effect of the soldiers (*terret oculos*) in order to enhance the drama of the scene. The passage is transitional because in it Cicero uses the element of fear from the opening sentence and carries it forward to characterize himself, Milo, and the *iudices*. And it is this fear that Cicero uses in his transition to the next appeal, to the *corona* (*ab auditorum persona*):

> 1.7-2.13: Non enim corona consessus vester cinctus est, ut solebat, non usitata frequentia stipati sumus, non illa praesidia, quae pro templis omnibus cernitis, etsi contra vim collocata sunt, non adferunt tamen aliquid quo, ut in foro et in iudicio, quamquam praesidiis salutaribus et necessariis saepti sumus, tamen ne non timere quidem sine aliquo timore possumus.

In the accretive development of the argument Cicero carries forward the visual affront that Pompey's soldiers represent as he describes the scene of the forum that attends the trial of Milo. Cicero begins by explaining the fear he admitted in the opening passage, and ends by reassuring the jury that they should not be afraid. Here, as often in Cicero, the perfect passive verb forms (*cinctus est...stipati sumus...saepti sumus*) have an adjectival force, and when joined with *sum* form not a perfect tense, but rather vividly indicate the present state of things.[20] Cicero uses this construction to illustrate the relationship of the court to Pompey's soldiers who surround it. Cicero subtly shifts focus from the second person (*consessus vester cinctus est*) to the first person (*stipati sumus*) in order to insinuate that he and the *iudices* share the same fear: Cicero aims to win their *benevolentia* by getting the jury to identify with his own situation, and therefore with Milo's. The anaphora in the repetition of *non...non...non* adds to the dramatic effect of the ablatives *corona* and *frequentia*, and helps set up the abrupt shift from the passive voice to the active with the introduction of the nominative *praesidia* — an ambiguous term for Pompey's soldiers in the present context. Cicero immediately qualifies the presence of Pompey's soldiers, first in the following relative clause, and then in the *etsi* clause: although the *praesidia* that the *iudices* can see assembled *pro templis omnibus* frighten Cicero, he portrays them in a positive light.[21] They have been summoned as a *praesidium contra vim*, and

---

20. Cf. Leumann-Hofmann 2.2.2, 156-157

21. The temples are those of Castor, Concord, and Saturn; the last was occupied by Pompey (Asconius 41; Stangl, p. 40). Perhaps Cicero also means the rostra and the curia as well, both of which were innaugurated *templa*.

therefore pose less of a threat to Cicero (*non adferunt tamen oratori terroris aliquid*) than to the Clodians. Still, Cicero portrays them as a necessary evil (*praesidiis salutaribus et necessariis saepti sumus*), and because he would like to find some safety in the fear they inspire, he renders the paradox as a striking oxymoron: only fear can remove fear (*tamen ne non timere quidem sine aliquo timore possumus*). Although Cicero tries to interpret the presence of Pompey's soldiers in a positive light, he cannot divorce himself entirely from his surroundings, try as he will. Still, Cicero tries to convince his audience that the *praesidium* is not to be interpreted as *contra Milonem*.

> 2.13-2. Quae si opposita Miloni putarem, cederem tempori, iudices, nec inter tantam vim armorum existimarem esse oratori locum; sed me recreat et reficit Cn. Pompei, sapientissimi et iustissimi viri, consilium, qui profecto nec iustitiae suae putaret esse, quem reum sententiis iudicum tradidisset, eundem telis militum dedere, nec sapientiae, temeritatem concitatae multitudinis auctoritate publica armare.

The focus of this passage is one of contrast, in which Cicero describes his fears awakened, and his fears removed. The passage contains two main characterizations, each of which contains two sub-groups. In the first, Cicero's characterization of Pompey is based on his description of his soldiers; in the second, Cicero's characterization of Milo's supporters depends upon his description of his opponents. But because Cicero does not make a clear distinction between those Clodians who are onlookers and those who make up the prosecution, his treatment of them will introduce the next appeal, *ab adversariorum persona*.

In the first characterization Cicero begins by addressing the military attendance at the trial, flatly denying that the soldiers' presence poses a threat either to Milo or himself.[22] Their role is purely a peace-keeping one, and the proof of this lies in Cicero's characterization of Pompey, the real power behind the troops. Cicero addresses Pompey indirectly, attributing his confidence in the military presence to Pompey's *consilium*, the subject that Cicero delays until after the

---

22. But note the use of *cedere*, often used by Cicero in the context of social and political warfare: cf. *Marc.* 7 (*cedat forma castris*). The phrase *cedant arma togae* is a famous line from Cicero's poem *de consulatu suo* (*Off.* 1.22.77; cf. *Pis.* 72; *Phil.* 20).

dramatic position and doubling of the verbs (*recreat et reficit*), whose
synynomy underlines the emphasis; furthermore, the superlative
construction (*sapientissimi...iustissimi*) is answered in chiastic
arrangement in the two noun clauses that follow (*iustitiae... sapientiae*)
linked by the *nec...nec* anaphora. Cicero characterizes Pompey in most
flattering terms and highlights the nature of his *auctoritas*, which does
not yield to mob rule. In the first part of the *qui* clause Cicero states that
it is not characteristic of Pompey's *iustitia* to subject a man, whom he
has delivered to the court, to the weapons of his soldiers to the weapons
of his soldiers (*tradidisset...dedere*: note the balance and paranomasia);
in the second part of the *qui* clause Cicero assures his audience that it
would also not be characteristic of Pompey's *sapientia* to arm the anger
of an excited mob with the sanction of the state. The balance of the
parallel clauses beginning with *nec iustitiae...nec sapientiae* is
strengthened by the periodic structure of the individual cola
(*qui...putarem esse :: quem...tradidisset :: eundem...dedere :: nec
sapientiae...armare*). Cicero plays on the idea of the offensive presence
of the soldiers (*telis*) versus the defensive posture and dangerous
exposure of the court (*armare*).[23]   Cicero concludes by returning to the
soldiers whom he characterizes now with the same detail he used in his
characterization of Pompey:

> 3.2-6: Quam ob rem illa arma, centuriones, cohortes non periculum nobis,
> sed praesidium denuntiant, neque solum ut quieto, sed etiam ut magno
> animo simus hortantur, nec auxilium modo defensioni meae, verum etiam
> silentium pollicentur.

Cicero builds his characterization of the soldiers around a series of
periodic parallel clauses, reminiscent of his treatment of Pompey in the
previous passage. Cicero first builds antithesis around a tricolon of *non*
(*modo*)...*sed* (*etiam*) clauses, but with variation moves from antithesis
to emphasis. In the first colon Cicero uses alliteration to enhance the
antithesis of the function of the soldiers (*non periculum...sed
praesidium denuntiat*), which then sets up the following two cola, in
which Cicero expands upon his view of the function and effect of
Pompey's soldiers in a different light. Cicero uses *variatio* as he shifts
construction from the active to the passive voice, and from antithesis to

---

23. Cf. Cicero, *Har. Resp.* 7: *si quod in me telum intenderit, statim me esse
adrepturum arma iudiciorum.*

emphasis. In the second colon Cicero explains the positive effect that Pompey's soldiers have on his own state of mind (*neque solum ut quieto...sed etiam ut magno animo simus hortantur*), which then leads into the third and final member of the tricolon (*neque auxilium modo defensioni meae, verum etiam silentium pollicentur*).[24] Cicero portrays the soldiers as a source of encouragement (*hortantur*) and aid (*auxilium*) that will ensure a peaceful trial (*silentium*).[25] By characterizing Pompey's soldiers as a purely peace-keeping force under Pompey's circumspect wisdom and keen sense of justice, Cicero is able to draw an even greater antithesis between the *personae* of Milo's supporters and the Clodians. Cicero begins with Milo's supporters:

3.6-11: Reliqua vero multitudo, quae quidem est civium, tota nostra est, neque eorum quisquam, quos undique intuentes, unde aliqua fori pars aspici potest, et huius exitum iudicii exspectantes videtis, non cum virtuti Milonis favet, tum de se, de liberis suis, de patria, de fortunis hodierno die decertari putat.

Cicero describes Milo's supporters as *reliqua multitudo*, in contrast to the preceding description of Pompey's soldiers. *Quidem* emphasizes that the great majority is made up of *cives Romani*, not Clodius' rabble, which also sets up the antithesis to Cicero's characterization of the Clodians below. Cicero describes the *multitudo* of onlookers in terms of their ability to see what is really going on (*intuentes, aspici, exspectantes*), just as he reminds the *iudices* that they too have eyes and are capable of such perceptive and informed observation (*videtis*). What should be obvious to all is that Milo's fate is linked to the welfare of the common *civis* because Milo stands for all the things that are sacred to all right-minded men (*cum virtute Milonis ... tum de se, de liberis suis, de patria, de fortunis hodierno die decertari putat*). These are all such things as all *boni* should hold dear and defend, as Cicero urged the senate at the end of the Fourth Catilinarian (4.24). By associating Milo with these ideals and portraying him as their champion, Cicero is alluding to those consular qualities that Milo shares with Cicero.

---

24. For the dramatic shift of construction within a single tricolon, see E. Vereecke (1991), 171-178, esp. 173.

25. It was Pompey, after all, who had helped Milo win the praetorship in 55 (*Mil.* 68; Cass. Dio 39.32; Plutarch, *Cat. Min.* 42; *Pomp.* 52.2; Livy, *Epit.* 105)

Cicero repeats the preposition (*de*) for emphasis as he describes the trial as a physical battle (*decertari*) — and we can well imagine that in delivery his emphasis on the preposition was picked up by his stressing of the first syllable of the verb. By portraying the onlookers as aware of this fact Cicero can contrast them with the Clodians. His characterization of the *multitudo* forms the transition from Cicero's portrayal of Milo's supporters to the appeal *ab adversariorum persona* as he focuses on the Clodians:

> 3.12-15: Unum genus est adversum infestumque nobis eorum, quos P. Clodi furor rapinis et incendiis et omnibus exitiis publicis pavit; qui hesterna etiam contione incitati sunt, ut nobis voce praeirent quid iudicaretis.

With the opening words of this characterization Cicero establishes the dramatic contrast between the members of the two opposing factions, out of which emerges the violent intensity of the conflict between them. By portraying the Clodians as a violent and criminal mob, Cicero isolates his opposition as the enemy not only of himself and Milo, but also of the rest of the *cives* who make up the *multitudo* of spectators, as well as Pompey and his soldiers, whose presence Cicero has already characterized as peaceful and lawful and therefore on the side of the defense.   Cicero described Milo's supporters as *cives*, and his characterization of the Clodians here as falling short of that dignity further isolates them from the rest of the audience. While Cicero implies that the followers of Clodius are largely runaway slaves, certainly riffraff, he states in no uncertain terms that they are, in fact, the enemy (*unum genus...adversum infestumque nobis*).   Cicero characterizes the Clodians as a gang of criminals whose main concern is the opposite of all that Milo stands for. In contrast to Cicero's characterization of Milo as the champion of the *salus rei publicae, furor* has become the trademark of the Clodians.[26] Cicero describes Clodius' followers as being fed (*pavit*) by this *furor*, which nourishes them with the destruction of the very things that Milo stands for

---

26. Cf., e.g., *furere* (26), *furiosus* (14), and similar vocabulary such as *amentia* (12), *insania* (22), and *insanus* (45). In two passages from the speech Cicero contrasts *salus* with *furor* and its synonyms: *Quae quidem si potentia est...dum modo ea nos utamur pro salute bonorum contra amentiam perditorum* (12); *Illi erat, ut odisset primum defensorem salutis meae, deinde vexatorem furoris* (35).

(*rapinis et incendiis et omnibus exitiis publicis*). The distinguishing feature of Cicero's characterization of the prosecution, however, is the *furor Clodi*, which feeds on the destruction of all that is dear to the *multitudo civium*. Cicero concludes the appeal *ab adversariorum persona* by comparing Milo's character with that of the *genus* of his accusers:

3.15-18: Quorum clamor, si qui forte fuerit, admonere vos debebit, ut eum civem retineatis, qui semper genus illud hominum clamoresque maximos prae vestra salute neglexit.

Here Cicero returns to the theme of the *salus rei publicae* which he used to identify Milo to his audience in the opening sentence, and again portrays him as its champion (*prae vestra salute*). Cicero also reminds his audience that Milo is a *civis*, as opposed to the questionable condition of the Clodiani, and therefore deserves the support of the *iudices*. Cicero states this again in the next passage, the appeal *a iudicum persona*, always the most important appeal and focal point of the *exordium*:

4.18-29: Quam ob rem adeste animis, iudices, et timorem, si quem habetis, deponite. Nam si umquam de bonis et fortibus viris, si umquam de bene meritis civibus potestas vobis iudicandi fuit, si denique umquam locus amplissimorum ordinum delectis viris datus est, ut sua studia erga fortes et bonos cives, quae vultu et verbis saepe significassent, re et sententiis declararent, hoc profecto tempore eam potestatem omnem vos habetis, ut statuatis, utrum nos, qui semper vestrae auctoritati dediti fuimus, semper miseri lugeamus, an diu vexati a perditissimis civibus aliquando per vos ac per vestram fidem, virtutem sapientiamque recreemur.

Quam ob rem links this sentence to the previous one, in which Cicero anticipated this appeal with the phrase *prae vestra salute*. This section is an example of the rhetorical figure *expolitio*, restatement with variation of a theme.[27] Cicero returns to the theme of fear with which he began, but now he asks the *iudices* to lay aside any fear that they might have because (*nam*) the cause is just and worthy of their attention (the defense of a *vir bonus*), and they alone have the *potestas* to uphold

---

27. Cf. *Rhet. ad Her.* 4.54, ff.

justice. Typically, Cicero uses the appeal *a iudicum persona* to move
the argument from the specific issues concerning his client to a more
general argument that involves the welfare of the entire state, an
approach anticipated by Cicero's characterization of himself and Milo
in the opening sentence, and developed accretively throughout the
course of the entire *exordium* through the introduction of a precise
thematic vocabulary. Cicero makes the transition from the specific case
of Milo versus Clodius, to the general contest between good and evil by
appealing to the *iudices* in terms of the tradition of their office.
Furthermore, through the use of plural verbs he broadens the focus of
his argument as well. The compound condition contains a tripartite
protasis:

(P$_1$) si umquam de bonis et fortibus viris

(P$_2$) si umquam de bene meritis civibus potestas vobis
                                                  iudicandi fuit

(P$_3$) si denique umquam locus amplissimorum ordinum
                                    delectis viris datus est

    ut sua studia erga fortis et bonos civis... (quae voltu et verbis
         saepe significassent) ...re et sententiis declararent

    (A) hoc profecto tempore eam potestatem omnem vos habetis

Through the tricola of the protasis, introduced each time by the
anaphora *si umquam*, Cicero stresses the importance of the role of the
iudices in the past. The first protasis (P$_1$) is incomplete and anticipates
the second (P$_2$) through the repetition *de bonis et fortibus viris* and *de
meritis civibus*. The second clause is then linked to the third (P$_3$) by the
periodic resolution of the verbs (*fuit :: datus est*) as Cicero again
stresses the historical role of the court (*potestas...iudicandi :: locus
amplissimorum ordinum*). Cicero's point is to remind the new members
of the jury that it is still their job to protect good citizens (*boni*). The
terms are universal. In the first two *si* clauses Cicero returns to his
initial characterization of Milo as a *vir fortissimus* with the phrase *de
bonis et fortibus viris*. Just as it was Cicero's duty to speak *pro
fortissimo viro* in the opening sentence, so now it is the jury's duty to

find that same man innocent. In the third *si* clause Cicero appeals to the class prejudice of the *iudices* (*amplissimorum ordinum*), and then in the *ut* clause repeats the same phrase (*fortis et bonos cives*) as in the first protasis, but the order of adjectives is reversed and *civis* has been substituted for *viri*. As Clark points out, the repetition is intentional to emphasize the point, and the chiastic arrangement *bonis ... fortibus ... fortes ... bonos*, and the substitution of *cives* for *viros* prevents monotony.[28] But by reversing the noun in the third protasis from *viri* to *cives* Cicero reminds the jury that Milo is a *civis*, one of a privileged class which the Clodiani fall short of. Furthermore, by characterizing the *iudices* as *viri delecti* who have been granted a seat with the *ordo amplissimus*, an epithet properly used by Cicero of senators and higher magistrates (cf. 5, 90), Cicero is obviously playing up to Pompey's special *iudices*, the *equites* and *tribuni aerarii*, whom he treats as a permanent fixture of the new judicial process and flatters by extending to them the dignity of the senatorial members of the jury.

In the apodosis (A) Cicero addresses the issue of the traditional power of the *iudices* and their responsibility in the trial by assuring them that if they fulfill the conditions he has specified in the tripartite protasis, then and only then (*hoc profecto tempore*) will they have complete power (*potestas omnis*) to decide what course to take. Cicero makes the appeal more personal through the alternative indirect question by contrasting the first person plural (*utrum nos*) with the second person plural of the *iudices* (*an...per vos*), a favorite rhetorical device of Cicero which in this passage is meant to heighten contrast to the generalizing terms given in the compound protasis. A further contrast is drawn in the apodosis by the phrase *a perditissimis civibus*, a direct antithesis to the *meriti et boni et fortes cives* of the protasis. Although no names are mentioned either in the protasis or the apodosis, the distinction between Milo and the Clodiani is apparent. The comparison is implied because Cicero is using general terms in order to impress upon the jury that much more than the fate of a single man depends upon their verdict.

In conclusion Cicero returns to the appeal *a nostra persona*:

5.29-2:   Quid enim nobis duobus, iudices, laboriosius, quid magis sollicitum, magis exercitum dici aut fingi potest, qui spe amplissimorum

---

28. A. C. Clark (1895), 4 n.5.

praemiorum ad rem publicam adducti metu crudelissimorum suppliciorum
carere non possumus?

Enim links this series of questions to the previous sentence, and once
again Cicero returns to the theme of fear. Cicero maintains the first
person in this passage, but clarifies it with the dual *nobis duobus*, which
serves both to associate Cicero with his client, and to show that Cicero
and Milo's predicament is linked to that of the *iudices*: just as the
authority of the *iudices* will determine the fate of Milo, so the fate of
Milo will determine the authority of the *iudices*. Cicero clarifies this
distinction in the *qui* clause in which he characterizes himself, Milo,
and the *iudices* as men who are *spe amplissimorum praemiorum ad rem
publicam adducti*, but who run the risk of not achieving this because of
their fear of suffering harsh punishment (*metu crudelissimorum
suppliciorum*). This also is a double-edged allusion that applies to both
Cicero and Milo: Cicero's execution of the Catilinarian conspirators in
63 B.C. resulted in his own exile, and he does not want to see Milo
suffer a similar fate. Through the interrogative cast of the question,
and the insistent repetition *quid ... quid magis ... magis*, along with the
personal reference *nobis duobus* and the direct address of the *iudices*,
Cicero not only commands his audience's attention but also compels
their participation.

Cicero now returns to the appeal *a nostra persona* where he treats
Milo's character alone:

5.2-9: Equidem ceteras tempestates et procellas in illis dumtaxat fluctibus
contionum semper putavi Miloni esse subeundas, quia semper pro bonis
contra improbos senserat, in iudicio vero et in eo consilio, in quo ex
cunctis ordinibus amplissimi viri iudicarent, numquam existimavi spem
ullam esse habituros Milonis inimicos ad eius non modo salutem
exstinguendam, sed etiam gloriam per talis viros infringendam.

Equidem, used by Cicero only with first-person verbs, places emphasis
on the personal view of the speaker.[29] In the present context the sense
is as ironic as it is emphatic, for Cicero is using Milo's perseverance in
past difficulties (*ceteras tempestates*) as a means of measuring or
defining his client's ability to overcome the present judicial danger (*et
procellas in illis...fluctibus contionum semper putavi Miloni*

---

29. Cf. Leumann-Hofmann 2.2.2, 174, 486.

subeundas).   Cicero qualifies his opinion with a characteristic *quia* clause in which he states Milo's political sympathies (*senserat*) as *pro bonis contra improbos*, a phrase that recalls Cicero's emotional and politically charged appeal to the *iudices* at 4.18-29.   Cicero uses his confidence in Milo to attack the credibility of the Clodiani in the eyes of the court by going on to characterize them in completely opposite terms.   But the effect of the contrast goes beyond Milo and the Clodiani.   Cicero effectively excludes the opposition from the court by undermining their importance in this setting (*in iudicio vero et in consilio...numquam existimavi spem ullam esse habituros Milonis inimicos*).   Cicero creates tension between the opposition and the *iudices* by portraying them as working against each other, and his description of the members of the court (*in quo ex cunctis ordinibus amplissimi viri iudicarent*) recalls the description of the court in his previous appeal to the *iudices* (*locus amplissimorum ordinum*).   The repetition is meant to be inspiring, as is also the phrase *per tales viros*, the insertion of which after *sed etiam* is highly emphatic because Cicero's first description of the jury would apply to both the *non modo* and *sed etiam* clauses.

Although Cicero speaks here of Milo's *salus* as being threatened, he employs the term to remind the *iudices* of the theme with which he began the *exordium*, the *salus rei publicae*, and to associate Milo directly with that cause.   This return to the opening theme signals that Cicero is bringing the *exordium* to a close, as does the dramatic cadence of homeoteleuton in *non modo exstinguendam...sed etiam infringendam*.[30]   Cicero now returns to the point at which he began, his opening characterization of Milo in which he described him in similar terms (*T. Annius ipse magis de rei publicae salute quam de sua perturbatur* [1.2-3]).   The only other place in the *exordium* where Cicero uses the formal address of his client:[31]

> 6.9-11:   Quamquam in hac causa, iudices, T. Anni tribunatu rebusque omnibus pro salute rei publicae gestis ad huius criminis defensionem non abutemur.

---

30. As Quintilian notes (9.77).

31. Cicero refers to Milo in the formal form of address only four more times in the course of the speech (77; 83; 100).

Cicero dismisses Milo's performance during his tribuneship, a time when he was working for Cicero's recall, so that his defense of Milo does not appear to be motivated by his own personal animosity toward Clodius, which was well known, and his personal debt to Milo, who was instrumental in securing Ciceo's recall from exile. Cicero's aim in characterizing Milo as a *civis bonus* and Clodius and his supporters as *viri improbi et perditissimi* throughout the *exordium* has been to convince the court that Clodius was not only the personal enemy of Milo and himself, but a public enemy of the state, and by killing him Milo was acting in the interest of the *salus rei publicae*.

> 6.11-16:　Nisi oculis videritis insidias Miloni a Clodio factas, nec deprecaturi sumus, ut crimen hoc nobis propter multa praeclara in rem publicam merita condonetis, nec postulaturi, ut, quia mors P. Clodii salus vestra fuerit, idcirco eam virtuti Milonis potius quam populi Romani felicitati adsignetis.

Having established the conflict between Milo and Clodius, Cicero now introduces the specific grounds for his defense, and in this passage he reveals what the plan of his defense will be. Through *praeteritio* he states that: he will not base his defense on the grounds that murder was committed for the good of the state (*nec deprecaturi sumus ut...condonetis*); nor will he ask that the court excuse his client because the death of Clodius was in fact an act of benefit for the citizenry (*mors P. Clodi salus vestra fuerit*). Because *deprecatio* was hardly appropriate in a judicial proceeding such as this (*Rhet. ad Herenn.* 1.24), Cicero must prove that Milo acted within the law (*iure fecit*). But although he claims that his defense will not include such arguments, they have constituted a major portion of the *exordium* thus far and will appear later as his second line of defense *extra causam* (72-91). Cicero's *constitutio causae* will be to answer the question *uter utri insidias fecerit* (30-31) by showing that it was Clodius who plotted against Milo, and that Clodius' death was the result of self defense on Milo's part. Cicero, however, is careful to delay the *constitutio causae* until late in the speech in order to color the facts through character, the chief aim of the *exordium*.

Cicero began the *exordium* by stating that Milo was risking his own life *pro rei publicae salute* by standing trial for the murder of Clodius, and in this passage Cicero describes Clodius' death in terms of the same image (*mors P. Clodi salus vestra fuerit*), while he draws a strong parallel between the *virtus* of Milo and the *felicitas* of the state. Cicero is not asking the jury to view the death of Clodius as an act of salvation purposely conferred upon the Roman people by Milo, but rather to see that Clodius' death was merely an example of the good fortune that attends the nation. The chiastic arrangement of the phrase *virtuti Milonis potius quam populi Romani felicitati*, however, implies that there is a definite cause and effect relationship between the *virtus Milonis* and the *felicitas populi Romani*. Cicero weaves a chiastic pattern through the homeoteleuta of the verbs of the main and dependent clauses:

(A) nec deprec*aturi* (sumus)

    (B) ut crimen...condo*netis*

(A) nec postul*aturi*

    (B) ut eam (mortem)...adsig*netis*

Other themes recur in this final passage that were introduced at the beginning of the *exordium*, most important of which is the theme of "vision," which, clouded by the *insolentia* of the circumstances in the opening sentence (*novi iudici novo forma terret oculos qui quocumque inciderent, consuetudinem fori et pristinum morem iudiciorum requirunt*), now has been freed to see clearly the true guilty party (*nisi oculis videritis insidias Miloni a Clodio factas*). This idea is also carried over into the final sentence of the *exordium*:

6.17-20:   Sin illius insidiae clariores hac luce fuerint, tum denique obsecrabo obtestaborque vos, iudices, si cetera amisimus, hoc saltem nobis ut relinquatur, ab inimicorum audacia telisque vitam ut impune liceat defendere.

In this passage Cicero proposes an alternative condition (*sin*) in response to the condition of the preceding sentence (*nisi*). The main point is one of identifying the true guilty party, and the emphasis is once again on "vision" and how it reveals the *insidiae Clodi*. Cicero now appeals to the jury that the crimes of Clodius can be clearly seen (*clariores hac luce*), before concluding with the plea for Milo's life (*vitam ab inimicorum audacia telisque ut impune liceat defendere*).

Because Cicero has already linked Milo's *salus* with the *salus rei publicae* in the opening sentence, his plea to the *iudices* for the protection of his client (*defendere*) takes on a greater significance than simply the salvation of a single individual.

Conclusion

Although the *Pro Milone* belongs to Cicero's post-consular period, the insecurity he professes to feel in the face of the *insolentia* of the trial hardly resembles the confidence of his consular *persona* in the *exordium* of the *Pro Murena*. This is in large part due to the chaos of the times, in which the consular qualities that Cicero relied upon in the *Pro Murena* had to yield to the violence of characters like Clodius. Cicero uses the *insolentia* of the trial to build the antithesis around which he structures the opening sentence of the *exordium*, an approach that recalls the *exordium* of the *Pro Roscio Amerino*. Cicero extols the virtues of his client at the risk of his own ethos, using the insecurity and apprehension he feels about his ability to speak on Milo's behalf to build up the character of his client: unlike the *Pro Roscio Amerino*, in the *exordium* of the *Pro Milone* Cicero uses the weaknesses of his own *persona* as a rhetorical vehicle to throw into relief the strengths of Milo's. Milo's patriotism will be the cornerstone of Cicero's defense, and Cicero uses it to introduce the theme of *salus rei publicae*, whose preservation, Cicero argues, was Milo's motive for killing Clodius. Although Cicero had represented the *salus rei publicae* as consul in 63 B.C., now he portrays Milo as the champion of that ideal. The theme of *salus rei publicae*, to explain Milo's motivation for killing Clodius, operates much as *iniquitas temporum* does in the *Pro Roscio Amerino*, to explain Cicero's motivation for defending Roscius. Although delivered some 28 years apart, both *exordia* also revolve around the *insolentia* created by external *personae*: in the case of the *Pro Roscio Amerino*, it was the *iniquitas temporum* created by the dictatorship of Sulla; in the case of the *Pro Milone*, it is the *nova forma iudici* arranged by Pompey for the specific purpose of trying and condemning Milo. In both speeches, however, Cicero attempts to turn the disadvantage of the *insolentia* to his advantage. Just as Cicero used Sulla as a foil to condemn the actions of Chrysogonus, so in this speech Cicero portrays

Pompey and his soldiers as a presence intended to protect his client (*non periculum nobis, sed praesidium*) while it condemns the presence of the Clodians.

CHAPTER FIVE

Pro Rege Deiotaro

Introduction

In 45 B.C. Cicero defended king Deiotarus, tetrarch of Galatia, against the charge of having plotted the murder of Caesar when Caesar was a guest in his house after the battle of Zela in August, 47 B.C. (*Fam.* 9.12.2), the accusation brought by Deiotarus' grandson, Castor. King Deiotarus, the hereditary tetrarch of the Tolistobogii, who had eventually absorbed nearly all of Galatia into his kingdom, had long been an ally of a succession of Roman *imperatores*, most notably Pompey, in the war against Mithridates (*Phil.* 11.33). Once the civil war was under way, Pompey used his extensive clientela in the East in order to muster military and political support for the Republican cause, and among the eastern kingdoms from which Pompey obtained this support was Galatia. Deiotarus, who was indebted to Pompey because his rule of Galatia, and perhaps also of Lesser Armenia, had been ratified by the senate in 59 B.C. in large part due to Pompey's backing, had virtually no choice but to support his old ally even if it meant opposing Caesar.[1] While we have no complete account of Pompey's settlement of Asia Minor following his defeat of Mithridates in 62 B.C., it seems likely that in return for Deiotarus' services during the war, he not only confirmed him in his ancestral position of King of Galatia, but also awarded him a considerable additional territory, including the district of the Gadilonitis (on the Halys) and the region around Pharnaceia and Trapezus.[2]

According to Cicero (*Deiot.* 12-13), Deiotarus supported Pompey in the civil war, although with some reluctance, by bringing a contingent of cavalry to Pompey which he himself commanded. Serving as an officer in this contingent was Deiotarus' grandson and future *accusator*, Castor. Following the defeat of the Republican forces at Pharsalus, Deiotarus fled with Pompey and accompanied him as far as Mytilene, but shortly thereafter returned to his kingdom. With Pompey's death, according to Cicero, his loyalty shifted from Pompey to Caesar, where it remained (*Deiot.* 13-14).

During the political upheaval in Rome in the years leading up to the civil war, Pharnaces, the ambitious son of Mithridates Eupator, had been slowly and methodically recovering the territories his father had lost to Pompey:[3] Pharnaces first occupied Colchis and then Armenia Minor and Cappadocia (Caesar, *BA* 34-41; Cass. Dio 42.45.1-46). Caesar had dispatched Domitius Calvinus to Asia after the battle of Pharsalus, while he himself pressed on Pompey's trail toward Egypt. Deiotarus, who also feared Pharnaces' advance, sent a force to aid Calvinus, no doubt as a possible good-will gesture to Caesar, as well as a defensive maneuver. In a pitched battle in Armenia Minor, however, Calvinus was defeated by Pharnaces, and Caesar, as soon as he could settle affairs in Egypt, moved swiftly through Syria and Cilicia into Cappadocia and the territory of central Pontus, near Zela (*BA* 66-69; cf. Strabo 12.35, 558). Caesar had with him less than a full legion and was

---

1. Caesar, *BA* 67; cf. also Cicero, *Div.* 2.37, 79; *Phil.* 2.37, 94. For a discussion of Pompey's settlement of the East and the difficult question of when Deiotarus came into possession of Lesser Armenia, see F. E. Adcock (1937), 12-17.

2. Strabo, 12.547; cf. Appian, *Mithr.* 105, 114; Eutropius 6.14. See also A. H. M. Jones (1971), 157-158.

3. For a good study of Pharnaces' strategies to recover his father's kingdom, see A. N. Sherwin-White (1984), 298-307.

joined by the forces of Deiotarus and what was left of the forces of Calvinus, and with this aid defeated Pharnaces at Zela (*BA* 72-76; Cass. Dio 42.47.4-5).[4] Although Deiotarus had taken Pompey's side in the civil war, Caesar allowed him to retain control of the Armenian territories of his kingdom, but he took from him his rule of Galatia.[5] Caesar also imposed upon Deiotarus a contribution of a large sum of money, partly as punishment, partly because he needed the funds to cover the expenses of his campaign against Pompey. Deiotarus was understandably unhappy with the reduction of his kingdom, and in a conversation with Caesar (*BA* 67-68; cf. Cicero, *Deiot.* 9) Deiotarus pleaded that he had no choice in his decision to support Pompey, since his kingdom lay in Pompey's sphere; Caesar is said to have responded that in his view Deiotarus owed him debts of *amicitia* above and beyond those he owed to Pompey, for it was in Caesar's consulship in 59 B.C. that Deiotarus' rule had been ratified by the senate.[6] Sometime in March or early April of 45 B.C., when Caesar was in Spain after the battle of Munda, the king sent Caesar a letter through an embassy consisting of Hieras, Blesamius, and Antigonus, the charge of which was to try to persuade Caesar to restore to Deiotarus the territories of which Caesar had deprived him after Zela. While Caesar did not grant Deiotarus' request at that time, he sent a letter back to the king that offered him some encouragement. Later in the same year, after Caesar had returned to Rome, Deiotarus sent a second embassy with the same object as before. In attendance on the ambassadors Hieras, Blesamius, and Antigonus were a number of slaves, among whom was Phidippus, Deiotarus' personal slave and *medicus*. Also in Rome at that time was

---

4. For a brief review of Deiotarus' relationship with Caesar in the years leading up to their joint effort in the battle of Zela, see H. W. Ritter (1969), 255-256. There is also the account in Magie (1950), 411-413.

5. But see G. J. Acheson (1965), 82, who cites frontier security as an alternate reason for the reduction of Deiotarus' kingdom: Deiotarus lost lesser Armenia to the neighboring kingdom of Cappadocia, and the land of the Trocini to Mithridates.

6. For the circumstances of this account, see D. Braund (1984), 56-57. In a letter to Atticus written in April of 44 (*Att.* 14.1.2) Cicero mentions a speech made by Brutus the conspirator to Caesar at Nicaea on his way back to Rome after the battle of Zela in 47. Cicero praises the speech at *Brut.* 21, but cf. Tacitus, *Dial.* 21.6.

Castor, who seized this opportunity to bring a capital charge against his grandfather, alleging that Deiotarus had plotted to assassinate Caesar while Caesar had been his guest in Galatia after the defeat of Pharnaces at Zela, and he induced Phidippus to serve as witness against his royal master.   Cicero undertook the defense of Deiotarus at least in part out of a sense of personal obligation.   During his governorship in Cilicia in 51 B.C.   Cicero entrusted both his son and his nephew to the care of Deiotarus (*Att.* 5.17.3), who also provided Cicero with military reinforcement during that year (*Att.* 5.18.2, 20.9), putting his entire army at Cicero's disposal as soon as the threat of a Parthian invasion loomed (*Att.* 6.1.14; *Fam.* 15.4.5, 15).[7] Cicero seems to have had mixed feelings about his speech on behalf of Deiotarus, as he wrote to Dolabella (*Fam.* 9.12.2) from his villa at Cumae sometime in December of 45:

> Oratiunculam pro Deiotaro, quam requirebas, habebam mecum, quod non putaram. Itaque eam tibi misi. Quam velim sic legas ut causam tenuem et inopem nec scriptione magno opere dignam. Sed ego hospiti veteri et amico munusculum mittere volui, levidense crasso filo, cuius modi ipsius solent esse munera.

Cicero claims he did not think highly of his speech for Deiotarus, that it was short and insignificant (*oratiunculam*), and hardly worth setting down (*causam tenuem et inopem nec scriptione magno opere dignam*). We do not know whether the speech was a success, yet we can assume that it was, for Cicero probably would not have distributed it unless he was either proud of it, which he clearly states he was not, or because it was a success. Still, it is entirely possible that Caesar had not yet returned a verdict at the time of his murder, for in April of 44 Cicero wrote Atticus about the *causa Deiotari nostri*, at which time the king's restoration seems to have been in the hands of Antony (*Att.* 14.12.1).

The *Pro Rege Deiotaro* is the third and final oration of what are generally referred to as the *Caesariana*, which consist of the *Pro Marcello, Pro Ligario*, and *Pro Rege Deiotaro*. In the interval between his defense of Milo and the *Pro Marcello*, Cicero seems to have refrained entirely from public speaking. While there is considerable

---

7. Cf. also Cicero, *Fam.* 15.1.6, 2.2, 8.10.1-2.

evidence that Cicero was very active in the courts in 52 B.C., we have no extant speeches to bridge the gap between the *Pro Milone* of 52 B.C. and the *Caesariana* of 46-45.[8] This interval of some six years saw Cicero's proconsulship in Cilicia from 51 to 50 B.C., followed by the turmoil of civil war almost immediately upon his return to Italy in November of 50 B.C.[9] After the defeat of the Republican forces at Pharsalus and Caesar's eventual pardon of Cicero at Brundisium in October of 46 (*Fam.* 14.20), Cicero tells us he withdrew from public life and devoted his attention to rhetorical studies and the writing of philosophy (*Fam.* 4.3.4, 4.4., 7.28.2, 7.33.2, 9.20.3, 26.1).[10] As Mitchell says of Cicero during this period: "He continued therefore to participate in public life to the least possible extent. He felt he should stay in the city while Caesar was there to avoid giving offense, and he did attend the senate, but he decided that his presence should be purely passive and that he would take no part in the debates."[11] Cicero remained immersed in his private studies during this period until the opportunity came to speak in the senate in support of Caesar's decision to pardon his enemy M. Marcellus, consul of 51. Cicero seized this occasion as an opportunity to emerge from his silence in order to extol Caesar's *clementia* as well as to make an urgent appeal to Caesar to heal the *res publica*.[12] Cicero had found a new cause to espouse, and in a letter to Servius Sulpicius (*Fam.* 4.4.3) of September or October 46 he writes:

---

8. For a summary of the evidence for speeches that Cicero might have delivered at some time before or just after the *Pro Milone*, see J. W. Crawford (1984), 219-240.

9. Even before reaching Rome, Cicero wrote Atticus a troubled letter dated 9 December 50 B.C. (*Att.* 7.3), in which he expressed his concern over the conflict between Caesar and Pompey, and its possible disastrous effect upon the future of the *res publica*.

10. For Cicero's literary pursuits of this period of political inactivity, see K. Bringmann (1971). See the reviews of A. E. Douglas, *JRS* 65 (1975), 198-200, and M. Ruch (1973), 103-108.

11. T. N. Mitchell (1991), 278.

12. Perhaps to restore the power of the senate through espousing the dictatorship of Caesar, see M. Rambaud (1984), 43-56.

Fecerat autem hoc senatus, ut, cum a L. Pisone mentio esset facta
de Marcello et C. Marcellus se ad Caesaris pedes abiecisset,
cunctus consurgeret et ad Caesarem supplex accederet. Noli
quaerere: ita mihi pulcher hic dies visus est ut speciem aliquam
viderer videre quasi reviviscentis rei publicae.

It was, as Cicero goes on to say in the letter, the *magnitudo animi
Caesaris* that changed his mind and brought him out of his self-imposed
silence. The confidence he had in Caesar's clemency then inspired
Cicero to deliver two orations on behalf of Q. Ligarius, both in 46 B.C.
and the latter of which Cicero published (see below), followed by the
Pro Rege Deiotaro in 45. The style and structure of the *Pro Rege
Deiotaro*, unlike that of the *Pro Marcello* or the *Pro Ligario*, most
closely resembles that of Cicero's earlier judicial speeches and indicates
that perhaps, as time went on, Cicero felt his old confidence returning.[13]
The *Pro Rege Deiotaro* is not, as the *Pro Marcello* and the *Pro Ligario*
clearly are, a panegyric pamphlet extolling the extraordinary *clementia*
for which Caesar was known, especially in his treatment of the
survivors of the Pompeian forces (Suetonius, *Iul.* 75; cf. also 73-74).[14]
While Caesar figures prominently in the *exordium* of the *Pro Rege
Deiotaro*, this is largely because of the requirements of the rhetorical
structure of the appeals of the *exordium*: Caesar was, after all, both the
iudex and the alleged intended victim of the accused king — not to
mention the only real audience present — and therefore Cicero had to
appeal to him several times and in several capacities within the
exordium.[15] Another reason for Caesar's exceptional importance in the
exordium is the extraordinary setting of the trial: Cicero was defending
Deiotarus before Caesar as *iudex* in the house of the dictator.[16] To

---

13. But see G. Petrone (1978), 85-104, who sees in this speech the combination
of forensic and panegyric elements that would later characterize court oratory
under the empire.

14. For the content and intention of the *Pro Marcello*, see R. R. Dyer (1990),
17-30; for the speech as a *gratiarum actio* see G. Cipriani (1977), 113-125,
esp. 117-118.

15. For a cursory study of the rhetorical style of the three Caesarian speeches in
relation to Cicero's earlier forensic speeches, see H. W. Montague (1987).

16. The trial probably took place in the domus publica, where Caesar took up
residence after he became pontifex maximus in 63 B.C. (cf. Suetonius, *Iul.* 46;

complicate matters, Cicero was defending a *rex* before a dictator who had given himself the prerogatives of a *rex*. Cicero was well aware of Caesar's courtship of monarchy (*Phil.* 1.3-4), but makes no mention of his disapproval of Caesar's arrogation of supreme power in the speech, except for the possible hint of it that might have been present in the inflection he gave the personal address "C. Caesar," which in this speech replaces his accustomed address of the *iudices*.

Although the setting for the *Pro Rege Deiotaro* is unique among the extant speeches, it was not the first occasion on which Cicero delivered an oration *intra domesticos parietes Caesaris*. Some months earlier (toward the end of November, 46 B.C.) Cicero had delivered the first of the two speeches on behalf of Quintus Ligarius, *legatus* to C. Considius, governor of the province of Africa at the outbreak of the civil war, in Caesar's house (*Lig.* 6, 14). As Cicero wrote Ligarius in August or September of 46 (*Fam.* 6.13.3), the trial had been a great success, even if Caesar's pardon did not follow immediately:

> Sed si tardius fit quam volumus, magnis occupationibus eius a quo omnia petuntur aditus ad eum difficiliores fuerunt; et simul Africanae causae iratior diutius velle videtur eos habere sollicitos a quibus se putat diuturnioribus esse molestiis conflictatum. Sed hoc ipsum intellegimus eum cottidie remissius et placatius ferre. Qua re mihi crede et memoriae manda me tibi id adfirmasse, te in istis molestiis diutius non futurum.

Ligarius' restoration was then further delayed when Q. Aelius Tubero brought Ligarius to trial on a formal charge of treason (*perduellio*), a case which Cicero defended before Caesar in the forum;[17] the success of his second speech (*Fam.* 6.14.2) was probably the reason why he published that oration rather than the first.[18]

Platner and Ashby, see under *Atrium Vestae*, 58-61). For Caesar as judge, see K. Bringmann (1986), 72-88, esp. 81-88.

17. *RE*, see under Aelius no. 156, Klebs 1.1, 1900, 537-538.

18. For a discussion of the evidence for the publication of the first *Pro Ligario*, see J. W. Crawford (1984), 241-243.

Commentary

Cicero begins the *Pro Rege Deiotaro* in a fashion similar to many of the *exordia* already examined: the structure of the opening sentence establishes the conflict in a rhetorical structure that illustrates the disadvantage Cicero feels he and his client face. In keeping with his rhetorical doctrines and the accretive format of the *exordia* of his earlier speeches, Cicero underscores this disadvantage by establishing an antithesis through the contrast of the appeals *a nostra persona* and *ab adversariorum persona*, and as always the aim of both, the climax or culmination of the *exordium*, is the appeal *a iudicum persona*. Furthermore, the opening sentence sets the tone of the *exordium* and lays out the *ratio* or framework for much of the rest of the speech:

> 1.1-6:   Cum in omnibus causis gravioribus, C. Caesar, initio dicendi commoveri soleam vehementius quam videtur vel usus vel aetas mea postulare, tum in hac causa ita multa me perturbant ut, quantum mea fides studi mihi adferat ad salutem regis Deiotari defendendam, tantum facultatis timor detrahat.

Cicero begins the *Pro Rege Deiotaro* with an *apologia* for his apprehension despite his age (*aetas*) and experience (*usus*). The rhetorical framework of the opening sentence of the *exordium* is structured around a temporal comparison in which Cicero contrasts his performance in the past (general) with his present (specific) situation, an approach reminiscent of the *exordium* of the *Pro Murena*, where Cicero contrasted the past specific circumstances surrounding the *precatio* with the present general conditions of the *causa* of his defense. In this speech, however, Cicero reverses the order by beginning with a characterization of himself in general terms of his past performances, and then applying that characterization to his specific present situation:

PAST (general):

cum in omnibus causis gravioribus

> initio dicendi commoveri soleam vehementius quam
> videtur vel usus vel aetas mea postulare

PRESENT (specific):

tum in hac causa

ita multa me perturbant ut

> quantum mea fides studi mihi adferat ad salutem
> regis Deiotari defendendam tantum facultatis timor
> detrahat

The opening sentence is also reminiscent of the *exordium* of the *Pro Roscio Amerino*, where Cicero's initial characterization of himself centered around his feelings of inadequacy. Here Cicero conveys this inadequacy through the opening correlative construction in which he contrasts his accustomed initial nervousness at speaking publicly in the past (*cum in omnibus causis gravioribus*) with his present feelings about speaking on behalf Deiotarus (*tum in hac causa*).[19] Cicero is probably sincere with this admission, as he wrote Ligarius (*Fam.* 6.14.2):

> Nam si quisquam est timidus in magnis periculosisque rebus semperque magis adversos rerum exitus metuens quam sperans secundos, is ego sum et, si hoc vitium est, eo me non carere confiteor.

Cicero uses his confession about his past experience to introduce the issue of the *insolentia* of having to speak *intra parietis domesticos Caesaris*. Cicero first began using this tactic in his consular speeches, such as in the *exordium* of the *Pro Murena* — something he could not have done in the early speeches before he had the experience of almost forty years of public speaking behind him.

In the first clause (*cum*) Cicero states that whenever he begins speaking he is accustomed to be more agitated and nervous (*initio dicendi commoveri soleam*) than either his experience or his age should

---

19. The scholiast (Gronov., Stangl, p. 299) observes that Vergil uses the same technique in Sinon's speech before the Trojans (*Aen.* 2.69-144).

demand (*vehementius quam videtur vel usus vel aetas mea postulare*).[20]
Usus and *aetas* in the present context are significant, especially when
comparing this *exordium* with the earlier *exordia*, such as that of the
Pro Roscio Amerino (1.2-4), where Cicero based his *apologia* on his
lack of *ingenium* and *aetas* (*ego surrexerim, is qui neque aetate neque
ingenio neque auctoritate sim cum his...comparandus*). But now *usus*
(experience) has replaced *ingenium* (natural talent, ability), one of the
primary features of the *apologia* of Cicero's early speeches, and Cicero
now speaks of his *aetas* not to emphasize his youth but for the opposite
effect — to underscore his maturity.[21] Cicero relies upon his age and
experience (*vel usus vel aetas*), rather than his youth and lack of ability,
to establish the *auctoritas* of his ethos and ask for the *benevolentia* of
his audience. But while the vocabulary Cicero uses has changed over
the forty years he has spent in public speaking, the purpose of the
apologia in the *exordium* remains the same, to throw into relief the
disparity of the situation facing him and the disadvantage that he feels
he must overcome to secure justice for his client.

The second clause (*tum*) of the opening correlative construction
contains within it a subordinate correlative construction
(*quantum...tantum*) through which Cicero contrasts his accustomed
fides with the *timor* brought on by his present situation: because of the
insolentia of the circumstances, the confidence (*quantum studi*) he
should derive from his *usus* and *aetas* is cancelled by the fear that any
possibility of using it (*tantum facultatis*) will be denied him. Whereas
fides ought to aid him in his defense (*adferat*), a shaken confidence in
his *facultas* due to his timidity (*timor*) robs him (*detrahat*) of the very
confidence that his age and experience ought to ensure. Cicero
illustrates the difference between his past experiences and the present
case first through *variatio* and synonymy with *commoveor* in the *cum*
clause and *perturbant* in the *tum* clause, followed by the chiastic
construction of the *quantum...tantum* clauses (*fides studi...facultatis
timor*) each of which is resolved through the periodic parallel verbs that
convey the antithesis of the temporal theme (*adferat...detrahat*).

---

20. For this construction, cf. *Sest.* 119: *quid aetas, quid honos meus postulet.*

21. For an earlier example of an *apologia* for *usus* and *ingenium* in the
exordium, cf. *Balb.* 1: *Quae sunt igitur meae partes? Auctoritatis tantae
quantum vos in me esse voluistis, usus mediocris, ingeni minime voluntati
paris*; cf. also *Quinct.* 1; *Rosc. Am.* 1; *Verr.* 1.1, 2.1; *Caec.* 1.

The theme of fear (*perturbare, timor*) also recalls Cicero's opening statements in the *Pro Quinctio*, the *Pro Roscio Amerino*, and the *Pro Milone*. Just as Cicero used his own fear of the opposition in the *Pro Quinctio* to characterize its members, so also he used the fear of the silent orators in the *Pro Roscio Amerino* to throw his own bold championship into relief; and in the *Pro Milone* he used his own admission of fear as a foil for the courage of Milo. Here Cicero uses his admission of fear as a means of transition to the appeal *a iudicum persona* by introducing and establishing the *clementia Caesaris*, which will compose the centerpiece of the *exordium*. But because Caesar is both the intended victim of the crime charged by the prosecution, and the *iudex*, Cicero is in a delicate position: he must introduce Caesar in different ways, both of which reflect the *insolentia* of the trial, and both of which are central to the progression of appeals within the *exordium*:

> 1.6-9: Primum dico pro capite fortunisque regis, quod ipsum, etsi non iniquum est in tuo dumtaxat periculo, tamen est ita inusitatum, regem reum capitis esse, ut ante hoc tempus non sit auditum.

Cicero begins (*primum*) by focusing on the *insolentia* of the circumstances of the trial, an approach reminiscent of the *exordia* of both the *Pro Roscio Amerino* and the *Pro Milone*. Cicero is speaking on behalf of the life and future of a king (*pro capite fortunisque regis*), and although he does not make immediately clear the nature of the charges against his client, he conveys the seriousness of the case through the *etsi...tamen* construction. In the protasis Cicero introduces Caesar's role in the trial as victim and in the apodosis juxtaposes him as defendant to Deiotarus as the accused. Cicero maintains that although (*etsi*) it is not unjust (*non iniquum est*) that such a charge be brought against Deiotarus in view of the fact that Caesar was the intended victim (*in tuo dumtaxat periculo*), nevertheless (*tamen*) the fact that a king stands accused of a capital crime (*regem reum capitis esse*) is extraordinary (*ita inusitatum...ut ante hoc tempus non sit auditum*). Cicero carries this antithesis forward as he explains *inusitatum* in preparation for his description of the *insolentia* of the circumstances surrounding the trial:

> 2.9-12: Deinde eum regem quem ornare antea cuncto cum senatu solebam pro perpetuis eius in nostram rem publicam meritis, nunc contra atrocissimum crimen cogor defendere.

Deinde signals the conclusion of the appeal *a persona nostra* along with the periodic resolution of the sentence (*cogor defendere*). The sentence is constructed around the same past/general :: present/specific contruction as the opening sentence. Not only are the circumstances of the trial extraordinary, so are the charges on which the *causa* is based. Cicero begins with the accusative *eum regem*, which sets up a verbal expectation that is suspended until the resolution of the *quem* clause, in which Cicero contrasts Deiotarus' loyalty to the state in the past (*antea*), which Cicero describes in general terms (*pro perpetuis eius in nostram rem publicam meritis*), with the specific disgrace of his present situation (*nunc atrocissimum crimen*). Through the contrast between past/general and present/specific circumstances Cicero not only throws the reversal of Deiotarus' previous good fortune into vivid relief, but also draws a parallel between himself and his client by contrasting his own customary laudatory treatment of Deiotarus in the past (*ornare...solebam*) with the new and unaccustomed situation of having to defend him (*cogor defendere*) in the present.[22] Antithesis is drawn from the contrast between both *ornare* and *defendere*, and *solebam* and *cogor*. The complete reversal of Deiotarus' relationship with the *res publica* mirrors the reversal of Cicero's relationship to Deiotarus as his *patronus*: the fact that Cicero describes himself as "forced" (*cogor*) to defend him strongly suggests that Cicero is acting on the conviction that his client is innocent of the charges, and therefore, despite the fact that Caesar is both the intended victim and *iudex*, he is representing Deiotarus entirely and altruistically because of the *fides* of his past relationship with the king.

Cicero now moves from the appeal *a nostra persona* to the appeal *ab adversariorum persona*, in which he introduces the *personae* of the prosecution:

> 2.12-13: Accedit ut accusatorum alterius crudelitate, alterius indignitate conturber.

The *personae* of the opposition consist of two individuals, the first of whom Cicero characterizes in terms of his *crudelitas*, the second in terms of his *indignitas*. Both *crudelitas* and *indignitas* beg for explanation and help keep the audience in suspense; but *crudelitas* has

---

22. For *cogere* cf. *Phil.* 1.11: Cicero did not like to be forced to do anything against his will, and considered it a form of *iniuria*.

more shock value, for it is generally used by Cicero and others to identify one of the worst characteristics of a man, worse than barbarity.[23]

2.13-19: Crudelis Castor, ne dicam sceleratum et impium, qui nepos avum in capitis discrimen adduxerit adulescentiaque sua terrorem intulerit ei cuius senectutem tueri et tegere debebat, commendationemque ineuntis aetatis ab impietate et ab scelere duxerit; avi servum corruptum praemiis ad accusandum dominum impulerit, a legatorum pedibus abduxerit.

Cicero carries forward his initial description of Castor (*crudelis*). And although he includes Deiotarus' *servus*, Phidippus, as one of the *accusatores*, it is Castor that Cicero focuses on as the *auctor* of the charge. Cicero contrasts Castor's youth (*adulescentia*) with Deiotarus' old age (*senectus*) in order to illustrate the criminality and outrage (*sceleratum et impium*) of his action: Castor is using this case in order to win a name for himself (*commendationemque ineuntis aetatis ab impietate et ab scelere duxerit*). This marks a significant shift in strategy from Cicero's early *exordia*, where he always portrayed himself as younger, more inexperienced than his opponents. By characterizing Castor in terms of his age, Cicero recalls his characterization of himself in the opening sentence (*vel usus vel aetas mea postulare*) and establishes a clear contrast between himself and his opponent while anticipating a later reference to the *aetas* of Deiotarus (6.2), which sets up an important aspect of his defense of the king.

Cicero then goes on to assert that Castor is not only guilty of falsely accusing his grandfather, but also of corrupting his grandfather's slave Phidippus in the process. Through parallel clauses and direct verbal echoes Cicero further demonstrates that it is Castor's coveting of his grandfather's throne that is the real motivation behind the prosecution: the case of the prosecution stems not only from the greed of Castor, but also from the greed of Deiotarus' slave, whom he does not name here but who, like Castor, is testifying against Deiotarus for personal gain. The chiastic verbal structure helps to illustrate the relationship between Castor and Phidippus:

---

23. Cf. Cicero, *Phil.* 11.6: *cuius taeterrima crudelitate omnis barbaria superata est*; also: *Verr.* 5.115; *Sulla* 93.

(A) avum in capitis discrimen **adduxerit**

(B) terrorem **intulerit**

(B) servum corruptum...ad accusandum...**impulerit**

(A) a legatorum pedibus **abduxerit**

The strong, active verbs Cicero uses underline the active role that Castor played in the indictment of his grandfather. Cicero then focuses on the *persona* of Phidippus and attacks him on the ground of the validity of his testimony against his *dominus*:

> 3.19-4: Fugitivi autem dominum accusantis et dominum absentem et dominum amicissimum nostrae rei publicae cum os videbam, cum verba audiebam, non tam adflictam regiam condicionem dolebam quam de fortunis communibus extimescebam.

Just as Cicero emphatically characterized Castor as the true criminal (*sceleratus*) because he was betraying the familial obligation of a *nepos* toward his *avus*, so here Cicero characterizes Phidippus as a criminal with the contemptuous condemnation implicit in the term *fugitivus*: Phidippus has betrayed the obligations of a *servus* toward his *dominus*. Cicero uses repetition and polysyndeton in conjunction with alliteration to emphasize that the testimony of Phidippus against Deiotarus is a violation of the loyalty of a *servus* to his *dominus*, which he uses in contrast to Deiotarus' steadfast loyalty to the *res publica* (*fugativi* d**o***minum* **a**cc*usantis et* d**o***minum* **a**b*sentem et* d**o***minum* **a***micissimum rei publicae*). Cicero calls into question Phidippus' motives and the validity of his testimony to show that the specific dangers threatening Deiotarus are not his primary concern. Although Cicero began the *exordium* by confessing that he was nervous because his defense was *pro capite fortunisque regis*, he now claims that the injustice that Deiotarus is suffering causes him to be concerned about the *fortuna communis* (*non tam adflictam regiam condicionem dolebam quam de fortunis communibus extimescebam*). By using the injustice of the plight of Deiotarus as an indicator of some larger evil impending for the common good, Cicero uses his own fear to shift the conflict from the appeals *a nostra persona* and *ab adversariorum persona* to the appeal *a iudicum persona*, in this case an appeal to Caesar alone:

> 4.8-11: Perturbat me, C. Caesar, etiam illud interdum quod tamen, cum te penitus recognovi, timere desino: re enim iniquum est, sed tua sapientia fit aequissimum.

Perturbat me echoes and recalls the opening sentence of the *exordium* (*me perturbat*), and allows Cicero to use his fear and lack of self-possession in order to introduce the *aequitas* of Caesar as *iudex*. Cicero begins by stating that because he knows Caesar well (*cum te penitus recognovi*), he need no longer fear (*timere desino*). This marks a significant reversal of the strategy of uncertainty that he used in the *exordium* of the *Pro Roscio Amerino*, where he expressed sincere doubt as to whether justice could and would be served under Sulla's newly organized judicial system. In this passage, Cicero characterizes Caesar in terms of his *sapientia*, which recalls the *exordium* of the *Pro Milone*, where Cicero used his apprehension in confronting the *insolentia* of the circumstances surrounding the trial in order to praise Pompey in a similar vein as the champion of justice (*Mil.* 2.16 ff.: *Sed me recreat et reficit Cn. Pompei, sapientissimi et iustissimi viri, consilium...*). Cicero contrasts the injustice of the circumstances with the supremely just nature of Caesar (*iniquum* versus *aequissimum*); throughout the *exordium* Cicero refers to Caesar as representative of *aequitas*, in direct contrast to his characterization of Castor, whom he describes as *crudelis*.[24] He then goes on to expand upon his characterization of Caesar:

> 4.11-15: Nam dicere apud eum de facinore contra cuius vitam consilium facinoris inisse arguare, cum per se ipsum consideres, grave est; nemo enim fere est qui sui periculi iudex non sibi se aequiorem quam reo praebeat.

The situation in which Cicero finds himself is difficult (*grave est*), because he is presenting his defense before Caesar who was the intended victim of the alleged crime (*dicere apud eum de facinore contra cuius vitam consilium facinoris inisse arguare*). But Cicero feels confident because Caesar's clement nature makes him a *iudex*

---

24. *Aequus* is an adjective Cicero also uses of Caesar in the *Pro Sestio*, 71: *aequus nobis fuerit.*

aequus, an impartial and unbiased mediator despite the fact that the alleged actions of the defendant would have threatened his life. It is this aspect of Caesar's nature that Cicero focuses on:

> 4.15-18: Sed tua, Caesar, praestans singularisque natura hunc mihi metum minuit. Non enim tam timeo quid tu de rege Deiotaro, quam intellego quid de te ceteros velis iudicare.

Cicero characterizes the *persona* of Caesar in terms of his exceptional nature (*praestans singularisque natura*) and emphasizes its ability to diminish his own fear (*mihi metum minuit*: note the alliteration of the period). Because Cicero opened with his fear, this characterization of Caesar sets up the final appeal of the *exordium*.

Having established the *persona* of Caesar in terms of his *aequitas* and *clementia*, Cicero uses this as a basis for establishing a favorable relationship between himself and his *iudex*, because the fear, with which he opened, can only be relieved by Caesar (*tua...praestans singularisque natura hunc metum minuit*):

> 5.18-25: Moveor etiam loci ipsius insolentia, quod tantam causam quanta nulla umquam in disceptatione versata est dico intra domesticos parietis, dico extra conventum et eam frequentiam in qua oratorum studia niti solent: in tuis oculis, in tuo ore voltuque acquiesco, te unum intueor, ad te unum omnis spectat oratio: quae mihi ad spem obtinendae veritatis gravissima sunt, ad motum animi et ad omnem impetum dicendi contentionemque leviora.

Cicero now focuses on the *insolentia* of the circumstances of the trial which disturbs him (*moveor*), because he is pleading a case of such magnitude as has never been argued before (*tantam causam quanta nulla umquam in disceptione versata est dico*) and he is forced to do so *intra domesticos parietis*, which is at variance with all his former experience (*dico extra conventum et eam frequentiam in qua oratorum studia niti solent*). The *insolentia* of the trial denies Cicero the responsive audience of the forum, the lack of which would be detrimental and daunting indeed, were it not for the fact that he is pleading before Caesar, whose very presence inspires a new kind of confidence which Cicero expresses emphatically (*in tuis oculis, in tuo ore voltuque acquiesco*).

We can see Cicero's accretive style at work here as he carries forward the issue of *insolentia* and expands upon it. As he brings the *exordium* to its conclusion, Cicero heightens the drama of his appeal:

> 6.25-31: Hanc enim, C. Caesar, causam si in foro dicerem eodem audiente et disceptante te, quantam mihi alacritatem populi Romani concursus adferret! Quis enim civis ei regi non faveret cuius omnem aetatem in populi Romani bellis consumptam esse meminisset? Spectarem curiam, intuerer forum, caelum denique testarer ipsum.

This passage is linked to the previous one thematically, drawing on the contrast between Cicero's past experience of speaking before an audience and the closed room in which he is at present forced to plead his case. The circumstances must have called for an emotional delivery that certainly would have heightened the drama of the moment. By characterizing Deiotarus in terms of his *aetas*, which has been spent in wars on behalf of Rome (*omnem aetatem in populi Romani bellis consumptam*), a direct contrast to the way Castor is using his *aetas* against Deiotarus, Cicero returns briefly to the appeal *a nostra persona*. Cicero links this passage to the previous one, in which he used the repetition of the second-person pronoun to emphasize Caesar's role as *iudex*, by showing that Caesar is an adequate alternate for the accustomed forensic setting by verbal repetition and the substitution of *curia* and *forum* for the emphatic repetition of *te unum*: all power rests with Caesar. The structure is chiastic:

[5.22-23] (A) te unum *intueor*

　　　　　(B) ad te unum omnis *spectat* oratio

[6.30]　　　(B) *spectarem* curiam

　　　(A) *intuerer* forum

There is a secondary emphasis here in the progression of the accusatives that moves *curia* (a), *forum* (b), *caelum* (c), which Cicero then carries forward and uses in the next passage in reverse order:

6.31-2:   Sic, cum et deorum immortalium et populi Romani et
senatus beneficia in regem Deiotarum recordarer, nullo modo mihi
deesse posset oratio.

The progression of the three genitives, *deorum immortalium, populi
Romani, et senatus*, corresponds to the three accusatives of the previous
sentence in reverse order (A B C :: C B A). The images that the *curia* (=
senatus), *forum* (= *populus Romani*), and *caelum* (= *di immortales*)
bring to Cicero's mind images that allow him to move from his own
situation and the *insolentia* he is faced with, to that of Deiotarus and the
beneficia due to the loyal king. Indeed, Cicero concludes with the
assurance that his defense of Deiotarus will be based on his ability to
demonstrate that his client has been a faithful servant of the *res publica*.
The character of Deiotarus is best shown by the fact that he enjoys the
beneficia not only of the immortal gods, but also of the Roman people
and the senate as well. This is the highest endorsement that Cicero can
bestow upon his client, and it is also one of the most powerful
rhetorical devices of the *exordium*, for it serves to impress upon the
audience that the matter at hand is of the greatest importance, for it
pertains to the Roman people and to the immortal gods (*Inv. Rhet.*
1.23); relying on the power of this endorsement Cicero asserts that
were he granted his accustomed audience, his eloquence would be
invincible (*nullo modo mihi deesse posset oratio*).

Cicero concludes by uniting the main elements of the *exordium* in a
final appeal to Caesar as *iudex*. As in all the *exordia* thus far examined
in this study, the culmination of the *exordium* is an appeal *a iudicum
persona*:

7.2-7:   Quae quoniam angustiora parietes faciunt actioque
maximae causae debilitatur loco, tuum est, Caesar, qui pro multis
saepe dixisti, quid mihi nunc animi sit ad te ipsum referre, quo
facilius cum aequitas tua tum audiendi diligentia minuat hanc
perturbationem meam.

Cicero continues the theme of *insolentia* created by the *parietes* of the
domus Caesaris, which he introduced above (5.1), by explaining that he
feels confined by the narrow parameters (*angustiora*) of this strange
forum, and therefore sees himself at a considerable disadvantage. The
nature of this disadvantage lies in the fact that because Cicero has been
denied his accustomed audience — the *iudices*, the *corona publica* —
his ability to sway his audience through a dramatic performance is

greatly diminished (*actioque maximae causae debilitatur loco*). As in past *exordia*, however, Cicero does his best to turn disadvantage to advantage and weakness to strength: since he has been robbed of his accustomed theatre setting, he appeals to Caesar to sympathize with his plight: the judgment rests with Caesar alone (*tuum est, Caesar...ad te ipsum referre*) who, Cicero claims, can sympathize because he has defended many men just as Cicero has (*qui pro multis saepe dixisti*) and therefore can identify with what Cicero is feeling (*quid mihi nunc animi sit*). Cicero began the *exordium* by admitting his fear (*me perturbat*) in the face of the *insolentia* of the circumstances, and now ends by identifying Caesar as both judge and audience (*quo facilius cum aequitas tua tum audiendi diligentia minuat hanc perturbationem meam*): Caesar is by virtue of his position the one man who can counterbalance Cicero's fear by fulfilling his role in the rhetorical equation of the *exordium* by being both a fair judge and an attentive audience.

Conclusion

Cicero's rhetorical strategy in the opening sentences of the *exordium* of the *Pro Rege Deiotaro* reflects a confidence and a program lacking in the other two "Caesarian" orations, one that is in many ways reminiscent of the *exordia* of earlier speeches delivered before an audience of the Roman people. But given the specific dynamics of the *causa* of his defense of king Deiotarus — the fact that he has been deprived of an audience and must defend his client *intra domesticos parietis Caesaris* — Cicero handles himself in classic form. In the face of circumstances he had not yet encountered in his career Cicero applies the same rhetorical techniques and principles prescribed in his rhetorical works and demonstrated throughout his career, masterfully adapting the elements of the *exordium* to accommodate a situation that finds no parallel in any of the other speeches examined in this study. Instead of extolling the *magnitudo animi* of his client, as he had once done in his defense of Milo, Cicero must now praise Caesar in these terms. Because by his own definition the purpose of the *exordium* has always been to establish conflict between his client and the opposition, Cicero must adapt: Caesar is not only judge, with whom all power rests, but also the intended victim and therefore a member of the opposition. Because of this unique situation, Cicero's *persona* no longer has the authority that it once had in the days when *quaestiones* were conducted *sub divo*; still, Cicero finds the room to manoeuvre rhetorically despite the circumstances. As in the *exordia* of the *Pro Roscio Amerino* and the *Pro Milone*, Cicero exploits the *insolentia* of the conditions in which the case is being heard in order to secure Caesar's *benevolentia*. Cicero begins with an *apologia* to win the sympathy of his audience, but now the basis for the *apologia* has changed. Instead of trying to explain how his youth and inexperience hinder him from defending his client, Cicero uses the *apologia* to explain that despite his mature age (*aetas*) and advanced experience (*usus*), the circumstances of the trial have left him at a loss for words.

One gets the impression that Cicero felt his hands were tied in this speech, and in many ways this was certainly the case. But his ability to adapt his rhetoric to the specific circumstances of a given case enabled him to proceed with his defense of Deiotarus despite the awkwardness of the situation.

CHAPTER SIX

Conclusions:

The Second Philippic In Perspective

In order to understand the *exordium* of the Second Philippic in terms of its rhetorical structure, it is necessary to view it in the perspective of the other speeches of this study. In all the *exordia* examined so far we have observed how Cicero followed his own stated *ratio exordiendi*, which was straightforward and explicit: *reddere auditores benevolos, attentos, dociles* (*Inv. Rhet.* 1.20). The three-fold function of the *exordium* dictated that the orator: 1) secure the goodwill (*benevolentia*) of his audience through the effective delineation and exploitation of character (*persona*); 2) focus their attention (*attentio animi*) by presenting the facts of his case (*causa*) in a way that made it seem urgent and of wide importance; and 3) make them receptive (*docilitas*) to hear and be persuaded by what he has to say by removing any prejudice against him or his client that might be the work of the opposition. Because the circumstances and individuals involved in each speech would naturally change from case to case, the two primary components of the *exordium*, treatment of *persona* and *causa*, were the most important as they were the most mercurial. As we have seen, *persona* encompasses not only the ethos of Cicero, his client, and sometimes even his client's *advocati*, but also that of the corresponding members of the opposition, as well as the character of the *iudices*, the *iudex quaestionis*, or whoever is presiding over the proceedings, including eventual *assessores*. *Causa*, a much broader category, can embrace not only the alleged misdoing, but also the circumstances leading up to it, often including the political atmosphere surrounding the trial itself — what Cicero customarily calls the *tempora*. Because the *personae* and *causa*, though inextricably linked, changed dramatically from speech to speech, Cicero's handling of these elements differs significantly from *exordium* to *exordium*. The *exordia* of the speeches of this study are representative not only of the different ways in which Cicero combines these two variables in order to achieve the aims of the *exordium*, but also of the effect that the chronological development of Cicero's own ethos had on his *ratio exordiendi*.

According to his rhetorical treatises, the main elements of the Ciceronian *exordium* are the appeals *a persona nostra, ab adversariorum persona, a iudicum persona*, and *a causa*. While there is no single, fixed paradigm that Cicero follows at all closely in his arrangement of these elements, we have observed that he tends to follow certain general patterns. Once again, these patterns are not based on the guidelines found in his rhetorical works dealing with *insinuatio* and *principium*, but rather they are based on practical expediency. Unlike his Greek predecessors, Cicero relied heavily upon his own ethos in the *exordium*, and in most speeches Cicero begins the *exordium* with an exposition of his own *persona*, characterizing himself in a way that will reflect positively, even glowingly, on his client, whose character he presents in direct contrast to that of the opposition. A sample schema of an *exordium* might look like this:

1) Establishment of Theme, Character, and Conflict:

   a nostra persona $\Rightarrow$

        $\Rightarrow$ *ab adversariorum persona*

2) Central Exposition: Development of Theme:

a persona et a causa $\Rightarrow$

3) Conclusion:

$\Rightarrow$ *a iudicum persona*

We can talk about the Ciceronian *exordium* as containing three "movements:" in the first (1) Cicero uses the antithesis of the juxtaposition of the appeals *a nostra persona* and *ab adversariorum persona* to develop the contrast and conflict that springs from the characters of the defense and prosecution, and in this way he establishes the main themes of his case; in the second (2) Cicero carries forward and develops these themes through an accretive rhetorical progression using key "concept words" to exploit the relationship between the appeals *a persona* and *a causa*; this accretive argumentation leads to the third movement (3), the conclusion of the *exordium*, where Cicero makes the impassioned, often overtly emotional, appeal *a iudicum persona*. The progression of the three movements always starts with Cicero, his duty as an orator and advocate, and ends with the *iudices* and their duty as judges.

In the evaluation of Cicero's use of his own ethos within the context of the *exordium*, we must take into consideration not only the chronological development of Cicero's career as an orator and statesman, a development that is certainly reflected in the various *personae* he projects in the speeches, but also in the circumstantial issues of the *causa*. For instance, in the pre-consular speeches Cicero tends to characterize himself in terms of his inexperience, and in the speeches of the consular period he uses his consular office to lend authority to his *persona*. In the post-consular speeches, however, because of the uncertainty of the *tempora*, Cicero allows his *persona* to play a supporting role to the external circumstantial issues of the *causa*, of which he often portrays himself as a victim, as is his client. But in all the speeches Cicero is careful to establish immediately a close bond between himself and his client.

In the *exordium* of the *Pro Quinctio*, Cicero focuses immediately on the *potentia* of the opposition in order to contrast his own *persona*, and that of his client, with that of the members of the opposition. Although the occasion for the speech was not a *quaestio* but a *praeiudicium*, Cicero's strategy is direct. He immediately focuses on the *gratia et eloquentia* of the opposition in order to associate himself closely with Quinctius in terms of their shared lack of political and judicial sophistication. Because neither Cicero nor Quinctius possesses those advantages that the opposition commands, Cicero uses the strengths of the opposition and his own professed weakness to prejudice his hearers against the opposition. It is a strategy aimed at winning *benevolentia* by soliciting an emotional response from his audience. Cicero describes himself as: *ego qui neque usu satis et ingenio parum possum (Quinct.* 2). The *contentio* that Cicero constructs between himself and Quinctius versus Hortensius and Naevius is one built purely on *persona*, and Cicero devotes the entire *exordium* to establishing and embellishing this contrast. This singular focus was especially important in the case of the *Pro Quinctio* because Cicero was placed in the uncomfortable position of being the *accusator*; by emphasizing his disadvantage in comparison with his opponents, Cicero manages to reverse the situation and assume the more accustomed and sympathetic role of *defensor*.

   Cicero adopts a similar approach in the *exordium* of the *Pro Roscio Amerino*. As he does in the *Pro Quinctio*, Cicero still exploits his own inexperience in contrast to the opposition in order to win the *benevolentia* of his audience: *ego...qui neque aetatis neque ingenio neque auctoritate sim cum his qui sedeant comparandus (Rosc. Am.* 3). But unlike his approach in the *Pro Quinctio*, in this speech Cicero combines *causa* with *persona* in his characterization of Roscius and himself as victims of an unjust political system, and the opposition as its profiteering champions and privileged darlings. Cicero uses the autocracy of the Sullan regime to establish a bond with his client, which in turn forms the basis of the conflict between the defense and the prosecution. Using the arbitrary brutality and cruelty of the Sullan proscriptions Cicero taps the emotion of fear in his audience and uses it to establish the conflict between Roscius and Chrysogonus. The *iniquitas temporum*, of which both Cicero and Roscius are victims, emerges as the main theme of the *exordium*.

   The ethos of fear, modest self-doubt, and uncertainty that Cicero exploits in the *exordia* of the early speeches of his career is replaced by a more confident, self-assured *persona* in the *exordia* of the speeches from the consular period. But even though his ethos has evolved, his approach to the structure of the *exordium* remains the same. Just as he combined his own inexperience (*persona*) with the political insecurity of the times (*causa*) in order to win the *benevolentia* of the *iudices* in the *Pro Roscio Amerino*, so in the *Pro Murena* Cicero combines *persona* and *causa*, but in this speech Cicero's consular *dignitas* allows him to project a more confident ethos. Before winning the consulship Cicero could never have adopted the *persona* of *conservator rei publicae* that he does in the *Pro Murena* and in all the other consular speeches. Moreover, after his exposure of the Catilinarian conspiracy and subsequent suppression of the threat of revolution, Cicero's ethos changed even further, and with it changed the rhetorical strategies of his consular, and his post-consular speeches as well. The *exordium* of the *Pro Murena* certainly reflects that change, because Cicero was in the unique position of defending a consul-elect while he himself was still consul. Understandably, he elects to make the case revolve around the implications of that office and the collegial solidarity it entailed with his client, and because Catiline was still on the loose as *hostis rei publicae*, the issues of the *causa* were also working in his favor.

In the two speeches that follow on the *Pro Murena* in this study, the *Pro Milone*, and the *Pro Rege Deiotaro*, Cicero found himself faced with new combinations of external circumstances that were far beyond his control. Unlike his *persona* in the speeches of the consular period, where the ethos Cicero projects is one of a magistrate in assured, though beleaguered control, through the *persona* Cicero projects in the *Pro Milone* and the *Pro Rege Deiotaro*, he impresses upon his audience the damaging and daunting effects of the *insolentia* of the circumstances under which he is forced to speak. While we observed how the *Pro Murena* marked a confident departure from the insecurity of the *Pro Quinctio* and *Pro Roscio Amerino*, we find the external circumstances of this later period forcing Cicero to return to many of the themes of the *exordia* of his earlier career. In the *Pro Milone* Cicero once again projects an ethos that is characterized by doubt and insecurity. While this approach recalls the *exordia* of both the *Pro Quinctio* and the *Pro Roscio Amerino*, the emphasis of his defense is that Milo was acting out of a sense of *officium* for the good of the *res publica*, and this emphasis marks a stage in Cicero's development that clearly stems from his consular period. In the *exordium* of the *Pro Milone* Cicero characterizes both himself and Milo as lone champions of the *res publica*. By describing Milo as *magis de rei publicae salute quam de sua perturbatur* (*Mil.* 1), Cicero portrays Milo as a patriot in an appeal that recalls his defense of Murena: just as Cicero felt compelled to defend Murena out of a sense of patriotic *officium*, so in the *Pro Milone* Cicero stresses the *salus rei publicae* as the primary reason for Milo's involvement in the death of Clodius and Cicero's decision to defend him.

Of all the judicial speeches in this study perhaps the most unusual is the *Pro Rege Deiotaro*, in which Cicero had to defend a client king of Rome *in absentia* before a court that consisted of Julius Caesar as the sole *iudex quaestionis*. To Cicero's further disadvantage was the fact that Caesar was also the plaintiff. Cicero begins the *Pro Rege Deiotaro* with an elaborate *apologia*, and in a fashion similar to all the *exordia* already examined, the structure of the opening sentence establishes the conflict at issue in a rhetorical structure that illustrates the disadvantage Cicero feels he and his client face. Once again we find Cicero apologizing for his fear, but now it is not because of his youth and inexperience, but in spite of his advanced age and experience: *initio dicendi commoveri soleam vehementius quam videtur vel usus vel aetas mea postulare* (*Deiot.* 1). Cicero relies upon his age and experience to establish the *auctoritas* of his ethos to move his audience, as he can no longer rely on his youth and lack of experience. An evaluation of the *exordium* of the *Pro Rege Deiotaro* shows how the progress of Cicero's career naturally influenced the *persona* he projected in his *exordia*, but despite the changes in his *persona* throughout his career, his approach to the *exordium* remained largely consistent. And even as his rhetorical skills and political adroitness grew over the course of his career — from the pre-consular insecurities of the *Pro Quinctio* and the *Pro Roscio Amerino*, through the emergence of the consular ethos of the *Pro Murena*, and finally the post-consular diffidence of the *Pro Milone* — we can see the same patterns at work in the *exordia* of the speeches of the final period of his career.

The Second Philippic, hailed by Juvenal as Cicero's masterpiece (*conspicuae divina Philippica famae*, 10.125), is the longest speech of the corpus of the fourteen Philippics, all of which were delivered between 2 September 44 and 21 April 43 B.C. The title *Philippicae*, after Demosthenes' orations in the face of the threat of the invasion of Philip of Macedon, was first used by Cicero of the speeches collectively in a letter to Brutus (*Ad M. Brut.* 2.3.4, 4.2; cf. Plutarch, *Cic.* 24, 48).[1] The closest parallel to Cicero's Second Philippic in the *Philippicae* of Demosthenes is Demosthenes' *De Corona*, in which Demosthenes, like Cicero, delivers an elaborate and spirited character assault upon his

---

1. Plutarch (*Cic.* 48) also calls them Philippics; although Aulus Gellius (22.17; 6.11.3-6; 13.1; 22.1.6) refers to the speeches as *Antonianae*.

opponent while defending his own career.[2] If one looks for parallels between these two speeches by Cicero and Demosthenes, perhaps the most relevant to the present study is the similarity between the traditional social and political ideals to which both men clung, and which are reflected elsewhere in the oratory of their final years. As Wooten observes, "like Demosthenes, [Cicero] portrayed himself as a man of destiny, struggling valiantly against evil and corruption for traditional ideals. However, we see in his later career, as in his earlier life, a man who really did not think deeply about the basic political, social, economic, and administrative problems of the age in which he lived and who, like Demosthenes, often preferred to idealize the past than to face the present realistically."[3] Although Cicero jokingly called the final speeches of his career *Philippicae*, they are in no way copies of Demosthenes' speeches of the same name.

If we analyze the *exordium* of the Second Philippic in the perspective of the other speeches treated earlier, we can see it as a direct outgrowth of the rhetorical strategies that served Cicero so well throughout his career. Of the three categories of types of speeches identified by Cicero in his rhetorical works (*Inv. Rhet.* 1.7; cf. *Rhet. ad Her.* 1.2; Aristotle, *Rhet.* 1.3.1-3), the Second Philippic most closely resembles epideictic, for it concerns itself with the censure of an individual. The speech contains many of the stock elements that Cicero uses in his invectives against such enemies as Catiline, Vatinius, Piso, and Gabinius: the speech is studded with references to Antony's questionable pedigree, dubious sexual proclivities, and generally excessive and outrageous *libido*. This speech is included in this study because through an analysis of the *exordium* we can observe how Cicero continued to apply the same rhetorical principles to a different type of speech from the judicial. Although the speech is a direct reply to Antony's speech of 19 September in the senate (cf. *Phil.* 2.3, 36), and not an effort to sway a jury, the *exordium* of the Second Philippic still serves the same purpose as the *exordia* of the other speeches examined thus far: it sets the tone of the speech to follow, it lays the groundwork for what is to come, and it serves to prejudice the audience to adopt a specific point of view against the opposition by establishing

2. See G. Rowe (1967), 184-192; also, C. Wooten (1979), 321-327.

3. C. Wooten (1983), 16. Wooten disagrees with Martin van den Bruwaene's eulogistic view in his essay "Démosthène et Cicéron" in *Études sur Cicéron* (Brussels 1946), 80-107.

antithesis through certain key words describing clear lines of conflict between Cicero and Antony.[4]

The enmity between Cicero and Antony began in the weeks and months following the murder of Julius Caesar on the Ides of March, 44 B.C., when Cicero's hopes for the restoration of the *res publica* through the leadership of the conspirators were sorely and summarily disappointed. On 5 April Cicero left Rome for his villas in Campania, from there planning a trip to visit his son, who was studying in Athens. But after several failed attempts to leave Italy, promising news from Rome of a reconciliation between Antony, now sole consul, and Brutus and Cassius the conspirators, reached him in Leucopetra on 7 August (*Att.* 16.7.1-2), and Cicero abruptly abandoned his plans of leaving Italy and returned to Rome, arriving on the last day of August. The senate met the following day in the temple of Concord, but Cicero chose not to attend because he disapproved of Antony's intended proposal for a day of public thanksgiving (*supplicatio*) in memory of Caesar (*Phil.* 1.11-13, 5.18-20).[5] Although Cicero sent Antony a message excusing himself as fatigued from his journey, Antony chose to take his absence as a personal insult, and publicly threatened to have Cicero hauled bodily into the senate if he would not come voluntarily. Cowed by Antony's violent language, his threats to burn down Cicero's house, and the presence of his armed bodyguard, the senate passed his proposal for the *supplicatio* in Caesar's honor.   Report of Antony's invective directed against him reached Cicero, and on the next day, 2 September 44 B.C., Cicero appeared in the senate and delivered what would become the First Philippic, a defiant, but still somewhat restrained speech, in which Cicero explained his reasons for returning to Rome and then criticized Antony's conduct in the aftermath of Caesar's death. Antony had conveniently decided not to appear in the senate on the occasion of Cicero's response, and when news of the speech reached him he retired immediately to his villa at Tibur to prepare his reply (*Phil.* 5.19).   On 19 September, 44 B.C., Antony delivered his reply to the First Philippic before the senate, what

---

4. For a reconstruction of Antony's speech based on what Cicero says see H. Frisch (1946), 133-140.

5. Cicero's objection was that the appropriate festival was the *parentalia*, not a *supplicatio*. Cicero himself had been awarded a *supplicatio* by the senate for his handling of the Catilinarian conspiracy, an honor he was very proud of: *qui honos togato habitus ante me est nemini* (*Cat.* 4.5).

amounted to a violent attack on Cicero's entire career. Again, Antony's soldiers were on prominent display and Cicero avoided the spectacle. After Antony left Rome on 9 October to receive the four Caesarian legions that had landed at Brundisium from Macedonia, Cicero issued his reply, the Second Philippic.

While the accepted view is that Cicero did not deliver orally, but rather chose to publish the Second Philippic as a pamphlet, there seems to be no actual support in the sources for this assumption. In his recent edition of Cicero's Philippics, D. R. Shackleton Bailey accepts the widely held view that Cicero did not deliver the Second Philippic, but rather published it as "a pamphlet in oratorical form supposed to have been delivered in Antony's presence on 19 September [44 B.C.]."[6] The idea that Cicero never delivered the Second Philippic, however, seems to be based entirely on certain remarks in three of Cicero's letters to Atticus, written between 25 October and 5 November of 44 (*Att.* 15.13, 15.13a, 16.11); but these are concerned only with the publication of the speech, and not with its delivery. Indeed, because the question of the delivery of the Second Philippic is inextricably linked with the question of its publication, one cannot address the former question without also addressing the latter. But Cicero's remarks in the letters concerning the publication of the Second Philippic are in themselves enigmatic and open to such a wide range of interpretation that some scholars have even doubted whether Cicero even published the speech in his lifetime.[7] James N. Settle, for instance, in his unpublished dissertation, *The Publication of Cicero's Orations* (Chapel Hill 1962), accepts without question that the Second Philippic was not delivered (p. 275), but concludes that "In view of the delivery and/or publication of the subsequent Philippics, there is surely no reason to assume a continued suppression of the Second Philippic" (p. 279). If Settle can argue that Cicero's publication of the subsequent Philippics is grounds for

---

6. D. R. Shackleton Bailey (1986), 31, in conjunction with the apparatus of P. Fedeli's Teubner text (Leipzig 1982); for this view see also: C. Craig (1993), 147-149; T. N. Mitchell (1991), 303; W. K. Lacey (1986), 19; J. D. Denniston (1926), xvii; H. Frisch (1946), 143.

7. For example, T. Rice Holmes (1928), 198-199, writes: "There is no direct evidence that the lampoon was ever published — that is to say, offered for sale, like Cicero's other works — in Cicero's lifetime." In this he is followed by M. Gelzer (1969), 352, who also expresses similar doubts.

proposing that he must also have published the second, why, then, can we not argue for delivery based on the same reasoning, especially since nowhere does Cicero, or any other ancient source, say that the oration was not delivered? All the evidence on which the question of delivery and publication of the speech hinges seems to show that there was ample opportunity between the delivery of the First and Third Philippics for Cicero to have delivered the Second.[8]

One of the most striking characteristics of the Second Philippic that emerges in the *exordium* is the simplicity with which Cicero characterizes himself and his opponent. Cicero's intention in the *exordium* of the Second Philippic is to show the struggle between himself and Antony as one between representatives of the primary forces of good and evil, and in keeping with the rhetorical strategies of previous *exordia*, Cicero begins by identifying where the conflict between himself and his opponent lies, using specific thematic vocabulary to establish polar extremes:

> 1.1-4:   Quonam meo fato, patres conscripti, fieri dicam ut nemo his annis viginti rei publicae fuerit hostis qui non bellum eodem tempore mihi quoque indixit. Nec vero necesse est quemquam a me nominari: vobiscum ipsi recordamini.

Through a rhetorical question of a highly philosophical color Cicero introduces the conflict between himself and his opponent once again cast in a progression that moves from the general to the specific. Cicero employed a similar rhetorical structure in the *exordia* of the *Pro Murena* and *Pro Rege Deiotaro*. Cicero's purpose in this approach is to establish antithesis and conflict: on one side stand Cicero and the *res publica*, on the other all the *hostes* that he and the state have, or have had in common.

The progression from the universal (*nemo...fuerit hostis*) to the more specific (*qui non bellum...indixerit*), works on several levels and plays off the expectations of the audience. The shift from the broad temporal parameters of the first clause (*his annis viginti*) to the specific temporal reference of the second (*eodem tempore*) at first seems to support the progression established by the shift from *nemo* to *qui*, but the phrase *his annis viginti* is in itself a direct reference to his consulship of 63 B.C. With this temporal reference Cicero's allusion to

---

8. For an examination of the evidence for the publication and delivery of the Second Philippic, see my article (1994), 23-28.

the *hostis rei publicae* takes on a much more pregnant meaning: without having named anyone yet, Cicero has already drawn a direct comparison between Antony and Catiline. Furthermore, by the parallel placement of *rei publicae* in the first clause and *mihi* in the second, Cicero equates himself with the state, and isolates his opponents as *hostes rei publicae*. Although Cicero does not name either Antony or Catiline in the opening sentence, the audience is invited to make the obvious association.

The question with which Cicero opens the *exordium* recalls the opening sentence of the First Catilinarian (*Quo usque tandem...*); it is a rhetorical question whose answer is obvious, as Cicero states: *Nec vero necesse est quemquam a me nominari: vobiscum ipsi recordamini.* We must not forget that Antony is consul, and with his opening words Cicero is challenging Antony's consular authority and integrity by alluding to his own triumphant consulship twenty years earlier. Cicero's allusion to the Catilinarian conspiracy not only prepares his audience for the consular nature of the *contentio* between himself and Antony that is to come, but it also gives weight to the superior authority of his *persona* over Antony's. This emphasis on the consular *persona* is also reminiscent of the *exordium* of the *Pro Murena*, where Cicero portrayed the office of the consul as intrinsically vital to the well-being of the state. By reminding his audience here of his own consulship, Cicero achieves the same end, and prejudices his audience against Antony before he even identifies him by name, which he does not hesitate to do immediately:

1.5-7: Mihi poenarum illi plus quam optarem dederunt: te miror, Antoni, quorum facta imitere, eorum exitus non perhorrescere.

Cicero introduces Antony by carrying forward the concept of *hostis* (*illi*) from the opening sentence. Just as Cicero addressed the senators in order to draw his audience into the drama of the situation, so here he addresses Antony directly. Cicero conjures up the image of the defeated enemies of his past in an attempt to deter Antony from repeating their mistakes — another way in which he equates Antony to a *hostis rei publicae* without actually coming out and calling him one. Cicero begins the sentence by reminding Antony of the penalties paid by past revolutionaries (*mihi poenarum illi plus quam optarem dederunt*), and warns him against imitating their actions (*quorum facta imitere, eorum exitus non perhorrescere*); by directly addressing Antony (*te miror, Antoni*), Cicero shifts the focus of the sentence from himself and his previous enemies to Antony and the risk he is running. The periodic resolution of the sentence (*perhorrescere*) conceals a powerful warning for Antony: he should fear the consequences of the course of action he is choosing to take. By establishing Antony's *persona* through the *exempla* of his past enemies, Cicero associates Antony with them. Cicero now carries that comparison forward and explores it in more specific and emphatic terms:

> 1.7-12: Nemo enim illorum inimicus mihi fuit voluntarius: omnes a me rei publicae causa lacessiti. Tu ne verbo quidem violatus, ut audacior quam Catilina, furiosior quam Clodius viderere, ultro me maledictis lacessisti, tuamque a me alienationem commendationem tibi ad impios civis fore putavisti.

Before Cicero accuses Antony outright of being another Catiline or Clodius, he is first careful to qualify the comparison between Antony and the enemies of his past. Through his initial self-characterization as the *defensor rei publicae* in the opening sentence Cicero has already shown what Antony has in common with his past enemies (that is, by being the *hostis rei publicae* he is also Cicero's enemy as well). Now Cicero shows how Antony is a *hostis* by reversing the argument to point out how he differs from the enemies of his past. The movement from general to specific repeats the progression of the opening sentence.

Nemo...fuit :: *tu...putavisti* echoes the opening sentence (*nemo...fuerit* :: *qui indixerit*). Cicero repeats the construction here only now with the direct second person address that focuses the audience's attention specifically on Antony. The point of the comparison is not so much to show how similar Antony is to Catiline or Clodius, but now how he is dissimilar and why; it is the difference between them that is the most telling blow to Antony's character. Once again the focus of the comparison is on motive: Cicero wants to expose Antony's sinister *persona*. None of Cicero's enemies in the past became an enemy voluntarily (*nemo...voluntarius*), but because Cicero challenged them (*omnes a me...lacessiti*), a point Cicero is careful to qualify by giving his motivation for doing so (*rei publicae causa*).[9] The distinction Cicero makes between Antony and Catiline and Antony and

---

9. Cicero was very proud of his proclivity for being the first to challenge his enemies who were also enemies of the *res publica*, as he admits at the end of the Third Catilinarian (3.28): *Est enim nobis is animus, Quirites, ut non modo nullius audaciae cedamus sed etiam omnis improbos ultro semper lacessamus.*

Clodius is an important one and is the pivotal point of the comparison. Antony has attacked Cicero of his own accord, without any provocation (*ultro me maledictis lacessisti*), although Cicero never even abused him verbally (*ne verbo quidem violatus*). Cicero is taking great care to develop his characterization of Antony as a *hostis* by showing that he is not only the complete antithesis of Cicero, but also of the enemies he is trying so hard to live up to. The culmination of the characterization comes with the final clause, in which Cicero delivers the most humiliating and condemning blow of all: Antony's motivation for wanting to alienate himself from Cicero stems from his desire to ingratiate himself with the enemies of the state (*tuamque a me alienationem commendationem tibi ad impios civis fore putavisti*). This statement confirms what Cicero asserted in the opening sentence, that any enemy of the *res publica* was, by definition, an enemy of his. Cicero has, in effect, used Antony as a working model for this hypothesis.

We must not forget, however, that Antony is consul, for Cicero surely has not. By characterizing him as an *inimicus* surpassing the likes of Catiline and Clodius — because unlike them he has assumed the role of aggressor willingly, without provocation — Cicero draws the ultimate contrast between himself and Antony by comparing the conduct of their respective consulships. Cicero uses the signal victory of his own consulship, his defeat of Catiline, to throw into relief every shortcoming of Antony's behavior while holding the same office. The irony is painfully obvious: while in his consulship Cicero defeated Catiline, Antony as consul has tried to be another Catiline — and could not even succeed at that:

> 2.12-15: Quid putem? contemptumne me? Non video nec in vita nec in gratia nec in rebus gestis nec in hac mea mediocritate ingeni quid despicere possit Antonius.

The rhetorical questions (*quid putem? contemptumne me?*) serve to expose the frivolity of Antony's conduct. Cicero delays the second *quid* clause, the object of the main verb of his response (*video*), with the insertion of four consecutive prepositional phrases, each emphatically introduced with the repetition of *nec in*, through which he dismisses all basis for Antony's contempt of him. Cicero expands the length of the first three phrases by one syllable consecutively (4, 5, 6), but employs *variatio* in the fourth, expanding it to 14 syllables, nearly the sum of the parts of the first three, thereby giving it added emphasis. For further emphasis Cicero withholds Antony's name until final position. Cicero is not only appalled that Antony should attempt to call into question his *vita, gratia, res gestae,* and *ingenium* (which he characteristically qualifies with *mediocritas*), but especially the setting in which he chose to do so:

> 2.15-18: An in senatu facillime de me detrahi posse credidit? qui ordo clarissimis civibus bene gestae rei publicae testimonium multis, mihi uni conservatae dedit.

The fact that Antony chose to challenge Cicero before the senate simply gives Cicero all the more ammunition to fire back at him, for it allows him yet another opportunity to recall to the minds of his audience the triumph of his consulship. It was only with the complete backing of the senate that Cicero was able to expose the Catilinarian conspiracy, and then follow through with his punishment of the conspirators; and, as he reminds his audience, it was also the senate that honored him for his actions by bestowing upon him the title of *conservator patriae*.[10]

Cicero continues to explore the possibilities of Antony's motivation for attacking him in public with another and final rhetorical question:

> 2.18-1: An decertare mecum voluit contentione dicendi? Hoc quidem est beneficium. Quid enim plenius, quid uberius quam mihi et pro me et contra Antonium dicere?

Having explored and exhausted all possible motives for Antony's invective against him, Cicero settles on the possibility that what Antony must be after is a *contentio dicendi* between the two of them. Cicero confidently states that this would be a boon to be sure (*hoc quidem est beneficium*). Having taken care from the beginning of the *exordium* to establish the contrast between himself and Antony in terms of how they conducted themselves in their respective consulships, Cicero is suddenly inspired by the rhetorical possibilities that a *contentio dicendi* between him and Antony presents (*quid enim plenius, quid uberius quam mihi et pro me et contra Antonium dicere?*). The self-confidence that Cicero exudes in the face of this challenge shows how far Cicero's *persona* has evolved since the delivery of the *Pro Quinctio* and the *Pro*

---

10. Of which Cicero was very proud, cf. *Cat.* 4.20: *ceteris enim semper bene gesta, mihi uni conservata re publica gratulationem decrevistis.*

Roscio Amerino almost forty years prior to the writing of the Second Philippic. In the *exordia* of both of those early speeches Cicero's inexperience as a public speaker was the focal point of the *exordium*, and he used it effectively to win the *benevolentia* of his audience: in the *exordium* of the *Pro Quinctio*, Cicero acknowledged the superiority of Hortensius' *eloquentia* over his own in order to win the sympathy of his audience; likewise, in the *exordium* of the *Pro Roscio Amerino*, Cicero admitted that while he had decided to represent Roscius, he was by far the least experienced orator available to do so. In fact, the confidence that Cicero displays in his eagerness to confront Antony on whatever ground Antony chooses marks not only the development of his *persona* from the pre-consular speeches, but also a self-confidence absent from the *Pro Milone* and the *Pro Rege Deiotaro* as well. In both of those speeches Cicero was pleading his case in the face of extraordinary circumstances (*insolentia*) — in the case of the *Pro Milone* it was Pompey's soldiers and the *nova quaestio*; in the case of the *Pro Rege Deiotaro* it was the fact that Cicero was pleading his case in Caesar's house before Caesar as both intended victim and sole *iudex*. While the circumstances of the Second Philippic are equally extraordinary, given Antony's power as sole consul and Cicero's status as a private citizen, Cicero shows no reservations whatsoever in confronting Antony publicly and challenging him. Cicero's eagerness to confront Antony demonstrates his conviction that the enmity between him and Antony is both professional and personal, and therefore absolute and irreconcilable:

> 2.2-3: Illud profecto: non existimavit sui similibus probari posse se esse hostem patriae, nisi mihi esset inimicus.

Illud profecto signals that Cicero is bringing the *exordium* to a close by returning to the argument with which he began. Cicero qualifies his evaluation of Antony's character and motivation by asserting that his ultimate ambition is to become another Catiline or Clodius (*sui similibus probari posse se esse hostem patriae*), which can only be realized by becoming Cicero's enemy as well (*nisi mihi esset inimicus*). His condemnation of Antony as both a public enemy (*hostis patriae*) and a personal foe (*inimicus*) brings the argument of the *exordium* full circle and confirms his initial characterization of Antony in the opening sentence, where Cicero alluded to Antony in similar terms. By his beginning and ending with the theme of *hostis rei publicae* (Antony) versus *conservator rei publicae* (Cicero), we can see how Cicero is using essentially the same strategy here that he has used in all the *exordia* of past speeches. Indeed, the heroic *persona* that Cicero adopts in the opening statement of the Second Philippic is a direct extension of the development we have seen that began in the *Pro Quinctio* and reached its apogee in the consular *Pro Murena*. Cicero isolates the opposition by characterizing himself as the champion of the state. This leaves his audience no choice but to see whoever is on the side of the opposition as an enemy of the state — as their enemy. Cicero uses the *exordium* to capitalize on this contrast by employing rhetorical devices that are designed to exploit the antithesis between him and his side and those who are lined up against him.

BIBLIOGRAPHY

The abbreviations for dictionaries and encyclopedias, reference works, and learned journals used throughout this book are a combination of those recommended in the "Notes for Contributors and Abbreviations" of the *American Journal of Archaeology* and those used in the *Oxford Classical Dictionary*[2] (Oxford 1970), ix-xxii. Abbreviations for secondary works frequently cited in the text are given below following their complete bibliographical reference.

Adamietz, J., *Pro Murena*. Darmstadt: Wissenschaftliche Buchgesellschaft, 1989.

Adcock, F. E., "Lesser Armenia and Galatia after Pompey's Settlement of the East." *JRS* 17 (1937): 12-17.

Austin, R. G., ed. *M. Tulli Ciceronis Pro M. Caelio Oratio.* 3rd ed. Oxford: Oxford University Press, 1960.

Axer, J., *The Style and Composition of Cicero's Speech Pro Q. Roscio Comoedo: Origin and Function.* Warsaw, 1980.

Ayers, D. M., "Cato's Speech against Murena." *CJ* 49 (1954): 245-254.

_____, "The speeches of Cicero's Opponents: Studies in *Pro Roscio Amerino*, *In Verrem*, and *Pro Murena*." Ph.D. Diss., Princeton University, 1950.

Bailey, D. R. Shackleton, ed. and trans. *Cicero's Letters to Atticus*. Cambridge: Cambridge University Press, 1965-1970. 7 vols. (= *Att.* vols. 1-7).

_____, *Cicero: Epistulae ad Familiares*. Cambridge: Cambridge University Press, 1977. 2 vols.

_____, *Cicero: Epistulae ad Quintum Fratrem et M. Brutum*. Cambridge, London, New York, New Rochelle, Melbourne, Sydney: Cambridge University Press, 1980.

_____, *Cicero: Philippics*. Chapel Hill and London: University of North Carolina Press, 1986.

_____, *Onomasticon to Cicero's Speeches*. Norman and London: University of Oklahoma Press, 1988.

_____, ed. *Quintilian, Declamationes Minores*. Stuttgart, 1989.

Bornecque, H., *Les clausules métriques latines*. Lille, 1907.

Braund, D., *Rome and the Friendly King*. New York, 1984.

Bringmann, K., *Untersuchungen zum späten Cicero*. Göttingen: Vandenhoeck & Reprecht, 1971.

Brunt, P. A., "*Amicitia* in the Late Roman Republic," *Proceedings of the Cambridge Philological Society* 191, n.s. 11 (1965): 1-20.

_____, "Der Diktator Caesar als Richter?" *Hermes* 114 (1986): 72-88.

Bruwaene, M., "Démosthène et Cicéron," in *Études sur Cicéron*. Brussels, 1946: 80-107.

Buchheit, V., "Chrysogonus als Tyrann in Ciceros Rede für Roscius aus Ameria." *Chiron* 5 (1975): 193-211.

_____, "Ciceros Kritik an Sulla in der Rede für Roscius aus Ameria." *Historia* 24 (1975): 570-591.

Buckland, W. W., *A Text-book of Roman Law*. Cambridge: Cambridge University Press, 1963.

Buckley, M. J., "Philosophic Method in Cicero." *Journal of the History of Philology* 8 (1970): 143-154.

Canter, H. V., "Irony in the Orations of Cicero." *AJP* 57 (1936): 354-361.

Castorina, E., *L'atticismo nell'evoluzione del pensiero di Cicerone*. Catania, 1952.

Cerutti, S. and Richardson jr, L. "The *Retiarius Tunicatus* in Suetonius, Juvenal, and Petronius." *AJP* 110 (1989): 589-594.

_____, "Further Discussion on the Publication and Delivery of Cicero's Second Philippic." *CB* 70.1 (1994): 23-28.

Christes, J., "Realitätsnähe und Formale Systematik in der Lehre vom *Exordium* der Rede." *Hermes* 106 (1978): 556-573.

Cipriani, G., *Struttura retorica di dieci orazioni ciceroniana*. Catania, 1975.

_____, "La *Pro Marcello* e il suo significato come orazione politica." *A&R* 22 (1977): 113-125.

Clark, A. C., *Pro T. Annio Milone*. Oxford: Clarendon Press, 1895.

Clark, M. E., and Ruebell, J. S., "Philosophy and Rhetoric in Cicero's *Pro Milone*." *RhM* 128 (1985): 57-72.

Clarke, M. L., "Ciceronian Oratory." *G&R* 14 (1945): 72-81.

_____, *Rhetoric at Rome*. London: Cohen & West, 1953 (reprinted with corrections, 1966).

Classen, C. J., "Cicero's Kunst der Überredung," Chap. 4 in *Éloquence et Rhétorique chez Cicéron*, edited by W. Ludwig, 149-184. Entretiens sur l'Antiquité Classique. Vol. 28. Vandoeuvres-Genève: Fondation Hardt, 1982, with discussion, 185-192.

_____, *Recht, Rhetorik, Politik: Untersuchungen zu Ciceros Rhetorischen Strategie.* Darmstadt: Wissenschaftliche Buchgesellschaft, 1985.

Cope, E. M., *An Introduction to Aristotle's Rhetoric.* London, 1867.

Cowles, F. H., "Cicero's Debut as Prosecutor." *CJ* 24 (1929): 429-448.

Craig, C. P., "The *Accusator* as *Amicus*: An Original Roman Tactic of Ethical Argumentation." *TAPA* 111 (1981): 31-37.

_____, "The Central Argument of Cicero's Speech for Ligarius." *CJ* 79 (1984): 193-199.

_____, "Cato's Stoicism and the Understanding of Cicero's Speech for Murena." *TAPA* 116 (1986), 229-239.

_____, "Cicero's Strategy of Embarrassment in the Speech for Plancius." *AJP* 111 (1990): 74-81.

Crawford, J. W., *M. Tullius Cicero: The Lost and Unpublished Orations*. Göttingen: Vandenhoeck & Reprecht, 1984.

Crawford, M. H., *Roman Republican Coinage,* 2 vols. Cambridge: Cambridge University Press, 1974 (= *RRC*).

Davies, J. C., "Cicero, *Pro Quinctio* 77." *Latomus* 28 (1969): 156-157.

_____, "Molon's Influence on Cicero." *CQ* n.s. 18 (1968): 303-314.

Deligiorgis, S., "The Auxetic Mode in Ancient Rhetorical Theory and Practice." *Platon* 23 (1971): 311-318.

Denniston, J. D., ed., *M. Tulli Ciceronis in M. Antonium rationes philippicae prima et secunda*. Oxford: Clarendon Press, 1926.

DeWitt, N. W., "Litigation in the Forum of Cicero's Time." *CP* 21 (1926): 218-225.

Donnelly, F. P., *Cicero's Milo: A Rhetorical Commentary*. New York: Fordham University Press, 1934.

Douglas, A. E., "A Ciceronian Contribution to Rhetorical Theory." *Eranos* 55 (1957): 18-26.

_____, ed. *M. Tulli Ciceronis Brutus*. Oxford: Clarendon Press, 1966.

_____, *Cicero*. Oxford: Clarendon Press, 1968.

_____, "The Intellectual Background of Cicero's *Rhetorica*: A Study in Method." *ANRW* 1.3 (1973): 96-138.

Drexler, H., *Die Catilinarische Verschwörung*. Darmstadt: Wissenschaftliche Buchgesellschaft, 1976.

Dyer, R. R., "Rhetoric and Intention in Cicero's *Pro Marcello*." *JRS* 80 (1990): 17-30.

Earl, D. C., "*Sallust*." Amsterdam, 1966. In *The Moral and Political Tradition of Rome*. London, 1967:, 5-40.

Eisenhut, W., *Virtus Romana. Ihre Stellung im römischen Wertsystem*. Munich, 1973.

Enos, R. L., "The Epistemological Foundation of Cicero's Litigation Strategies." *Central States Speech Journal* 26 (1975): 207-214.

_____, "Audience and Image in Ciceronian Rome: Creation and Constraints of the *Vir Bonus* Personality." *Central States Speech Journal* 29 (1978): 98-106.

_____, *The Literate Mode of Cicero's Legal Rhetoric.* Carbondale: Southern Illinois University Press, 1988.

Epstein, D. F., "Cicero's Testimony at the Bona Dea Trial," *CP* 81 (1986), 229-235.

_____, *Personal Enmity in Roman Politics, 218-43 B.C.* London, New York, Sydney: Croom Helm, 1987.

Ernout, A., "Les noms latins en -*TUS.*" *Philologica Classica* (1946): 36-43.

Fantham, E., "Ciceronian *Conciliare* and Aristotelian *Ethos.*" *Phoenix* 27 (1973): 262-273.

Ferguson, J., *Moral Values in the Ancient World.* London, 1958.

Fortenbaugh, W., "*Benevolentiam conciliare* and *animos permovere*: Some remarks on Cicero's *De Oratore* 2.178-216." *Rhetorica* 6 (1988): 259-273.

Fraenkel, E., *Kolon und Satz I.* Munich, 1932: 197-213.

_____, *Kolon und Satz II.* Munich, 1933: 319-354.

_____, *Noch Einmal Kolon und Satz.* Munich, 1965.

_____, *Leseproben aus Reden Ciceros und Catos.* Rome, 1968.

Frisch, H., *Cicero's Fight for the Republic: The Historical Background of Cicero's Philippics.* Copenhagen: Glydendal, 1946.

Gelzer, M., *Cicero: ein biographischer Versuch.* Wiesbaden: Steiner, 1969.

Gilson, E., "Éloquence et sagesse selon Cicéron." *Phoenix* 7 (1953): 1-19.

Gottoff, H. C., *Cicero's Elegant Style: An Analysis of the* Pro Archia. Urbana: University of Illinois Press, 1979.

_____, "Cicero's Analysis of the Prosecution Speeches in the *Pro Caelio*: An Exercise in Practical Criticism." *CP* 81 (1986): 122-132.

Grant, W. L., "Cicero on the Moral Character of the Orator." *CJ* 38 (1942): 472-478.

Greenidge, A. H. J., Infamia: *Its Place in Roman Public and Private Law*. Oxford: Clarendon Press, 1894.

_____, *The Legal Procedure of Cicero's Time*. Oxford: Clarendon Press, 1901.

Gruen, E., *Roman Politics and the Criminal Courts, 149-78 B.C.* Cambridge: Harvard University Press, 1968.

_____, "Some Criminal Trials of the Late Republic: Political and Prosopographical Problems," *Athenaeum* n.s. 49 (1971): 54-69.

_____, *The Last Generation of the Roman Republic*. Berkeley: University of California Press, 1974.

Halm, C., ed. *Rhetores Latini Minores*. Leipzig: Teubner, 1863.

Hardy, E. G., "The Catilinarian Conspiracy in its Context: A Re-study of the Evidence." *JRS* 7 (1917): 153-228.

Haury, A., *L'ironie et l'humeur chez Cicéron*. Leiden: Brill, 1955.

Hauschield, W., "*De Sermonis Proprietatibus Quae in Philippicis Ciceronis Orationibus Inveniuntur*." Diss. Halle, 1886.

Heibges, U., "Religion and Rhetoric in Cicero's Speeches." *Latomus* 28 (1969): 833-849.

Hendrickson, J. L., "Origin and Meaning of the Characters of Style." *AJP* 26 (1905): 249-290.

Hinard, F., "Le *Pro Quinctio*, un discours politique?" *REA* 77 (1975): 88-107.

Hubbell, H., *The Influence of Isocrates on Cicero, Dionysius and Aristides*. New Haven: Yale University Press, 1913.

Hughes, J. J., *Comedic Borrowing in Selected Orations of Cicero.* Ph.D. Diss., University of Iowa, 1987.

Humbert, J., "*Les plaidoyers écrits et les plaidoiries réelles de Cicéron.* Paris: Presses Universitaires de France, 1925.

Hunt, H. A. K., *The Humanism of Cicero*. Melbourne: Melbourne University Press, 1954.

Husband, R. W., "Election Laws in Republican Rome." *CJ* 11 (1915/6): 535-545.

_____, "The Prosecution of Murena." *CJ* 12 (1916): 102 - 118.

Imholz, A. A., "Gladiatorical Metaphors in Cicero's *Pro Sex. Roscio Amerino.*" *CW* 65 (1972): 228-230.

Johnson, W. R., *Luxuriance and Economy: Cicero and the Alien Style.* Berkeley: University of California Press, 1971.

Jones, A. H. M., *The Cities of the Eastern Roman Provinces* Oxford: Clarendon Press, 1971.

_____, *The Criminal Courts of the Roman Republic and Principate*. Oxford: Blackwell, 1972.

Jones, R. E., "The Accuracy of Cicero's Characterizations." *AJP* 60 (1939): 307-325.

Kelly, J. M., *Roman Litigation*. Oxford: Clarendon Press, 1966.

Kennedy, G. A., *The Art of Persuasion in Greece*. Princeton: Princeton University Press, 1963.

_____, "The Rhetoric of Advocacy in Greece and Rome." *AJP* 89 (1968): 419-436.

_____, *The Art of Rhetoric in the Roman World*. Princeton: Princeton University Press, 1972.

_____, *Quintilian*. New York, 1969.

Kinsey, T. E., "A Dilemma in the *Pro Roscio Amerino*." *Mnemosyne* 19 (1966): 270-271.

_____, "Cicero, Hortensius and Philippus in the *Pro Quinctio*." *Latomus* 29 (1970): 737-738.

_____, ed. *M. Tulli Ciceronis Pro P. Quinctio Oratio*. Sydney: Sydney University Press, 1971.

_____, "Cicero's Case Against Magnus, Capito, and Chrysogonus in the *Pro Sex. Roscio Amerino* and its Use for the Historian." *AC* 49 (1980): 173-190.

_____, "A Problem in the *Pro Roscio Amerino*." *Eranos* 79 (1981): 149-150.

_____, "The Political Insignificance of Cicero's *Pro Roscio*." *LCM* 7 (1982): 39-40.

_____, "The Case Against Sextus Roscius of Ameria." *AC* 14 (1985): 188-196.

_____, "The Sale of the Property of Roscius of Ameria. How Legal Was It?" *AC* 57 (1988): 325-332.

Kirby, J. T., *The Rhetoric of Cicero's* Pro Cluentio. Amsterdam: Gieben, 1990.

Kroll, W., "Studien über Ciceros Schrift *De Oratore*." *RhM* 58 (1903): 552-597 (= Kroll 1903A).

_____, "Cicero und die Rhetorik." *NJA* 11 (1903): 681-689 (= Kroll 1903B).

Kuklica, P., "Ciceros Begriff *virtus* und dessen Interpretation." *Graecolatina et Orientalia* 7-8 (1975-76): 3-23.

Kumaniecki K., "Ciceros Rede `Pro Murena'." In *Acta Conventus XI "Eirene*," *Diebus xxi-xxv mensis Octobris Anni MCMLXVIII Habiti*, 161-179. Wratislaviae, Varsaviae, Cracoviae, Gedani, 1971.

Lacey, W. K., *Cicero: Second Philippic Oration*. Warminster: Aris & Philipps, 1986.

Landgraf, G., ed. *Kommentar zu Ciceros Rede Pro Sex. Roscio Amerino*. 2nd ed. Berlin: Teubner, 1914.

Laughton, E., *The Participle in Cicero*. Oxford: Clarendon Press, 1964.

_____, "E. Fraenkel's *Leseproben aus Reden Ciceros und Catos*." *JRS* 60 (1970): 188-194.

Laurand, L., *Études sur le Style des Discours de Cicéron*. 4th ed. Amsterdam: A. M. Hakkert, 1965. Three volumes in one; reprint of the 1936-1938 Paris edition.

Leeman, A. D., *Orationis Ratio: The Stylistic Theories and Practice of the Roman Orators, Historians, and Philosophers*. Amsterdam: A. M. Hakkert, 1963.

_____, "The Technique of Persuasion in Cicero's *Pro Murena*." Chap. 5 in *Éloquence et rhétorique chez Cicéron*, in W. Ludwig, ed., 193-228. Entretiens sur l'Antiquité Classique. Vol. 28 Vandoeuvres-Genève: Fondation Hardt, 1982). with discussion, 229-236.

Lengle, J., *Untersuchungen über die sullanische Verfassung*. Freiburg, 1899.

Leon, H. J., "The Technique of Emotional Appeal in Cicero's Judicial Speeches," *CW* 29 (1935): 33-37.

Leumann, M., Hofmann, J. B., and Szantyr, A., *Lateinische Laut- und Formenlehre, Lateinische Syntax und Stilistik* (2 vols.) (*Handbuch der Altertumswissenschaft*). Munich, 1963, 1965 (=Leumann-Hofmann).

Loutsch, C., *L'exorde dans les discours de Cicéron.* Brussels: *CollLatomus* 224, 1994.

Magie, D., *Roman Rule in Asia Minor.* Princeton: Princeton University Press, 1950.

Marshall, B. A., "*Excepta Oratio*, The Other *Pro Milone* and the Question of Shorthand." *Latomus* 46 (1987): 730-736.

May, J. M., "The *Ethica Digressio* and Cicero's *Pro Milone*: A Progression of Intensity from *Logos* to *Ethos* to *Pathos*." *CJ* 74 (1979): 240-246.

_____, "The Rhetoric of Advocacy and the Patron-Client Identification: Variation on a Theme." *AJP* 102 (1981): 308-315.

_____, *Trials of Character.* Chapel Hill and London: University of North Carolina Press, 1988.

Mentz, A., "Die Entstehungsgeschichte der römischen Stenographie." *Hermes* 66 (1931): 369-86.

Merguet, H., *Handlexicon zu Cicero.* Leipzig: Teubner, 1962.

Michel, A., ed., *Rhetorique et Philosophie chez Cicéron.* Paris: Presses Universitaires de France, 1960.

_____, "La théorie de la rhétorique chez Cicéron," in *Éloquence et rhétorique chez Cicéron,* in W. Ludwig, ed., 109-147. Entretiens sur l'Antiquité Classique. Vol. 28 Vandoeuvres-Genève: Fondation Hardt, 1982). with discussion, 229-236.

Mitchell, T. N., *Cicero: The Ascending Years.* New Haven: Yale University Press, 1979.

_____, *Cicero the Senior Statesman.* New Haven: Yale University Press, 1991.

Montague, H. W., "Style and Strategy in Forensic Speeches, Cicero's Caesarians in Perspective." Ph.D. Diss., Harvard University, 1987.

Montefusco, L. C., Exordium, narratio, epilogus: *studi sulla teoria retorica greca e romana delle parti del discorso.* Bologna, 1988.

Norden, E., *Die antike Kunstprosa.* Stuttgart, 1958 (reprint).

Packard, D., *A Concordance to Livy.* Cambridge: Harvard University Press, 1968.

Petrone, G., "La parola e l'interdetto. Nota alla *Pro rege Deiotaro* e alle orazioni cesariane." *Pan* 6 (1978): 85-104.

Prill, P., "Cicero in Theory and Practice: The Securing of Good Will in the *Exordia* of Five Forensic Speeches." *RH* 4 (1986): 93-109.

Primmer, A., "Historisches und Oratorisches zur ersten Catilinaria." *Gymnasium* 84 (1977): 18-38.

Rambaud, M., "Le *Pro Marcello* et l'insinuation politique." *Caesarodonum* 19 (1984): 43-56.

Richardson jr, L., "The Tribunals of the Praetors of Rome." *MDAI(R)* 80 (1973): 219-233.

Ritter, H. W., "Caesars erstes Zusammentreffen mit Deiotarus." *Historia* 18 (1969): 255-256.

Sarsila, J., "Some Notes on *Virtus* in Sallust and Cicero." *Arctos* 12 (1978): 135-43.

Scaillet, A., "Cicéron, *Pro Milone*: La théorie oratoire appliquée à l'exorde et à la narration," *Études Classiques* 59 (1991): 345-347.

Schulz, F., *Classical Roman Law*. Oxford: Clarendon Press, 1951.

Settle, J. N., "The Publication of Cicero's Orations." Ph.D. diss., University of North Carolina, 1962.

_____, "The Trial of Milo and the other *Pro Milone*." *TAPA* 94 (1963): 268-280.

Sherwin-White, A. N., *The Letters of Pliny: A Historical and Social Commentary*. Oxford; Clarendon Press, 1966.

_____, *Roman Foreign Policy in the East: 168 B.C. to A.D. 1*. London, 1984.

Schuetrumpf, E., "Platonic Elements in the Structure of Cicero's *De Oratore* Book One." *Rhetorica* 6 (1988): 237-258.

Solmsen, F., "Aristotle and Cicero on the Orator's Playing upon the Feelings." *CP* 33 (1938): 390-404. Reprinted in kleine Schriften II (Hildesheim: Olms, 1968), 216-230.

_____, "Cicero's First Speeches: A Rhetorical Analysis." *TAPA* 69 (1938): 542-556.

_____, "The Aristotelian Tradition in Ancient Rhetoric," *AJP* 62 (1941): 35-50, 169-190. Reprinted in kleine Schriften II (Hildesheim: Olms, 1968), 178-215.

Stangl, T., ed. *Ciceronis Orationum Scholiastae*. Hildesheim: Georg Olms, 1964. Reprint of the 1912 Vienna edition (= Stangl).

Stone, A. M., "*Pro Milone*, Cicero's Second Thoughts." *Antichthon* 14 (1980): 88-111.

Syme, R., *The Roman Revolution*. Oxford: Clarendon Press, 1939.

Taylor, L. R., *The Divinity of the Roman Emperor*. American Philological Association Press, 1931.

_____, *Party Politics in the Age of Caesar*. Berkeley: University of California Press, 1949.

Vasaly, A., "The Masks of Rhetoric: Cicero's *Pro Roscio Amerino*." *Rhetorica* 3 (1985): 1-20.

Vereecke, E., "Le rythme binaire et terniare dans l'argumentation. Cicéron, *Pro Milone*, 1-31." *Études Classiques* 59 (1991): 171-178.

Walde, A., and J. B. Hofmann, eds. *Lateinisches Etymologisches Wörterbuch*. Heidelberg, 1965. 2 vols.

Wilamowitz, U. von, "Asianismus und Atticismus." *Hermes* 35 (1900): 1-52.

Winkel, L. C., "Some Remarks on the Date of the *Rhetorica ad Herennium*." *Mnemosyne* 32, 4th series (1979): 327-332.

Wooten, C., *Cicero's Philippics and Their Demosthenic Model: The Rhetoric of Crisis*. Chapel Hill and London: University of North Carolina Press, 1983.

_____, "The Nature of Form in Demosthenes' *de Corona*." *CW* 72 (1979): 321-327.

Zielinski, T., *Clauselgesetz in Ciceros Reden*. Leipzig: Teubner, 1904.

_____, *Der Constructive Rhythmus in Cicero's Reden*. Leipzig: Teubner, 1914.

Zumpt, A. W., *Das Criminalrecht der Römischen Republik*. Berlin: Teubner, 1.2 1865; 2.1 1868; 2.2 1869.

GLOSSARY

Grammatical Terms and Rhetorical Figures

ALLITERATION — the device of beginning several consecutive or parallel words or phrases with the same sound, usually the consonant (example: *mihi metum minuit* [*Deiot.* 4.16]).

ANTITHESIS — the opposition, or contrast, of terms or grammatical units for emphasis (example: *hinc pudicitia, illinc stuprum; hinc fides, illinc fraudatio...* [*Cat.* 2.25.31-32]).

ANAPHORA — the repetition of an initial word (with the same or different inflection) to link consecutive units (example: *qui...quos...in quibus* [*Rosc. Am.* 2.13-14]).

APODOSIS — the conclusion, or main clause, of a conditional sentence (see BIPARTITE CONSTRUCTION).

ASYNDETON — the arrangement of two or more coordinate words, phrases, or sentences without conjunctions or connectors (example: *putant oportere defendi, defendere...non audent* [*Rosc. Am.* 1.6-7]).

BIPARTITE CONSTRUCTION — simply a construction consisting of two parts, ranging from words and phrases to clauses and sentences. The device is most often used by Cicero to strike antithesis between the two elements in parallel construction (example: *Eloquentia Q. Hortensi ne me in dicendo impediat...gratia Sex. Naevi ne P. Quinctio noceat...* [*Quinct.* 1.4-6]).

CHIASMUS — the cruciform reversal of the order of words in corresponding pairs of phrases (ABBA), often used by Cicero to achieve antithesis (example: *Credo ego vos...mirari* [*Rosc. Am.* 1.1]).

CLAUSULA — rhythmical cadences strategically arranged by Cicero to mark the resolution of periods (example: *esse videatur* [*Leg. Agr.* 1.24.11])

HENDIADYS — the use of two parallel items, generally nouns, with a conjunction, where the sense strictly demands a single modified noun (example: *vim et gratiam...solitudine atque inopiae* [*Quinct.* 5.6-7]).

HOMEOTELEUTON — an echoing effect created by the arrangement of words of similar ending (example: *non electus unus...maximo ingenio...sed relictus ex omnibus...minimo periculo* [*Rosc. Am.* 5.11-13]).

ISOCOLON — correspondence of word order and syntactic function among parallel clauses.

LITOTES — the affirmation of something by the denial of its opposite (example: *non nihil commoveor :: non mediocriter pertimesco* [*Quinct.* 1.4-6]).

PARATAXIS — the arrangement of ideas or sentences into syntactically coordinate clauses without subordination (example: *Accusant ii...causam dicit is...* [*Rosc. Am.* 13.13-14]).

PARANOMASIA — the use of words of like sound, often involving, but not limited to, internal rhyming (example: *tradidisset...dedere* [*Mil.* 2.18-1]).

PROTASIS — the dependent, or "if" clause, of a conditional sentence that anticipates resolution in the main clause, or apodosis (s.v.).

TRICOLON — the arrangement or grouping of three words, clauses, or sentences, often in Cicero with an increase in the length of the members (example: *neque aetate neque ingenio neque auctoritate* [*Rosc. Am.* 1.3-4]).

VARIATIO — Any deviation from verbal or structural expectation for the sake of avoiding predictable symmetry (example: *si qui...dixisset...si verbum...fecisset* [*Rosc. Am.* 2.13-15]).

GENERAL INDEX

INDEX OF QUOTATIONS

Mil. 6.9-11 (125)
Mil. 6.11-16 (126)
Mil. 6.17-20 (127)
Mil. 12.15-18 (104)
Mil. 13.2-6 (103)

Pro Murena
  Mur. 1.1-10 (93)
  Mur. 1.10-15 (197-8)
  Mur. 2.15-21 (99)

Philippics
  Phil. 2.1.1-4 (160)
  Phil. 2.1.5-7 (161)
  Phil. 2.1.7-12 (162)
  Phil. 2.2.12-15 (163)
  Phil. 2.2.15-18 (164)
  Phil. 2.2.18-1 (164)
  Phil. 2.2.2-3 (165)
  Phil. 2.2.27-2 (104)

Pro Quinctio
  Quinct. 1.1-3 (24)
  Quinct. 1.4-6 (27)
  Quinct. 2.6-12 (29-
                30)
  Quinct. 4.19-3 (31-2)
  Quinct. 4.3-5 (32)
  Quinct. 5.6-11 (32)
  Quinct. 5.12-14 (36)
  Quinct. 5.15-18 (36)
  Quinct. 6.18-24 (37)
  Quinct. 7.24-2 (38)
  Quinct. 8.2-8 (40)
  Quinct. 8.9-14 (40)
  Quinct. 9.14-19 (41)
  Quinct. 9.19-24 (42)
  Quinct. 10.25-3 (43)

Pro Roscio Amerino
  Rosc. Am. 1.1-4 (57)
  Rosc. Am. 1.4-7 (59)
  Rosc. Am. 82 (53)
  Rosc. Am. 2.13-17
                (60)
  Rosc. Am. 5.11-15
                (62)
  Rosc. Am. 5.16-19
                (63)
  Rosc. Am. 5.19-21
                (65)
  Rosc. Am. 6.21-26
                (65)
  Rosc. Am. 59.3-60.8
                (67)
  Rosc. Am. 6.26-5 (68)
  Rosc. Am. 6.5-8 (70)
  Rosc. Am. 7.9-11 (71)
  Rosc. Am. 7.11-15
                (71)
  Rosc. Am. 8.27-4 (72)
  Rosc. Am. 9.5-11 (74)
  Rosc. Am. 11.21-24
                (76)
  Rosc. Am. 12.5-12
                (77)
  Rosc. Am. 13.13-22
                (79)

Rhetorical Works:

Brutus
  Brut. 290 (6)

De Officiis
  Off. 1.4 (90)
  Off. 3.43 (90)